W9-BYH-526

Advance Praise for *Embedded With Organized Labor*

"This is an exciting collection that respects workers enough to engage them in desperately needed discussions about union strategy. It presents a radical defense of the working class and an uncompromising critique of the labor movement as it exists today."
—SAM GINDIN, Professor, York University and Former Research Director
Canadian Auto Workers

"Steve Early's collected works is a real treasure trove. The author's astute analysis of labor's historic struggles, its achievements and shortcomings, is spiced by a lively writing style and enriched by years of personal involvement in unions. This is a book that every labor activist should read and think about."
—HARRY KELBER, Editor, *The Labor Educator*

"For those of us who continue to believe that a revitalized labor movement remains the last best hope for social change in America, Early's reporting is simply irreplaceable."
—ROSE ANN DEMORO, Executive Director, California Nurses
Association/NNOC

"There aren't many people who could pull off Early's hat trick. Here's a full-time union representative with an academician's smarts and education—and he can write. The result is a volume that will have long-time labor activists nodding their heads in recognition, union observers scribbling footnotes and working people gaining a better appreciation of why unions are the way they are, for better and worse."
—ANDY ZIPSER, Editor, *The Guild Reporter*, The Newspaper Guild/CWA

" . . . contains some very timely reflections on labor law reform and enforcement. As American unions try once again to seek changes in the National Labor Relations Act, they'd be well advised to consult this author's account of how and why similar campaigns have failed in the past."
—LEE ADLER, Attorney and Labor Law Instructor,
Cornell ILR School and Labor Extension Program

"If organized labor is ever going to regain its clout in the era of globalization, it must, as this collection argues, embrace real cross-border solidarity and bottom-up organizing."
—ELLEN DAVID-FRIEDMAN, Research Associate, Harvard Labor
& Worklife Program Former Organizing Director, Vermont-NEA

"Steve Early has never left the front lines of labor. He challenges unions to trust in the members and their right to be heard. He's relentless about the importance of workers' power on the job and in the community."
—HETTY ROSENSTEIN, New Jersey Area Director, CWA

"This collection demonstrates Steve Early's status as one of the leading organic intellectuals in labor. Early's attention to what workers read, think, say, and do places them at the center of his work as the active agents of their own lives and futures."
—PETER RACHLEFF, Professor of History, Mcalester College, and labor activist

"Early combines a realistic understanding of union functioning with the passionate outrage of a union reformer."
—MIKE PARKER, co-author, *Democracy is Power:
Rebuilding Unions from the Bottom*

EMBEDDED WITH ORGANIZED LABOR

Journalistic Reflections on the Class War at Home

by STEVE EARLY

MONTHLY REVIEW PRESS
New York

Library of Congress Cataloging-in-Publication Data

Early, Steve.

  Embedded with organized labor : journalistic reflections on the class war at home / by Steve Early.

    p. cm.

  ISBN 978-1-58367-188-7 (pbk.) — ISBN 978-1-58367-189-4 (cloth)

  1. Labor unions—United States. 2. Labor movement—United States. 3. Labor—United States. I. Title.

  HD6508.E34 2009

  331.880973—dc22

                                    2009007931

Monthly Review Press

146 West 29th Street, Suite 6W

New York, NY 10001

5 4 3 2 1

Contents

To Hector Giraldo of Colombia, Hashmeya Muhsin Hussein of Iraq, Yang Lieming of China, and Rafael Feliciano Hernandez of Puerto Rico, four workers of the world whose courage and persistence never cease to inspire.

Confessions of a Participatory Labor Journalist

Nearly thirty years ago, United Auto Workers president Doug Fraser—who was no radical—wrote a much-quoted letter in which he lamented the "one-sided class war" being waged against workers by leading corporations. Fraser was clearly fishing around for some sort of cease-fire. But I can accurately report that the shooting still hasn't stopped. Corporate America's multifaceted assault on the pay, benefits, and job conditions of millions of workers continues to this very day. When I first got involved in the labor movement in the early 1970s, unions still represented almost a quarter of the country's workforce. Now, unionization is down to 12.4 percent overall and only 7.6 percent in private industry.

This dramatic decline in "density" has had one salutary effect. Within organized labor, an institution not always known for the richness of its intellectual life, the marketplace for new ideas has greatly expanded even as unions have shrunk. Labor activists trying to reverse this trend are eager for information, insight, and inspiration that can aid the difficult task of rebuilding union organization. The challenges facing 16 million union members—and eight times as many unorganized workers—are the product of past workplace struggles, won and lost, and powerful economic and political forces. While much union education still focuses on training shop stewards, local officers, and union staffers to handle grievances, negotiate contracts, and organize new members, many activists realize they need to think critically and analytically about "the big picture" in their occupation, industry, and society. As British solidarity activist Eric Lee argues, trade unionists can even find out "what works and what doesn't" by studying "the experience of others in our globalized world."[1]

This collection of essays by a longtime "embedded" labor journalist reflects the search for answers that accelerated in the mid-1990s. John Sweeney's election as AFL-CIO president and defeat of the federation's old Cold War leadership markedly improved the intellectual climate in labor, while fostering a mini book-publishing boom. Since 1995, trade publishers like Houghton-Mifflin, Monthly Review Press, New Press, and Verso, plus university presses like Cornell, Princeton, Temple, and Wayne State, have all issued collections of labor-related essays inspired by the AFL-CIO shake-up or published book-length assessments of the state of labor and the forces for change within it. One such title was Sweeney's own call to arms, *America Needs a Raise: Fighting for Economic Security and Social Justice.* Another contemporaneous volume, with multiple contributors, was inspired by the labor "teach-ins" organized by Scholars, Artists, and Writers for Social Justice (SAWSJ), a group of left-wing academics and public intellectuals previously estranged from the union officialdom. At its founding, SAWSJ hailed "the new wave of hope and energy surging through the AFL-CIO." It also pledged to support Sweeney's "New Voice" leadership with more campus solidarity activity, plus supportive research and writing on the "remobilization" of unions and the transformation of work in America.

As more trade unionists joined labor historians, sociologists, industrial relations experts and worker educators in a wide-ranging debate about new strategies for labor, additional books have appeared that highlight model campaigns. On my own bookshelf I can count nearly a dozen such titles, all containing case studies in how to "remake," "reshape," "revitalize," "reorganize," or "restructure" unions. Frustrated with the actual pace of these efforts, the Services Employees International Union (SEIU) and six allies broke with the AFL-CIO in 2005 and formed a new labor federation. This contentious development initially aroused great concern among some union-oriented academics around the country. Yet the public criticism (and self-criticism) aired in connection with the AFL-CIO split has now inspired a new round of publishing activity—just like Sweeney's own election did a decade before. Books appearing recently (several of which are reviewed herein) explore what went wrong with Sweeney's reform project and whether Change to Win offers a real alternative to it.

Long before this literature of change emerged in several recent waves, I must confess that I had my own nose buried in more than a few labor-related books. For me, reading has always been fun, not work—even when I've been paid to review a book that I would have read anyway. Writing about labor—and, more recently, what others have to say about that subject—has been a sideline of mine for thirty-five years. As a college student in the sixties, I initially turned to books on labor history to understand why most unions were "missing in action" from key political struggles of that era—for civil rights and peace in Vietnam. My own summertime job experience, in high school and college, had made me a grateful, well-paid member of the Retail Clerks International Union (a predecessor of the United Food and Commercial Workers today). But during my entire career as an unloader of trucks and stocker of shelves for the A&P Company, not once did I ever meet a shop steward or receive any information about the union. (Even my RCIU initiation fee was paid to the store manager!) After college, when I was serving as Vermont Field Secretary for the American Friends Service Committee, I had my first encounter with a real workers' organization—the independent United Electrical Radio and Machine Workers (UE), then the largest industrial union in the state. My early 1970s contact with the UE introduced me to some hardy left-wing survivors of McCarthyism and a heritage more inspiring than mainstream labor's. (In the first section of this collection, the broader cross-generational encounter between New Left and old, in labor, is explored at greater length.)

I got my first union staff job—as a reporter for the *United Mine Workers Journal*—while completing law school in Washington, D.C. At the UMW, I had the privilege of working with and learning from Don Stillman (later a UAW editor and ghostwriter for Doug Fraser), Matt Witt, and Earl Dotter on a publication uniquely enlivened by the 1972 election victory of Miners for Democracy (MFD), a pioneering reform group. While writing for coal miners, I first encountered the two cardinal rules of business unionism: "Thou shall not criticize another union," and its even more important corollary, "Thou shall not meddle in the internal affairs of another union." In large part due to my experience with the miners' reform movement (and its later counterparts in steel and trucking), I became a repeat violator of both commandments for the next three decades.

My initial infraction, which created a minor uproar involving the United Steel Workers of America (USWA), was the product of mere naïveté. In 1975, I was writing a *Journal* column called "Labor Letter," which informed miners about important developments in other unions. It struck me as particularly newsworthy that a young dissident named Ed Sadlowski had just won a federally supervised union election (much like the MFD's), making him the new director of USWA's 130,000-member Chicago-Gary District 31. (My editorial judgment was influenced by the covert role played by *Journal* editor Stillman in producing Eddie's campaign literature.) The resulting upbeat item in "Labor Letter" asserted that Sadlowski had campaigned successfully against "union corruption, election fraud, and dues increases." According to no less a labor expert than me (at age twenty-five), Sadlowski's victory provided "new encouragement to rank-and-filers throughout the labor movement who were struggling for union democracy and reform."

Needless to say, this bit of reporting (and editorializing) was not well received by I. W. Abel, then president of the USWA, or other members of his International Executive Board, to which Brother Sadlowski was a most unwelcome addition. When a copy of the *Journal* reached Pittsburgh, Abel's office called UMW president Arnold Miller to complain. With complete candor and typical befuddlement, Miller professed ignorance of this journalistic faux pas, claiming truthfully that he was not a close reader of the publication in question. Not satisfied with Miller's response, the Steelworkers' Board then adopted and sent the UMW a formal resolution of condemnation. This document called my article a threat to "the historic relationship" between mine and mill workers, which dated all the way back to the mid-1930s, when UMW money and foot soldiers helped organize "basic steel" for the CIO. I was impressed, beyond words, by the power of the pen in the labor movement. Had I really torn asunder, with a mere four paragraphs, what the great John L. Lewis had personally wrought thirty years before?

Later in the 1970s—after assisting Sadlowski's unsuccessful but exciting campaign to succeed Abel—I became an organizer and legal advisor for Teamster dissidents. My duties included editing *The PROD Dispatch*, national newspaper of the Professional Drivers Council. (The mission of that feisty rag is still carried on by *The Convoy-Dispatch*, a product of the 1979 merger between PROD and Teamsters for a Democratic Union; see www.tdu.org, for the latest online edition.) Like TDU's newspaper today, the *Dispatch* had thousands of Teamster road driver readers. Mixed in with more typical articles about truck safety, Teamster corruption, and violations of the National Master Freight Agreement were some of my first labor book reviews. To this day, I have no idea how many PROD members, after reading these pieces, then proceeded to order books by authors like Trotskyist Farrell Dobbs, the famous Teamster organizer and 1934 Minneapolis general strike leader.[2] But at *The PROD Dispatch*—unlike official IBT publications—we tried to keep the rank and file informed about books that might add to their understanding of Teamster history, strike strategy, union politics, and pension fund management.

In 1980, I began my long tour of active duty as a Boston-based organizer and international representative for the Communications Workers of America (CWA). Twenty-seven years later, when I left CWA to work as a full-time writer, I was serving as an assistant to the vice president of 175,000-member CWA District One, which covers eight states. This meant I was in charge of education programs, organizing coordination, the district newsletter, and international solidarity in CWA's largest region. While serving as a Boston-based staffer for CWA, I wrote—in my spare time—nearly 300 articles, columns, essays, reviews, or op-ed pieces about workplace trends, labor politics and culture, organizing and bargaining, strikes, and union democracy struggles. This freelance work appeared in major metropolitan dailies, liberal and left-wing magazines, official and unofficial labor publications, academic journals, and as chapters in five or six books. The pieces collected and reedited for this book thus represent a small fraction of a much larger clipping pile—from *The Nation, The Progressive, In These Times, The Guardian, Mother Jones, American Prospect, Z Magazine, Labor History, New Politics, The Progressive Populist, New Labor Forum, Social Policy, Labor Notes, WorkingUSA, Labor Research Review, Monthly Labor Review, Technology Review, Boston Review, Socialism and Democracy, The Guild Reporter, Tikkun, CounterPunch, The Boston Globe, Boston Herald, New York Times, Washington Post, Los Angeles Times, Newsday, Wall Street Journal, Christian Science Monitor, Philadelphia Inquirer, USA Today, Toronto Globe & Mail,* and *The Berkshire Eagle* (among others).

Embedded with Organized Labor combines two genres—"literary journalism" and (because of my embedded condition) "participatory journalism" as well. Both are more familiar to readers in highbrow cultural settings than "The House of Labor." Literary journalism, in its normal milieu, tends to be a low-status form of writing. That's why even such a renowned practitioner as George Orwell (who was no slouch as a participatory journalist either) once complained that "the prolonged, indiscriminate reviewing of books is an exceptionally thankless, irritating, and exhausting job."[3] Within the labor movement, I've found that readers tend to make fewer status distinctions about anything in print. Book chat—not to mention different categories of non-fiction—is rarely part of the day-to-day "discourse" of union grievance handlers and contract negotiators. So, to many of my fellow trade unionists, any book review, op-ed piece, Sunday feature article, or business page column appearing in the *Boston Globe* was always indistinguishable from a "letter to the editor." The most common feedback I've received over the years on my *Globe* freelancing was the remark, "Hey, I liked your letter in the paper the other day." This minor bit of reader confusion notwithstanding, I've always been gratified by any reader response, pro or con. Orwell notwithstanding, I've personally found reviewing to be a useful contribution to general labor commentary, most of which comes from academics or the remaining handful of full-time labor reporters.

As noted above, sympathetic sociologists, historians, economists, political scientists, labor relations professors, and "working-class studies" experts have produced almost all of the recent books about unions. Some of these writers once did hands-on union work themselves and a few even held blue-collar jobs. But, at some point in their life, they decided to distance themselves from the day-to-day labor-management fray and pursue quieter university-based careers instead (although, in their academic mode, some have become quite active faculty union members). In contrast, everything in this collection was written by someone who remained a full-time "union practitioner." If there's criticism of other unions or the behavior of fellow trade unionists in the book—and there's plenty of that in some sections—it's never in the form of potshots from the sidelines or "Monday morning quarterbacking" from an ivory tower.

In my freelance journalism, I've always tried to draw on the lessons learned during my continuing education as an organizer, negotiator, contract campaign coordinator, and strike strategist for CWA. Actually handling workers' grievances, dealing with their employers, training shop stewards, and recruiting new members keeps you rooted in practice, rather than becoming facile with prescription. From years of personal involvement with embattled local unions, I know what it's like to be part of a team—often not in the best organizational shape—taking the field against corporate adversaries displaying all the speed, bulk, and aggressiveness of first-round NFL draft picks. Writing and talking about how the game should be played is not the same as playing in it—and never will be.

If there's any other bias on display in this book, it reflects my experience in 1970s struggles for union democracy and reform.[4] Thanks to my subsequent CWA career, I was able to develop an insider's view of the difficulty of institutional change within national unions, while maintaining a not-always-popular connection to various "dissidents" (i.e., Teamsters for a Democratic Union, Labor Notes, the Association for Union Democracy, UAW New Directions et al.). This insider/outsider perspective has helped me identify in a personal way with the risks workers take when they stand up for their rights on the job. It has also given me an appreciation of the price that some trade unionists have paid for challenging the leadership of their own unions. Without a doubt, my particular background made me a stronger believer in union democracy than most staff members of CWA, a union with a better record in this area than many other AFL-CIO or CTW affiliates.

Let me end this Introduction with a brief summary of the book's structure:

Part 1, "Labor and the Left, Old and New," focuses on twentieth-century labor activists or organizations, whose work provided the historical backdrop for organizers, with a similar left-wing orientation, who came of age politically in the 1960s or 1970s.

Part 2, "Race, Class, and Gender," deals with the intersection of race, class, and gender in American labor, past and present.

Part 3, "Voices of Dissent and Reform," covers the period of hope, opportunity, and, in some cases, disappointment following the election of John Sweeney as AFL-CIO president in 1995.

Part 4, "Workers' Rights and Wrongs," assesses the state of American labor law—and union efforts to use or change it—via an examination of books by historian Nelson Lichtenstein and labor attorneys Tom Geoghegan, Lance Compa, Bob Schwartz, and William Gould, former chairman of the National Labor Relations Board.

In Part 5, "Organizing in the Global Village," we learn how union responses to immigration, foreign military intervention, trade deregulation, and corporate globalization have changed for the better in recent years, due to pressure from below and the need for real labor internationalism. This section also illustrates the importance of alternative organizational models—whether in the form of the cross-border solidarity networks described by Kim Moody, David Bacon, and Robert Ross or the immigrant worker initiatives studied or assisted by Janice Fine, Jennifer Gordon, Manny Ness, and Biju Mathew.

Part 6, "Changing to Win," examines the controversial 2005 split at the top of organized labor in the United States. It was precipitated by SEIU president Andy Stern, who soon faced growing opposition within his own union, a development analyzed in this section as well.[5]

Much of the writing collected here would never have made it into print initially if it were not for the existence of independent journals, on the left and in the labor movement. The challenge confronting these publications is not unlike that faced by labor-oriented authors, many of whom have engaged in heroic exercises in self-marketing to connect with even a few working-class readers. (For more on successful book promotion strategies, see the Afterword to this collection.) To survive, much less grow at a time when even daily newspapers with deep pockets are contracting, the alternative press needs more paid subscribers and/or institutional financial backing from sympathetic unions. At many of these publications (and several mainstream dailies as well), there are past or present editors to whom I am indebted for their commissioning of material contained in this book.

I would particularly like to thank Manny Ness at *WorkingUSA*; Paula Finn, Steve Fraser, and Sherry Linkon at *New Labor Forum*; JoAnn Wypijewski, Art Winslow and Adam Schatz, former editors at *The Nation*; Matt Rothschild at *The Progressive*; Andy Zipser at *The Guild Reporter*; Victor Wallis at *Socialism and Democracy*; David Finkel and Diane Feeley at *Against the Current*; Mike Schaeffer, former book review editor at the *Philadelphia Inquirer*; Lydia Sargent at *Z Magazine*; Yoshie Furuhashi at *MRzine*; Alex Cockburn and Jeffrey St. Clair at *CounterPunch*; Jim Green and Leon Fink at *Labor*; Julius and Phyllis Jacobson, former editors, and Marvin and Betty Mandel, current editors, at *New Politics*; Dave Denison at *American Prospect*; Amy Gluckman from

Dollars & Sense, Lorraine Endicott at *Our Times* in Canada, Michelle Osborn, former business section editor, at *USA Today*, and Chris Chinlund, former Focus editor of *The Boston Globe*. In addition, Mike Eisenscher at Solidarity Information Services, Chris Spannos at Znet, Eric Lee and Roy Nitzberg at LabourStart, Paul Garver and Stuart Elliott at Talking Union, Steve Zeltzer at LaborNet, Tony Budek at *CL News*, Jerry Tucker at The Center for Labor Renewal, and the moderators at Portside and Labor Portside have been most helpful with Internet recycling of my labor journalism.

Keeping a sixty-year-old socialist magazine afloat, and a left-wing publishing house as well, is a double challenge that has long been met by the dedicated, resourceful editorial staff and board members of *Monthly Review* and Monthly Review Press. As someone born in the same year as *MR*, who spent his youth playing sandlot baseball just a line drive away from the Larchmont and Mamaroneck, New York, homes of Marxist economist and *Monthly Review* founder Paul Sweezy, I feel like I grew up around the magazine (even before I knew it existed). In college, I found it an invaluable tool for understanding an economic system that continues to wage war on workers, at home and abroad. Forty years later, I am deeply grateful for the help received, on this book project, from Michael Yates, Martin Paddio, and Scott Borchert.

Last but not least (among indispensable publications) is *Labor Notes*. For three decades, this Detroit-based newsletter has been publishing all the news (and opinion) that the official labor press doesn't see fit to print. I've been a *Labor Notes* editorial advisory committee member or contributor since 1979. *Labor Notes* ran several of the pieces contained in this collection, and many others over the years. It has always been a pleasure to work with *LN* activists, writers, and editors like Jim West, Jane Slaughter, Kim Moody, Mike Parker, Martha Gruelle, Marsha Niemeijer, Chris Kutalik, Dan LaBotz, Mark Brenner, Mischa Gaus, Tiffany Ten Eyck, Paul Abowd, and all the others who have toiled in the "Plywood Palace" that *Labor Notes* shares with TDU in Detroit. For more information about *Labor Notes* and its crucial work, see www.labornotes.org.

In and around CWA, my extracurricular scribbling has long benefited from the feedback and input of my longtime friends (and sometime coauthors), Larry Cohen and Rand Wilson. My past writing about the Teamsters (and some work in this volume) reflects regular "reality checks" with TDU National Organizer Ken Paff, who has done more than anyone else to change the IBT over the past thirty-five years. Cal Winslow has been a valued co-worker in recent solidarity activity involving reformers within SEIU and efforts to preserve the history of rank-and-file movements of the 1970s. Paul Poulos, Ellen David-Friedman, and Torie Osborn have been continuing collaborators since that era as well. My many other brothers and sisters in struggle—from CWA, IBEW, the Teamsters, SEIU, Jobs With Justice, et al.—are no less important but far too numerous to list without missing somebody, so I'm not going to even try. You know who you are—and how this author's organizational work and labor-related writing was deeply enriched and/or greatly aided by our mutual association. Finally, I want to thank my wife, Suzanne Gordon— the "real writer" in the house—for her three decades of encouragement and support, plus our daughters, Alex and Jess, for carrying on, in their own ways, a nuclear family tradition of labor solidarity and activism, at home and abroad.

PART ONE

LABOR AND THE LEFT, OLD AND NEW

The eight chapters in this section focus on twentieth-century labor activists or organizations, whose work provided the historical backdrop for organizers with a similar left-wing orientation who came of age politically in the 1960s and '70s. The impact of this generational cohort on American unions is the subject of a work-in-progress (for Cornell ILR Press). It will recount the personal and political stories of "68-ers" who went into labor after being radicalized in the antiwar, feminist, civil rights, or black power movements. Almost all the essay/reviews here deal with biographies, autobiographies, or collections of autobiographical writings by earlier left-wing laborites, some of whom had an insider/outsider relationship to the labor movement similar to my own, thus arousing my interest in learning more about them while retelling their stories to others. Part 1 addresses the political challenges or personal dilemmas faced by union radicals whose courage, creativity, or tenacity remain worthy of emulation today, particularly by younger activists now being recruited from campuses or community groups. In this section, we meet men and women who campaigned for the Knights of Labor, Industrial Workers of the World, the Congress of Industrial Organizations, the Communist and Socialist Parties or various Trotskyist factions. Among the unions they built—or tried to change—were the United Mine Workers, Electrical Workers, Auto Workers, Oil, Chemical and Atomic Workers,

Longshoreman, Teachers, and District 1199, the organization of New York City hospital workers now affiliated with SEIU. Several essays also trace the strange trajectories of groups or individuals associated with the extreme left and right wings of the "labor left." Their histories are described humorously but with less no fondness or admiration.

From Rebel Pens to Pencil Hands

In the mid-1970s, I did a story for the *United Mine Workers Journal* about coal miners who'd been fired and blacklisted for union organizing in eastern Kentucky. One of the unemployed UMW supporters I visited, along with *Journal* photographer Earl Dotter, lived in a creek-side trailer at the end of a small hollow, accessible only by a narrow, winding mountain road. When Dotter and I arrived at this miner's house, we introduced ourselves and explained our mission. He greeted us politely but with a hint of wariness. As we shook hands, he looked me in the eye and said, knowingly, "Ah, pencil hands." I was taken aback by his observation but had to admit it was accurate. Our host had the hands of an experienced coal digger, rough and calloused from his years underground. My own, in contrast, were unmarked by hard physical labor of any kind—a sure sign that I was from an office in Washington, D.C., far removed from the blue-collar world of Appalachian mining.

To its credit, the *UMW Journal* of that era sought far greater connection to the membership than most union newspapers because it was the product of Miners for Democracy, a successful rank-and-file reform movement. In 1975, the *Journal* even won a National Magazine Award for its aggressive investigative reporting on workplace hazards and wide-ranging coverage of community issues in Appalachia—the only time that a labor publication has ever been so honored. Yet, as the Kentucky miner's remark indicated to me, there's still a big gap—even under the best of circumstances—between those who labor and those who write about labor. It's a cultural and political divide that has only widened in the intervening decades, as labor journalism has atrophied in the mass media, and union publications have abandoned the crusading role played by the labor press during the late nineteenth century and first half of the twentieth—a tradition revived ever so briefly, in the 1970s, by the *Journal*.

As *Washington Post* reporter Frank Swoboda has noted in his own union newspaper, *The Guild Reporter*, "The dwindling economic impact and shrinking membership of American trade unions has consigned the labor beat to the fringes of newspaper coverage."[1] Fifty years ago, there were still scores of labor editors and reporters, many from working-class backgrounds themselves, who specialized in the subject of unions, contract negotiations, strikes, and industrial relations generally. Today, "labor news"—such as it is—tends to be buried in the "business pages" of major dailies. White-collar workplace trends, as defined by newsroom Yuppies, receive far more ink than shop-floor struggles by blue-collar workers or even the activities of the institutional labor movement. There are only a few remaining experienced labor reporters (like Tom Robbins at the *Village Voice* or Richard Steier at *The Chief*) and virtually no labor-oriented columnists with the exception of Juan Gonzalez at the New York *Daily News*.

The dearth of labor coverage in the mainstream media leaves an informational and ideological void that should be filled by a vibrant union-backed or independent labor press. Unfortunately, official union publications—with a potential readership of millions—don't offer much of an alternative. Instead, most function merely as house organs—and, at their worst, as a "vanity press" for the union officialdom. Even when union newspapers today undergo glossy makeovers to improve their readability—or their contents get posted on a website—such changes tend to be "more cosmetic than substantive" and a "triumph of public relations values over journalistic ones," according to Andy Zipser, editor of *The Guild Reporter* and a leading critic of the labor press. Says Zipser: "We should be writing about real people dealing with real conflicts, both inside our union and out, so that, when working people see one of our publications, they see themselves and understand that we are writing about them too." Instead, much "coverage of issues . . . remains safely antiseptic" and driven by the "leadership agenda." Rarely does a union "actually want a crusading labor editor roiling the waters."[2]

Controversial topics and unfettered criticism have thus been relegated to outlets with limited circulation. Among them are the Detroit-based newsletter, *Labor Notes*; magazines with a largely academic or union staff readership such as *Working USA*, *New Labor Forum*, or *Labor Studies Journal*; and those few left-wing journals of opinion—*The Nation*, *The Progressive*, *In These Times*, *Against the Current*, or *Z Magazine*—which continue to publish labor journalism by modern practitioners like David Moberg, David Bacon, Jane Slaughter, Liza Featherstone, Esther Kaplan, or JoAnne Wypijewski. (The dean of this small school may be the feisti-est of them all—Harry Kelber, who self-published an I. F. Stone–style newsletter called *The Labor Educator* into his early nineties and then switched to Internet distribution of his still trenchant commentaries on the shortcomings of the AFL-CIO.)

Dee Garrison's multi-volume excavation of the life and work of Mary Heaton Vorse and Elizabeth Faue's new biography of Eva Valesh remind us that labor writing once had a much higher profile in the popular press—in periods when working-class struggle commanded greater soci-etal attention. The now little-known "rebel pens" of Valesh and Vorse were deployed to great effect, in overlapping fashion, beginning in the 1880s and continuing until the late 1930s, from the heyday of the Knights of Labor to the triumph of the CIO. These four books by or about the two women provide a rich sampling of participatory labor journalism (or, in the case of Vorse's novel *Strike!*, fiction closely based on it). Both writers were activists as well as observers, plying their trade as part of working-class organizations or political parties that mounted serious challenges to the status quo of their day. Although Valesh was "the daughter of a workingman" and Vorse hailed from a wealthy New England family, they were, in their prime, equally "embedded" in the movements they wrote about.

Born Mary Eva McDonald in 1866, Valesh was the product of Minnesota labor radicalism, rooted in the Knights of Labor and, later, the Populists. After finishing high school, she apprenticed as a newspaper compositor and did her first writing for the Twin Cities' then-flourishing labor press. Like a nineteenth-century Barbara Ehrenreich, Valesh was soon hired by the *St. Paul Globe*, a daily newspaper, to do undercover reporting on working women who were the "Nickel and Dimed" of her time. This whistle-blowing series was published under the pen name Eva Gay, when she was only twenty-two. It "introduced readers to the lives of garment workers, laundresses, cigar-makers, seamstresses, domestics, operatives in woolen knitting mills and boot and shoe factories, telephone and telegraph operators, bookbinders, stenographers, and shop women." According to Faue, a professor of history at Wayne State, Valesh's "abili-ty to enter workplaces, accept positions, and conduct interviews depend-ed on workers' willingness to confide in her and keep her identity secret." The resulting newspaper accounts "helped to spark the interest of both labor advocates and middle-class reformers in helping the working girl." Her articles also "stressed that the appalling conditions under which most women worked were amenable to change"—if the "working girls" themselves took action on their own behalf.

They did just that at Shotwell's, one of the garment sweatshops that Valesh had infiltrated. When workers there struck in 1888, it was "the first of many labor conflicts in which she would play the role of instigator, organizer, and reporter." Valesh's involvement in the struggle led her to become an organizer for the Knights and labor editor of the *Globe*. She also published *A Tale of the Twin Cities*, a popular novel about the street car motorman's strike that convulsed all of Minneapolis and St. Paul in 1889. Like Vorse's fictional account of the labor war in Gastonia fifty years later, *Tale* was "the medium for a political message about the necessity of class solidarity and the increasingly vicious conflict between the classes."

The trajectory of Valesh's subsequent career not only overlapped with Vorse's but diverged from it as well. Valesh rose to prominence "as an authentic working-class voice" but she ended up using her labor writing and local acclaim as a public speaker—on behalf of the Eight Hour League, the Farmers' Alliance, and other causes—as a vehicle for upward social mobility, of the personal sort. As a journalist, she soon left the *Globe* behind for "more lucrative endeavors" at the *Minneapolis Tribune* and, later, at William Randolph Hearst's *New York Journal*. Along the way, she acquired and subsequently shed a husband, cigar maker Frank Valesh. Both became "key players in the transition of Twin Cities labor to the more prudential and conservative trade unionism" espoused by Samuel Gompers as an alternative to the Knights in the 1890s. In 1900, Valesh's alliance with the American Federation of Labor (AFL) president resulted in her becoming an AFL general organizer. At federation headquarters in Washington, she served as Gompers's "right-hand man," defying the gender conventions of her era. Working behind the scenes as the editor of the *American Federationist* for the next decade—a role for which her boss claimed public credit—Valesh experienced the frustration of union headquarters wordsmiths ever since. Her "assigned duties were almost always performed in the shadow of the great man" (who considered the *Federationist* to be his "personal organ").

Valesh's association with Gompers put her in the orbit of the National Civil Federation. The NCF was an early twentieth-century vehicle for labor-management cooperation that Eugene Debs once described as "a beast of prey, which tells its victims, 'our interests are one,' and then devours them." For Valesh, it opened doors to an "elite network" of "wealthy club women and patrons." She quickly became a popular speaker in their social and political circles, acting as "an important link between the organized working-class and upper-middle-class activists" who wanted to improve factory conditions. The contradictions between Valesh's labor movement roots and what Faue calls her "new class identity" became painfully clear during a massive left-led strike by female garment workers in New York City. Offering her services to the reform-minded Women's Trade Union League, Valesh was put in charge of pickets and later served on the legal and publicity committees. She also helped organize "the Mink Brigade," a group of affluent female "picket-watchers" that was formed to stave off police brutality and "unwarranted arrests."

However, when the AFL brokered a settlement of the 1909 walkout, immigrant shirtwaist makers rejected the deal. Valesh condemned their decision, threatening to launch a "campaign against socialism" because it made "ignorant foreigners discontented, set them against the government, [and made] them want to tear it down." As Faue notes, Valesh's public denunciation of the strikers was "seen as a fundamental betrayal" and her labor career never recovered. On the rebound, she married Captain Benjamin Franklin Cross, "a broker on the cotton exchange and the playboy son of a wealthy Rhode Island family." Together, they retired to a farm in upstate New York and lived, for the next fifteen years, off his mother's money, while Valesh edited the *American Club Woman*, a journal for Progressive Era women's club members.

Despite her more privileged background, Vorse—in contrast—maintained her commitment to labor radicalism, a cause she did not embrace until she was already thirty-eight, the single mother of two children, and a well-known writer of "light romantic fiction." Vorse was a former art student who had been disinherited by her family for her bohemian tendencies. By 1912, she had become a leading denizen of Greenwich Village and an activist in the suffrage and women's peace movements, a founding editor of *The Masses*, and one of the founders of the Provincetown Players. What transformed her career was her involvement in the "Bread and Roses" strike—a largely spontaneous uprising by 25,000 immigrant textile workers in Lawrence, Massachusetts, aided by the Industrial Workers of the World (IWW). When that 1912 walkout began, Vorse reported, only a few millhands belonged to any union, radical or conservative; it was "not their strike . . . but the indignant expression of people who considered their wages had been cut below the living point." Out-of-town IWW organizers, including Big Bill Haywood, immediately

began to organize all of the textile workers into one great industrial
union. . . . Arrayed against the strikers, along with the mill owners, the
militia, and the police, were the officials of the Textile Union of New
England and the Central Labor Union of Lawrence. The American
Federation of Labor in Washington was also hostile, seeing in the ideal of
labor solidarity that was being preached at Lawrence an attack on craft
unionism. But it was a message which appealed strongly to the diverse
mass of men and women who made up the strikers, and it held them.

After Lawrence, Vorse managed to be at the scene of every major
union dispute for the next quarter of a century. On the labor beat, she
freelanced for mainstream dailies, mass circulation magazines, left-wing
journals, and labor publications—once even covering the same strike for
the *New York Globe* and the *Blast*, an anarchist paper. (It's hard to imagine any leftist today—with the possible exception of Ehrenreich—simultaneously writing for periodicals as diverse as *Cosmopolitan, McCall's,
Good Housekeeping, Harper's, Atlantic Monthly, The New Republic,* and
The Nation!) Thanks to the editorial work of Garrison, a history professor at Rutgers, *Rebel Pen* contains a vivid collection of Vorse's frontline
dispatches from around the country, many of which were distributed in
the 1930s by Federated Press, a labor news service.

Vorse's association with the IWW continued prior to World War I,
when she worked with its leading female organizer, Elizabeth Gurley
Flynn, during an iron ore miners strike in the Mesabi range of Minnesota.
In 1919, she served in Pittsburgh as a volunteer publicist for the nationwide work stoppage by 350,000 steelworkers led by William Z. Foster. As
an organizer for the Amalgamated Clothing Workers in 1920, she rallied
workers and exposed conditions in shirt factories in eastern
Pennsylvania. Throughout the 1920s, she covered the rank-and-file
insurgencies of coal miners attempting to overthrow the autocratic regime
of UMW President John L. Lewis. In 1926, she wrote about the "War in
Passaic"—a Communist-led textile workers' strike in New Jersey that featured the same police beatings, restrictions on free speech and public
assembly, and virulent red-baiting that Vorse had witnessed in Lawrence.

In 1929, she followed the southern wave of textile mill walkouts to the
Piedmont region of North Carolina, scene of the doomed uprising against
"industrial feudalism" so movingly described in *Strike!* In both this novel
about Gastonia and the reporting collected in *Rebel Pen,* Vorse captures
the behind-the-scenes tensions among radical organizers sent from the

North to support strikers faced with mass evictions from company housing, vigilante attacks on their tent colony, murder and conspiracy indictments, and the hostile intervention of the National Guard. When the Depression started, she covered militant protests by the Unemployed Councils and their national "Hunger March" on Washington in 1932. That same year, she was part of a delegation of New York authors and intellectuals that was run out of Harlan County, Kentucky, by sheriff's deputies trying to block supplies from reaching embattled members of the National Miners' Union.

Vorse returned to the "Steel Valley" in 1936 to cover the successful organizing drives of the Steel Workers Organizing Committee (SWOC) and was injured during the shooting of union pickets at Republic Steel in Youngstown. In February 1937 she was in Flint, Michigan, where her dispatches on the sitdowners' struggle against General Motors highlighted the crucial role played by the UAW's "women's auxiliary," with its "babies and banners." *Rebel Pen* also describes the terrifying mob violence unleashed against Victor Reuther and local UAW supporters during an organizing skirmish in Anderson, Indiana, right after the union's victory in Flint. In that gun battle, Vorse almost lost her son, Heaton, a Federated Press stringer who was badly wounded yet ended up being charged with trespassing and riot.

Despite her personal involvement in many of these fights, Vorse's writing was notably "free of political dogma and strident rhetoric"—in contrast to what Garrison calls "the crude *Daily Worker* style of harangues and exaggerations." She let the facts—and the workers—speak for themselves in her work, particularly in the pieces written for non-labor audiences. Despite considerable qualms about the behavior of the CP in some of the struggles she covered, Vorse, to her credit, "refused to publicly bait the Communist rank and file in the union trenches." According to Garrison,

> She never confused the embattled labor activist, many of whom were women, with the Communist office functionary, or the carping bystander, most of whom were men. She cared little for abstraction. She judged people by what they did, not by what they said, by their action, not their theory. She always understood the distinction between the immense club of official power and the tiny barb of the radical few.

Unfortunately, labor journalism—the field in which Vorse made her name—"effectively expired with the end of the great labor wars" and the onset of McCarthyism. In the 1950s, Vorse was forced into "semi-retire-ment." *Rebel Pen* contains only three articles from that decade and, reflect-ing the changing times, one of them deals with union corruption. Titled "The Pirates' Nest of New York," this 1952 piece from *Harper's* was an account of wildcat strikes that challenged "mob rule" and labor-manage-ment collusion on the waterfront. It was the last story she did that received any national attention.

In her final years, Vorse slipped into penurious obscurity while living in Provincetown, Massachusetts, on Cape Cod. There, she opposed the Vietnam War and supported local environmental causes until her death at age ninety-one in 1965. Valesh's period of withdrawal from public life was even more protracted before she died at ninety in 1956. After divorcing her debt-ridden second husband in the mid-1920s, she was unable or unwilling to resume a career in journalism. At age fifty-eight, she renewed her Typographical Union card and spent the remainder of her working life correcting galley proofs at the *New York Times*.

A modern reader who revisits the life and work of both women is struck by the richness of the material available to them as fiction and non-fiction writers. The American labor scene of the late nineteenth and early twentieth centuries was far more lively, dramatic, and political than it is today, albeit more chaotic and dangerous as well. Working-class struggles not only proved inspirational for workers themselves, they also raised "artistic consciousness" and fired the imagination of journalists and nov-elists. Between 1930 and 1934, the Gastonia strike alone was the subject of five other novels in addition to Vorse's (including one by Sherwood Anderson), a literary trend not much in evidence today amid a steady decline in strike activity. That's not to say, however, that modern labor relations is so lacking in confrontation and color that it's no longer of interest or concern to any serious writer outside of academic circles. At least one well-known author—the novelist and former newspaper reporter Barbara Kingsolver—produced an excellent 1983 book, *Holding the Line: The Great Arizona Mine Strike*, about the role of women in the Phelps-Dodge walkout.

For those still trying to bring workers' sacrifices and struggles, victo-ries and defeats, to life on the printed page, the challenge of labor journal-ism remains what it was in Valesh and Vorse's day. Labor-oriented writers should, in Garrison's words, seek to "faithfully render the messy com-plexities of human ideals and behavior" within the working class, "while also imparting a vision of a better, more democratic and egalitarian future." The pallid institutional propaganda put out by most unions today—plus their skimpy mainstream media coverage—usually does neither. So there's plenty of room for experimentation and improvement by new literary or journalistic voices. Whether they arise on the left or, better yet, from within the ranks of labor, let's hope they can soon revive the proud tradition of writing with a "rebel pen."

FROM CRIMSON TO COAL SEAM

I first heard about Powers Hapgood while working at the union he had tried to change fifty years earlier. The "Save the Union" movement in the United Mine Workers, which Hapgood and other left-wingers organized in 1926, did not succeed in toppling then-UMW president John L. Lewis. But, in the early 1970s, rank-and-filers campaigning under the banner of "Miners for Democracy" defeated his successor—the even more despotic W. A. "Tony" Boyle. Backing this new UMW reform effort was an energetic group of college-educated "outsiders" who, like Hapgood, were drawn to the miners' struggle because of its potential for triggering a broader transformation of organized labor and coalfield communities. The more radical among them took jobs in the mines, as did Hapgood, despite his Harvard pedigree. Others were propelled by the MFD victory directly into UMW staff positions, where union politics was also a severe, if less physically demanding, test for even the most committed idealist.

In the seventies, as in the twenties, almost every UMW battle with the coal operators had an internecine aspect. Loyalists to Boyle quickly regrouped and tried to undermine the new MFD leaders. The latter fell out among themselves, adding to the factionalism, infighting, and red-baiting. A growing wildcat strike movement in the coalfields—over unresolved workplace problems—put the reformers in the uncomfortable position of trying to curb the militancy of members frustrated with the pace of change. Despite the MFD's success in democratizing the union, many of the hopes and expectations it initially aroused were never fulfilled. A decade after the group's election win, almost none of the progressives associated with it— either as "colonizers" in the mines or appointed staffers—were still active in the UMW (although some went on to other unions).

It's too bad that Robert Bussel's excellent new biography of Powers Hapgood wasn't available sooner to help put their experience in historical perspective. A former trade unionist now employed as a labor educator, Bussel has both an academic's ability to scour the archives and an activist's feel for the real-life context of his subject. His book traces Hapgood's personal and political odyssey from a privileged WASP family to the coal mines of western Pennsylvania and then active engagement in some of the most high-profile labor struggles of the twenties, thirties and forties. A peripatetic organizer and frequent *Nation* contributor, Hapgood had a Zelig-like ability to be at or near the center of the action— whether in the UMW, the Socialist party, Sacco and Vanzetti defense campaign, Congress of Industrial Organizations (CIO) sit-downs, New Deal labor politics, or postwar conflict over reds and racism within unions.

Throughout it all, he was an unusually perceptive and self-critical participant/observer. His private journals represent, in Bussel's view, "a rich chronicle of the American working class, the labor movement, and the practice of radical politics." Heavily mined by the author, these diaries record Hapgood's "interactions with intellectuals, workers, labor leaders, and managers as he attempted to make sense of his experience and adapt to the changing cultural and political circumstances that occurred during his career." Hapgood's career reflected many of the same hopes and frustrations experienced by other labor leftists, before and since. He continually chafed at the institutional constraints imposed on him by a union movement whose economic and political agenda was far more limited than his own. Yet, during his various stints as a "freelance agitator," Hapgood often felt marginalized and ineffective because he was cut off from the resources, legitimacy, and popular base that only mass organizations can provide. His biggest compromise came in the mid-thirties, when he reconciled with Lewis, his onetime archenemy in the UMW. This permitted him to play an active role in the great organizing upsurge that built the CIO. However, within a few short years, "he found himself squeezed between the militancy of the workers, the demands of the wartime state, and the CIO leadership's increasing hesitation to offend the Roosevelt Administration."

Hapgood was, in short, someone who never stopped trying to reconcile the demands of his own conscience with the sometimes conflicting dictates of organizational policy and the day-to-day pressures of trade union work. While rooted in a particular era, his story is nevertheless relevant, as Bussel points out, to "succeeding generations of intellectuals . . . who have looked to the working class and the labor movement . . . [for] political fulfillment"—only to be "inspired and confounded." *From Harvard to the Ranks of Labor* should be required reading for the young Ivy Leaguers (and other recent college graduates) now being hired as organizers by several national unions. It might also stimulate some useful reflection among former sixties radicals who have, from their impressive new perches in the AFL-CIO, been promoting this student recruitment.

When Hapgood finished Harvard in 1920 (after prepping for it at Andover), he was an unlikely convert to union activism. He hadn't been a student radical or a critic of his own generation's imperialist war. His father was a boss, president of Columbia Conserve Company, an Indiana cannery widely hailed for its worker-ownership plan. Not surprisingly, Hapgood's background made him far more sympathetic toward Progressive Era experiments in labor-management cooperation than working-class struggle. His views began to change during a postgraduate tour of the West. There he met Wobblies, worked in a Montana mine, and joined the UMW. His initial stint underground led to a job researching hazardous conditions in the Pennsylvania coalfields, where he formed a lifelong friendship with John Brophy, a UMW district official who became his most influential mentor. Sixteen years Hapgood's senior, Brophy was a class-conscious, self-educated immigrant from Britain who cultivated ties with urban intellectuals and rallied the rank and file around demands for nationalization of the mines and democratization of the national union. Brophy's nemesis (and soon, Hapgood's as well) was John L. Lewis.

In his 1920s incarnation, the UMW president was autocratic, conservative, and very reluctant to confront the open-shop trend then developing in the coal industry. Brophy, on the other hand, took a hard-line approach in a walkout by more than 500,000 miners in 1922. This sixteen-month struggle provided Hapgood with his first and most formative strike experience. Sent by Brophy to Somerset County, Pennsylvania—a hotbed of UMW activity—Hapgood helped workers and their families resist injunctions, jailings, brutal evictions, and baton charges by the "coal and iron police." Because of these sacrifices (and Hapgood's impassioned PR work in liberal journals), the coal miner "achieved iconographic status, both as a symbol of an oppressed working class and as an agent capable of reforming an unjust economic system." Lewis, however, was not yet ready to buck that system. A "ruthless pragmatist," he ended the dispute with a settlement that failed to extend the union's national contract to the non-union miners who had joined the strike. Brophy, Hapgood, and other militants denounced this as a betrayal, launching a "Save the Union" movement to support Brophy's run against Lewis for the UMW presidency. Lewis had a formidable political machine that counted votes as deftly as it cut deals with employers. Marred by fraud and intimidation, the election ended in bitter defeat for the insurgents. Hapgood in particular was demonized as a radical disrupter and a tool of the Communist Party (to which he did not belong). Both he and Brophy were driven out of the UMW and forced, at one point, to seek work at the "model company" run by Hapgood's father.

Hapgood then spent several years at loose ends. He took up Socialist Party work, aided the defense of Sacco and Vanzetti, campaigned for civil liberties and workers' rights, and tried unsuccessfully to get back into mining (from which he had been blacklisted by labor and management). As a "lone wolf crying in the wilderness," he reached the low point of his career just as the Depression revived labor militancy and the election of Franklin Roosevelt created the conditions for successful mass organizing of industrial workers. This sea change passed others by in the American Federation of Labor, but not John L. Lewis. The UMW leader first used FDR's National Industrial Recovery Act to rebuild his own union. Then, in 1935, fearing that a historic opportunity was being squandered, he broke with labor's old guard over the role of his newly formed Committee for Industrial Organization (predecessor to the Congress). Lewis also knew that the CIO needed experienced organizers, including CP members and former dissidents in his own union like Brophy, Hapgood, and Adolph Germer. (When asked privately why he was hiring such people, Lewis told his associates to remember "Who gets the bird, the hunter or the dog?") Hapgood and many other former Lewis critics responded to the CIO's call for obvious reasons of their own: "Industrial unionism with its rallying message of inclusiveness, popular participation, and working-class power represented the kernels of a larger program that might yet be directed toward social transformation."

During the next few years, Hapgood was in the thick of many great victories. As an influential emissary of Lewis, he advised rubber and auto industry sit-down strikers in Akron and Flint and helped the United Electrical Workers win a key union-building fight at RCA in Camden, New Jersey. Bussel's biography also sheds light on Hapgood's role in several less successful but no less interesting ventures while he directed the CIO's Shoe Workers Organizing Committee. For anyone who thinks that the thirties were all about labor's "giant step" forward, it's instructive to read the book's detailed account of how a spirited strike by thousands of French-Canadian shoe workers in Maine was crushed by the combined efforts of management, local government, a hostile press, and the reactionary Catholic Church.

Hapgood was most in his element in strike situations, preferably ones that recalled his glory days among the miners in Somerset County. However, as Bussel observes, winning union recognition during the New Deal often involved "a delicate balancing act: ensuring that militancy did not degenerate into violence, staving off police intervention, attempting to maintain public sympathy, and defining union objectives in limited terms" to establish the organizational basis for future gains. The onetime union dissident "soon discovered the difficulty of reconciling his commitment to working-class mobilization with the complex demands of union leadership." According to the author, "The bureaucratic and managerial overtones of his new role distressed Hapgood. He feared that he was beginning to manipulate rather than mobilize workers, contradicting the democratic commitments that defined his political identity." Along with other radicals who were CIO functionaries, Hapgood came under pressure to keep his politics private. Sympathetic to Socialist Party presidential candidate Norman Thomas, Hapgood had little ability to promote SP critiques of the New Deal. ("We are all working for CIO unions but is our work helping socialism or not?" he wondered with good reason.) In the early forties, after being rejected for military service as a security risk, Hapgood was appointed CIO regional director in his home state of Indiana. There he helped organize black workers in the service sector and tried to find "alternatives to what he regarded as the pallid world of mature labor relations"—the "dense, legalistic system of industrial relations that was being cemented during World War II [which] threatened to erode the participatory activist orientation of the early industrial union movement."

Hapgood ended his career in tragic circumstances—alcoholic, unhappy, worn down by years of frenetic travel and high-pressure assignments. Nevertheless, he spent his final years resisting the creeping conservatism of postwar American unionism. He was an outspoken critic of discriminatory racial practices within labor, a stance that risked his local popularity. He also courageously resisted the CIO's first moves toward its eventual purge of left-led unions, fearing that "a new red scare would discredit all forces on the left, non-Communist and Communist alike, resulting in political sterility and conformism." Heavily red-baited himself, just as he had been in the twenties, he was forced out of his CIO post in 1948. Less than a year later, he was dead of a heart attack at forty-nine. Thanks to Bussel's skillful excavation and examination of Hapgood's life, his story didn't end there. It's now available for a new generation of labor activists to read and learn from. For any among them still struggling to reconcile loyalties to democratic socialist ideals and trade unionism, this book offers no simple answers or solutions. But it does suggest the need to find a middle way between selling out and dying so sadly.

RADICAL UNIONISM

When the Congress of Industrial Organizations (CIO) unleashed a great strike wave right after World War II, the United Electrical Radio and Machine Workers (UE) was its third-largest affiliate. It had a half-million members, contracts with corporate giants like General Electric and Westinghouse, and considerable political influence within the labor movement. Sixty years later, as battered as they are today, the two largest surviving CIO unions—the United Auto Workers and United Steelworkers—still represent more than 500,000 workers each. In contrast, the UE is down to 17,000. Belonging to neither the AFL-CIO nor its new rival, Change to Win, UE prefers to soldier on as a vital independent presence in a few states. In Illinois, for example, several hundred UE members made national news in late 2008 when they staged a dramatic six-day occupation of a factory. Their Chicago "sit-down"—triggered by a plant closing dispute—was hailed as the first industrial action of its kind since the late 1930s."

Despite its feistiness, the UE has, like most manufacturing unions, fared badly in the era of automation, globalization, and overseas outsourcing of production. Yet its decimation began long before capital flight weakened every industrial union from the 1970s onward and free trade nearly finished them all off in the last decade. Along with ten other unions representing more than one million workers, the left-led UE was forced out of the CIO in 1949. That purge, which predated the full-blown McCarthyism of the 1950s, became the opening shot in an internal war that left labor radicals on the run and the UE a shadow of its former self.

The story of the UE's rise in the 1930s, fall in the 1950s, and struggle to survive ever since has long been a favorite of portside labor history buffs. Two UE-friendly volumes—*Labor's Untold Story* by Richard Boyer and Herbert Morais and *Them and Us: Struggles of a Rank-and-File Union*, by UE national officer James Matles and journalist James Higgins—were required reading among student radicals who took a post-graduate plunge into blue-collar jobs and union politics three decades ago. Both books were also promoted within the UE to educate younger members about its distinctive heritage of struggle (and inoculate them against charges of "communist domination" that dogged the union from its inception).

In Matles and Higgins's account, the UE recognized—when few others in the CIO did—that the emergence of a "cold war" during the Truman administration and the first calls for a domestic anti-Communist crusade were linked to big business plans for expansion abroad and weakening of the National Labor Relations Act (NLRA) at home. Breaking ranks with the CIO, UE leaders refused to endorse Truman's reelection in 1948 and backed Henry Wallace's ill-fated third-party candidacy instead. They also tried to rally other union officials against signing affidavits denying membership in the Communist Party, as required by the 1947 Taft-Hartley Act, a crippling package of anti-union amendments to the NLRA.

The UE continued to resist the affidavit requirement and was punished by losing access to National Labor Relations Board (NLRB) representation elections and enforcement proceedings. Meanwhile, the CIO caved in to Taft-Hartley and then contributed to the growing anti-Red hysteria. Both its own affiliates and conservative craft unions from the American Federation of Labor (AFL) exploited UE's legal disability by raiding its membership. Like vultures, the UAW, USW, Teamsters, Machinists, and International Brotherhood of Electrical Workers wrested away many bargaining units, with the help of firms like GE who were only too happy to see their longtime nemesis ousted. During these inter-union conflicts, UE officers, local leaders, and active members were hauled before a variety of witch-hunting committees. Many rank-and-file militants were fired and blacklisted, plus burdensome criminal charges were lodged against UE officials. Due to the combined efforts of hostile employers, media red-baiters, congressional investigators, the FBI, and the International Union of Electrical Workers (IUE)—a right-wing replacement union chartered by the CIO—UE membership plummeted to 90,000 by the mid-1950s.

Amazingly, the union survived and even began to grow again, briefly, in the 1960s, while still clinging stubbornly to its independence. (All the other CIO affiliates kicked out nearly sixty years ago ceased to exist, were absorbed into larger unions by mergers, or, in the case of the West Coast Longshoremen's Union (ILWU), eventually rejoined the "house of labor" via affiliation with the AFL-CIO.) The UE continued to exhibit an unusual degree of internal democracy, emphasizing membership control over union finances and bargaining strategy. Until recently (due to the financial strain of annual conventions), elections for UE national officers were held every year, a rarity in the labor movement. To this day, no union official or staff member is paid more than the highest-paid workers in UE shops (to ensure, as Matles and Higgins explained, that full-time reps "feel *like* UE members" and not simply "feel *for* them").

For many in the old left and (now aging) "new left," the much-admired UE has always been a case study in "what might have been" if America's management-backed Red Scare hadn't been so successful in marginalizing militant, rank-and-file oriented, politically progressive unionism. In a typical academic tribute, *Left Out: Reds and America's Industrial Unions,* Judith Stepan-Norris and Maurice Zeitlin bemoan the lost influence of the UE (and other purged CIO unions) "that were most dynamic, egalitarian, democratic, class conscious and advanced on issues of women's rights and interracial solidarity."

Rosemary Feurer's valuable new book, *Radical Unionism in the Midwest, 1900–1950,* concentrates on an important slice of the UE's tragic history. Her sweeping (and somewhat misleading) title notwithstanding, the focus of Feurer's research and writing is the dramatic growth and then rapid demise of UE District 8, headed by William Sentner, an open member of the Communist Party. Openness about the CP's role in building and leading the UE was not a feature of *Them and Us* or the norm among its leading figures. The union's 1973 official history by Matles and Higgins barely acknowledges the role of past or present party members or the UE's complex and often strained relations with the party's officialdom. Instead, the CP appears to be just one of many groups whose members participated freely in the UE because the latter's constitution—unlike that of most other labor organizations—welcomed everyone regardless of "political belief."

The book's only significant reference to a party line shift that affected the UE is Matles and Higgins's unfavorable mention of CP enthusiasm about the AFL-CIO merger in 1955. Following this burying of the hatchet between craft and industrial unions, the CP wanted UE to rejoin the "mainstream of American labor." Matles and his fellow officers rejected the party's advice (because they viewed the merged federation to be a "polluted river," rife with racism, corruption, and conservative politics). While they stood fast, the union suffered what Stepan-Norris and Zeitlin describe as "grievous new wounds inflicted by its own erstwhile comrades responding to party orders." A large group of UE district presidents, staff members, and local business agents declared that the UE was "finished" and joined the exodus to other AFL-CIO unions, taking 50,000 members with them.

As this near fatal blow and Feurer's book on Sentner's career both show, there was a lot more to the story of CP-UE relations than meets the eye in *Them and Us*. Sentner, for example, was never one to kowtow to party headquarters in New York—like the union's mid-1950s defectors did— yet he paid a high price for his CP membership, during and after his ten years as president of UE District 8. In the middle of difficult 1952 contract negotiations with an Illinois manufacturer, he was arrested and charged under the Smith Act for "conspiracy to advocate the overthrow of the U.S. government by force and violence." ("The charge is ridiculous, " Sentner responded. "The only thing I have conspired in is to keep the Eagle Signal Corporation from installing an incentive system" at its plant in Moline.) At his St. Louis trial two years later, the UE leader "passionately defended his belief in democratic socialism, the U.S. Constitution, and non-violence." Nevertheless, he and his co-defendants were quickly found guilty and sentenced to five years in jail. Sentner remained free on appeal, but, two months after the Supreme Court invalidated these and other Smith Act convictions in 1958, he died of heart failure at age fifty-one, leaving his family penniless.

According to Feurer, Sentner had, by then, officially resigned from the party, while remaining "deeply committed to the need for a working-class party dedicated to socialist principles, the very impetus that had caused him to cast his lot with the CP more than twenty years before." The son of Russian-Jewish immigrants, Sentner was born in New York but grew up in St. Louis. After dropping out of college, he spent four years at sea where he discovered Marx and "the radical syndicalist milieu of the merchant seaman." Back in Missouri at the start of the Depression, he joined a CP-backed John Reed Club in St. Louis and, by 1935, was co-chair of the local party. Sentner's energetic organizing among the city's unem-

ployed workers and low-wage factory hands led to a job with the CIO's
Steel Workers Organizing Committee.

In 1936–37, the real action in St. Louis shifted to Emerson Electric
and other local electrical equipment manufacturers. CP "colonizers" at
Emerson united with indigenous militants to stage a 53-day-long sit-
down strike (the second longest in U.S. labor history), coordinated by
Sentner. This victory for the UE's fledgling Midwest organization led to
other successful union recognition battles and Sentner's election as president of District 8, which covered Missouri, Kansas, Iowa, Illinois, and
Indiana. The "militant minority" that built the CIO during this period
was not afraid to tackle either anti-union employers or worker attitudes
that weakened the union. Sentner was a critic of segregated practices in
St. Louis and a key labor ally of the March on Washington Movement,
which protested discrimination against blacks in the armed forces and
industry during World War II. By the war's end, Sentner's district had
more than 50,000 members (25 percent of them African-American in St.
Louis). The UE was in the forefront of progressive initiatives for labor-
oriented regional economic planning and its regional leader had been
profiled in *Fortune* magazine "as a 'Communist proud of his political
beliefs' whose trade unionism was not controlled by party interference and
who 'doesn't talk party jargon.'"

Feurer concludes, however, that Sentner could "never fully confront
or resolve the paradox that the CP was an organization based on authoritarian and hierarchical principles antithetical to democratic ideals." In
her view, CP ties ultimately "tarnished the strongly democratic radical
vision the Left promoted" in District 8 and gave its myriad enemies a
powerful weapon to use in dismantling the UE. Before Sentner's death,
he "spoke somewhat wistfully of workers having urged him to leave the
party, noting their promise that, if he did, they would support his right to
discuss socialism—'but as long as you are a Communist, we are afraid to
take a chance.'" Sentner did relinquish his elected union position in 1948
and became an appointed UE national representative—in a self-sacrificing
effort to make District 8 less of a political target. But, as Feurer recounts,
the mounting "focus on the Communist issue," locally and nationally in
the 1950s, still "overwhelmed the Left's efforts to continue an ideological
struggle that included commitment to militancy on the shop floor, a challenge to corporate power in the community and the larger political economy, the breaking down of racial divisions, and the right of political radicals to have membership and leadership in unions."

Its unhappy ending notwithstanding, *Radical Unionism* contains several important lessons for a contemporary labor left that faces far less red-baiting (since the fall of the Soviet Union) but also suffers from the absence of any broad, nonsectarian socialist organization with working-class adherents. First, Feurer's book makes a strong case for the enduring relevance of bottom-up organizing. It describes, for example, the critical role played by community-based worker organizations in the early 1930s. Like the network of local Jobs With Justice coalitions and immigrant "workers' centers" that operate around the country today, the CP-backed Trade Union Unity League and Unemployed Councils provided critical support in places like St. Louis for workplace struggles that paved the way for larger-scale union building later in the decade. Some of these early fights—such as a 1931 strike by hundreds of black and white women at an east St. Louis pecan-packing plant—involved workers in "submarginal industries" who were ignored by AFL unions or excluded from them on the basis of race. Then, as now, new forms of "community unionism," utilizing innovative tactics and grassroots mobilization, emerged to fill the void left by the contraction and decline of "organized labor," as traditionally defined.

Feurer's book also demonstrates the great power and potential of worker solidarity, developed at the grass roots, through one-on-one recruitment of activists and their subsequent experience of collective action on the job and in the community. In contrast, the "union revitalization" efforts promoted recently by some supposedly "visionary leaders" have relied primarily on bureaucratic consolidation, top-down control, and greater reliance on full-time union officials and staff. The mid-twentieth-century UE contract campaign and strike case studies in *Radical Unionism* illustrate how shop-floor initiatives, rank-and-file leadership development, and "horizontal networking" among union stewards can strengthen and politicize the labor movement at its base. As Feurer suggests, "this history may be useful to keep in mind" because the "current emphasis on the need for organizing at the national and global level may cause us to lose sight of how important community-level organizing is to the development and sustenance of new ideas and bonds of solidarity."

On Culturing a Union

American labor still pays lip service to the idea that it seeks "bread and roses too"—a higher standard of living, plus the chance for workers to enjoy some of the finer things in life. In reality, the famous rallying cry of the 1912 textile workers' strike in Lawrence, Massachusetts, is no more than a faint echo in today's unions. Few offer what anyone would call a rich cultural experience for their members. Much of the labor movement is no longer rooted in immigrant communities or working-class fraternal associations of the sort that once supported folk music, dance, theater, and even literature in foreign-language newspapers like *The Forward*, the Yiddish daily. Postwar assimilation and suburbanization, the decline of indigenous working-class radicalism, and the rise of "mass culture" and entertainment have left American workers with little claim to a culture of their own. Beset with many current problems (including threats to their very survival), unions are not inclined to embrace the additional challenge of making drama, poetry, or music—in new or old forms—part of their internal life again.

The one AFL-CIO affiliate that has attempted this, on a large scale, is the union of New York City hospital and health care workers best known by its number—1199. Now part of the Service Employees International Union, District 1199 launched a cultural program called "Bread and Roses" in 1978, with labor and foundation funding. Since then, B&R has sponsored an impressive stream of union musicals and documentary films, exhibits of paintings, poster art, murals, and photography dealing with workplace themes, poetry and writing classes for workers, oral histories of their struggles—all of which help foster membership solidarity and connection to the union. *Not For Bread Alone* is the story of that effort and a brief history of the union behind it, as told by 1199's longtime publicist, campaign strategist, and cultural impresario Moe Foner. The book also traces Foner's own career as a labor PR man, par excellence, and contains much useful advice for today's "union communicators." The author was a scrappy, streetwise hustler of the press who couldn't type himself but had, on his desk, one of the most formidable Rolodexes in the labor movement. A product of left-wing politics and CIO unionism in its Big Apple heyday, Foner was far more effective than the AFL-CIO's current crop of blow-dried, inside-the-beltway "media consultants" (whose idea of "party work" is introducing labor clients to the Democratic candidates served by their firms, so that union treasuries and political action funds can be milked simultaneously). Foner displayed a different kind of political savvy, in countless picket-line battles and major lobbying efforts. As journalist Jack Newfield observes, he "could publicize like P. T. Barnum, organize like Joe Hill, and network like Bill Clinton."

For example, Foner's pioneering work on 1199 campaigns among private nonprofit hospital workers—who didn't have the right to bargain with management forty years ago—provides a good model for any union trying to make organizing rights a higher profile issue today. *Not For Bread Alone* also reminds us about the important role played by the Labor Leadership Assembly for Peace—the anti–Vietnam War coalition launched by Foner, 1199, and their union allies in the late 1960s.

The author completed this memoir, with the assistance of former *1199 News* editor Dan North, shortly before his death in January 2002 at age eighty-six. As the book recounts, Foner was born into a Jewish working-class family in Brooklyn that produced not one but four radical activists. A member of the Communist Party from the mid-1930s "until the Khrushchev revelations in 1956 about what went on under Stalin," Moe—along with Jack and Phil, his twin brothers—was victimized by an early purge of leftists in higher education. All three were fired from teaching or administrative jobs at City College of New York in 1941. (The resulting controversy led the highly musical Foners to change the name of their dance band—already popular on the Catskill small hotel circuit—to Suspended Swing.)

Despite their dismissal, Phil and Jack went on to have distinguished careers as academic historians. Henry Foner, youngest of the four, joined the Furriers Union and later became its president. And the author, for much of his forty-year union career, became the living embodiment of the cultural politics that developed during the period of the Popular Front, when American liberals and radicals united to oppose fascism abroad and support Roosevelt's New Deal at home. Some of the best material in Foner's book is, thus, like a collection of old photos in a family album, faded but fascinating because of what it reveals about the social and political milieu of a now largely deceased generation of labor activists who managed to survive both McCarthyism and the self-inflicted wounds of the Communist Party. In the 1930s and '40s, Foner observes, the Left created "a vigorous cultural life that became part of its mass appeal."

The most famous writers . . . appeared in *The New Masses*, which was close to the Communist Party. The *Daily Worker* had great cartoons by people like Robert Minor, William Gropper, and Art Young, but artists from *The New Yorker* also appeared there.

This was the era of the experimental Group Theater and *Waiting for Lefty*, the Clifford Odets play about striking taxi drivers. The International Ladies Garment Workers Union had already put on its immensely successful musical review, *Pins and Needles*, and on a smaller scale, the American Student Union put on a Marx Brothers take-off called *Pens and Pencils*. There was the Theatre Arts Committee that had a cabaret to support the Loyalists in the Spanish Civil War. And the YCL [Young Communist League] was always putting on skits and shows.

Foner was hired in 1947 as education director for a department store union. Many Manhattan store clerks of that era, like waiters and waitresses today, were aspiring actors. So when Foner put out a call for auditions for the union's first theatrical venture—a seventeen-song musical review called *Thursdays 'Til Nine*—four hundred members showed up. Through his dance band and party connections, Foner also "had access to an unusually large number of creative people who were, because of their political beliefs, more than happy to participate for little or no money in union cultural events." For music, lyrics, or other help, he tapped show business talents like Millard Lampell, later a successful Hollywood screenwriter; playwrights Arthur Miller and Norman Rosten; film producer/director Martin Ritt (who went on to win an Oscar for *Norma Rae*); comedians Sam Levinson and Irwin Corey; actors Jack Gilford and Zero Mostel; and future TV writer Mel Tolkin. Although professionally written and produced, *Thursdays 'Til Nine* drew on the workplace experiences of store workers themselves and provided humorous commentary on contemporary labor issues (in numbers like "The Taft-Hartley Rumba"). Thousands of members applauded its performances and Foner's singular career was launched. The show cost only a few thousand dollars, but in return it "reaped immense rewards in good publicity, education on labor issues, and membership pride in their union."

These positive results became a hallmark of Foner productions for his later union employees as well. The store workers soon merged with "another center of left unionism in New York, District 65," whose stewards were deployed in Peekskill in 1949 to protect Paul Robeson when a right-wing mob attacked one of his concerts. At District 65, Foner ran educational, social, and cultural programs for 20,000 workers in retail, wholesale, or warehouse jobs. One of the first things he did was start a nightclub on the top floor of the union's lower Manhattan office building.

> Each week, a different group of members would be in charge of selling 400 tickets each. Rank-and-file committees would set up, check coats, wait on tables, serve drinks, etc. . . . I'd line up a band. And every Saturday night, I'd get a guest star to perform for free. . . . Harry Belafonte was just breaking in then, and he'd come down and sing in his dark glasses. We were packing them in, the place was always full.

On Saturday mornings, District 65 also had a "kiddy program," which featured sing-alongs with Pete Seeger and Woody Guthrie, dance programs conducted by Guthrie's wife, Margie, and magic shows by Doc Horowitz, who brought along his daughter, a "terrific ventriloquist and puppeteer" who acted as emcee. Her name? Shari Lewis, later the star of one of the fifties' most popular children's TV shows.

In 1952, Foner moved to 1199, where he spent three decades—editing the union newspaper, aiding strikes and organizing campaigns, advising union founder Leon Davis, and eventually creating Bread and Roses. At mid-century, the union looked quite different than it does today, with more than 200,000 members, many of whom are African-American, Hispanic, and/or female. When Foner was hired by Davis, a radical immigrant from Russia, 1199 had only 5,000 members and was overwhelmingly composed of Jewish men working as pharmacists or clerks in New York City drugstores. But, as Foner notes, 1199 had campaigned since the late 1930s for the hiring of black pharmacists and was one of the first unions anywhere to celebrate Negro History Week. When 1199 began organizing primarily non-white hospital workers in the late fifties—which led to its explosive growth over the next twenty years—the union already had a strong record of support for civil rights. Commitment to that cause was symbolized by 1199's close relationships with leading black artists and entertainers. Then relatively unknown as actors, Ruby Dee and Ossie Davis (who contributed a loving foreword to this book) became lifelong friends and collaborators with the author. The couple directed or performed in a series of productions at 1199's annual *Salute to Freedom*. Much later, they helped Foner create Bread and Roses' best-known musical review, *Take Care*, which used humorous songs and sketches to tell the story of hospital workers' daily lives, their frustrations on the job and hopes for the future.

In 1199's initial hospital organizing and strikes, the union tried to fuse civil rights and working-class consciousness. Several of the best chapters in *Not For Bread Alone* describe how its "Union Power, Soul Power" campaigns were built—first in New York, and then in Baltimore, Philadelphia, and Charleston, South Carolina, site of an epic 113-day walkout aided by Coretta Scott King, Ralph Abernathy, Andew Young, and other leaders of the Southern Christian Leadership Conference. The photographs accompanying Foner's memoir confirm the breadth of the union's political alliances—with Malcolm X, Martin Luther King Jr., Bayard Rustin, A. Phillip Randolph, Roy Wilkins, and Congressman Adam Clayton Powell.

If the 1960s and early '70s were years of triumph for 1199, they culminated in a decade of byzantine internal feuding. Leon Davis suffered a stroke in 1979 and decided, after nearly five decades as president, to turn over the reins to Doris Turner, an African-American and former dietary clerk who headed 1199's hospital division. At the same time, the union's founder tried to realize his longtime dream of creating "one big union of all health care workers" by merging 1199 with SEIU. Neither the merger nor the internal transfer of power proceeded as planned. Instead, the union was plunged into a terrible "civil war," replete with "bitter elements of racism, sexism, red-baiting, violence, and corruption."

For the majority of 1199 members, one thing eventually became clear: Turner was an incompetent autocrat and their union had become a "busted Stradivarius." Turner purged all staff critics, surrounded herself with goons, moved the union to the right politically, engaged in vote fraud to win reelection, and then, in 1984, led "one of the most inept, unplanned, and disastrous strikes in New York history." To get the union back on track, Foner and other 1199 veterans joined forces with Dennis Rivera, a staff organizer from Puerto Rico recently fired by Turner. They created a dissident group called "Save Our Union," which ran a slate headed by Georgianna Johnson in a federally supervised rerun election for 1199 officers. Johnson narrowly defeated Turner, but her presidency was only slightly less troubled. She was soon ousted by her former backer, Rivera, who has led 1199 ever since (and engineered its long-delayed affiliation with SEIU in 1999).

On matters related to 1199 internal factionalism—what Foner calls "the most heartbreaking experience" of his life—*Not For Bread Alone* is both unreflective and unrevealing. "To some extent, we all played out events based on our backgrounds, and mistakes were made. But the union survived," the author writes. Elsewhere, Foner admits that "the whole affair had disturbing overtones" but claims, unconvincingly, that during the union's 1989 leadership race he "was removed from the day-to-day running of 1199, and I have only a hazy idea of the details." As a history of 1199, then, *Not For Bread Alone* is best read along with Leon Fink and Brian Greenberg's *Upheaval in the Quiet Zone* (University of Illinois Press, 1989), which Foner, to his credit, helped the authors research, despite its dissection of various 1199 flaws. Upheaval appeared thirteen years ago, when the union's bloody and embarrassing leadership succession fight was still unresolved. Yet it remains the definitive study of what went wrong then—and its analysis is just as relevant today, in light of 1199's recent right turn, under Rivera, into the camp of Republican governor George Pataki, a questionable ally for any "progressive" trade union.

Fink and Greenberg criticize Davis not only for his disastrous choice of Turner as heir apparent but also for functioning as a "charismatic patriarch" whose "unquestioned authority verged on benevolent despotism." According to them, even the 1199 bylaws reforms championed by Save Our Union failed to address the problem of overly centralized decision making in a "local" union far larger than most national ones. "Without provisions for an elected 'chief delegate' at each hospital or elected area directors, there is still no structural accommodation to pluralistic power centers within the union and little place for leaders of the future to spread their wings," they contend. "Communication as well as decision making will still be formulated in a room at the top."

The local's history or internal politics aside, the main question raised by Foner's memoir is whether Bread and Roses offers a viable model for cultural programming elsewhere in labor. Or is it too much a product of New York City exceptionalism—a unique expression of 1199's interracialism and now fading political traditions, including its Popular Front alliance with artists and entertainers long in the orbit of the old left? B & R has, from the beginning, inspired other labor arts initiatives. Just as 1199 once tried to spread its unique brand of hospital unionism elsewhere in the country (with varying degrees of success), Foner helped organize, in 1980, the first in a series of Bread and Roses cultural festivals in Lawrence, Massachusetts, which have been held there on Labor Day weekends ever since. For almost as long, the Labor Heritage Foundation in Washington has hosted an annual "Arts Exchange and Conference on

Creative Organizing," which brings together union activists and enter-tainers. LHF also sells poster art, videos, and CDs of union music to help publicize the work of labor choruses and individual singer/songwriters. At the local level, however, few unions have the kind of membership base and staff support—or access to foundation funding—that has kept B & R afloat for nearly twenty-five years. (During his period of forced exile from 1199 during the mid-1980s, even Foner found it hard to reproduce his past successes while working part-time for a small Meat Cutters local in Queens.)

According to Esther Cohen, Bread and Roses' current director, the project continues to achieve its founder's goal of providing professional quality programming and opportunities for creative expression by 1199 members. B&R's permanent art gallery at union headquarters currently hosts eight exhibits a year, on topics ranging from Haitian culture and Dominican religion to the lives of Langston Hughes, Paul Robeson, and Pennsylvania coal miners, and the death row experiences of Mumia abu-Jamal. Once a month, Cohen reports, the gallery becomes "a cozy night-club" and cafe, with entertainment provided by 1199 rank-and-filers. More than 150 members recently signed up for a creative writing work-shop as well, and as part of an amateur photography program called "Unseen America," Bread and Roses is also helping scores of its mem-bers—and other immigrant workers—record and display scenes of work-place and community life rarely shown in the mass media.

However, in the issue of *New Labor Forum* that recently published Cohen's account of B & R activity, the Queens College magazine also bemoaned the fact that most professionals in the arts are no longer stirred by "the plight of working people and the intoxicating promise of their lib-eration." According to NLF's editors:

> For two centuries, until now that is, there was always a cultural alterna-tive, a point of opposition that said no to the callous calculations of the marketplace. . . . While many kinds of people and institutions have, at one time or another, joined the opposition, the labor movement was always part of the picture, sometimes at the center of the canvas. No more. . . . The labor movement is at a cultural dead end. It has been defeated in the struggle for the hearts and the minds of our fellow citizens.

Such funereal observations were not part of Moe Foner's game. He was ever the optimist, the union survivor and upbeat promoter of new ideas and causes. If still on the job at 1199, he'd be on the phone button-holing talent for its next production, badgering reporters to cover it and rallying members to fill every seat in the house. He'd also be applauding the role played by hip-hop stars in the mass rally of New York City teach-ers (and thousands of their music-loving students) held during 2002 con-tract talks between Mayor Bloomberg and the United Federation of Teachers (UFT). Better than some activists in his field, the author knew that if "labor culture" is going to be sustained, it must be periodically renewed—that Ossie and Ruby must finally give way to Sean (Puff Daddy) Combs, Jay-Z, LL Cool J, and Erykah Badu, all of whom graced the platform of the UFT. As New York City union historian Joshua Freeman observed, in another recent exchange about the future of labor-oriented art and entertainment: "There's no going back in time, and no reason to do so. The strength of mid-century New York left culture lay in its organic relationship to the needs and tastes of the city's working class. It remains for another generation, in its own way, to build a new culture of labor and the left."[1]

REVOLUTION IN THE AIR

In the interests of full disclosure, I must admit that I was never a big fan of the "new communist movement" (NCM), whose rise and fall is chron-icled so exhaustively in Max Elbaum's *Revolution in the Air*. The doctri-naire shenanigans of the NCM did little to build durable rank-and-file organization in any unions or industries targeted for colonization in the 1970s by its various alphabet soup groups. A number of "cadre organiza-tion" veterans continued to be active in unions after their enthusiasm for "Third World Marxism" waned and their respective sects imploded. Some have managed to secure comfortable careers for themselves within various union bureaucracies and the officialdom of the "new" AFL-CIO. Once big boosters of China's cultural revolution, their more recent polit-ical activity includes cheerleading for "cadre" from the centrist Democratic Leadership Council—Bill Clinton, Al Gore, and their innu-merable state and local clones.

During the heyday of the NCM, some actual third world Marxists were just beginning the process of building broad-based, multi-tendency anti-capitalist parties, rooted in militant unions and community groups. In Brazil, for example, the long, patient, and pragmatic march of the Workers Party has finally led to the election of former metal workers leader Luis Inacio "Lula" da Silva as president of the country. In contrast, 10,000 or so NCM adherents embarked, thirty years ago in the United States, on a much shorter march—this one to political marginalization, organizational disintegration, and, for many, personal estrangement from radical politics in any form. Much of the emancipatory spirit of the sixties, so full of hope and new political energy, ended up being channeled here into the dreary sectarianism of the 1970s and '80s—thanks in no small part to the NCM and its many little would-be Lenins, competitors all.

Elbaum's book explains, in great detail, what went wrong with the NCM and what today's generation of campus and community activists might learn from this sorry experience. A veteran of Students for a Democratic Society at the University of Wisconsin and now a volunteer staffer for the valuable West Coast peace publication *War Times,* the author is himself a recovering sectarian. For more than a decade, he was part of Line of March (LOM)—which, he now acknowledges, may have adopted "the worst name ever chosen by a party-building group." Previously known as the Rectification Network, Line of March quickly displayed the kind of dogmatism that earned it the derisive nickname, "March in Line!" As an aid to readers, Elbaum includes a "Glossary of New Communist Movement Organizations," most of which now, RIP (Rest in Peace); without this, it's very hard to keep track of the book's bewildering array of organizational acronyms—RCP, CLP, CP-ML, CWP, DWP, MLP, LRS, RWL, PRRWO, OCIC et al. Any reader with the good fortune not to have been around when many on the list were still active will need to consult this glossary early and often.

According to Elbaum, new communists' tendency to march in line— and right over the cliff—was one of the NCM's major weaknesses, along with being "disproportionately composed of individuals from the intelligentsia" who had little "sense of proportion about theoretical differences and fell into self-destructive infighting." Blinded by the light of Mao's shining path, NCM adherents linked their "never-ending quest for ortho- doxy" with "a constant suspicion of heresy." No sooner was the NCM born, when it got busy dying—via inter-organizational feuds, internal fac- tionalism, and eventual splitting over "minor points of doctrine" bor- rowed from "Cultural Revolution Maoism," "traditional Stalinism," or Cuban Communism. What Elbaum calls "the proliferation of ever-smaller vanguards" did, of course, create leadership opportunities for losers in various theoretical debates, because the latter invariably picked up their marbles and left, only to form their own group, based on a new and improved brand of "left purism."

Within the NCM, "democratic centralism" and party discipline became a cover for abuses of power by various ego-tripping males—and, apparently, a few out-of-control female authority figures as well. Here, for example, is Elbaum's memorable description of the not-so-democratic internal life of the Democratic Workers Party, a "secret cadre organization" formed by "thirteen women (all white) in the San Francisco Bay Area in 1974, under the influence of Marlene Dixon, a charismatic intellectual from a working-class background." Dixon had "a deep-rooted dictatorial streak and major substance abuse problems," a dangerous combination in any maximum leader:

> In its internal functioning, DWP was rigid and top-down to a degree unusual even by the hierarchical standards of the New Communist Movement. Members were subject to nearly 24-hour-a-day discipline and internal political debate was surpressed via the argument that it was "class standpoint" rather than political line that determined a cadre's mettle—with the precise definition and practical tests of class standpoint subject to constant change and leadership manipulation.
>
> Dissent was harshly dealt with, and purges and expulsions were commonplace. General Secretary Dixon ruled with an iron hand, and almost all major party documents were attributed to her or to other members working under her personal guidance. In practical campaigns, DWP rejected united-front cooperation with other left groups in favor of setting up mass organizations strictly under party control.

Not surprisingly, most normal people—regardless of their class background—did not last long in outfits like this. Many survivors of new communism, "like former cult members," experienced something resembling post-traumatic stress syndrome," Elbaum reports. The burnout and bitterness was so deep among some individuals that they "simply abandoned political work altogether" after leaving or being expelled from the hermetic world of the NCM. Though freely confessing the NCM's many sins of "ultra-leftism," Elbaum nevertheless expresses a certain lingering admiration for the movement's ability "to maintain itself as a militant, anti-capitalist current far longer than most other tendencies that came out of the upheavals of the 1960s." He even manages to find nice things to say about the DWP, calling it "a breath of fresh air" which produced "analytical work on women's oppression far more sophisticated than the mechanical perspectives that had dominated the pre-1973 party building movement."

The NCM's bizarre ideological contortions reached their zenith in the late 1970s, when various groups or their top commissars began "to see splitting controversies in every disagreement over international affairs." While proclaiming itself to be "new," the internal dynamic of the NCM was not unlike that of the old CPUSA, from the 1920s to the mid-1950s, in that party members were frequently torn apart by abrupt ideological flip-flops, decreed by the leadership in response to political developments abroad—in this case, splits between Russian, Chinese, and Vietnamese communists, Cuba and China over Angola, China and Albania, and even various Central American revolutionary factions. (Particularly jolting was Beijing's official recognition of the Pinochet dictatorship in Chile, just a year after thousands of leftists were killed, exiled, or imprisoned in that country's military coup.) As longtime Democratic Socialists of America (DSA) activist Tim Sears observes, "the basic political outlook of the new communists struck most people at the time—even most people inclined toward radical or progressive politics—as incredibly wacky." NCM ideas haven't improved with age. If anything, many Maoist conceptions of "anti-imperialism" seem more otherworldly today than they did twenty-five or thirty years ago. How many of us remember, for example, that "by 1975, the October League—having achieved premier status in the Maoist camp—was arguing that the main blow must be directed at the USSR and calling for steps to strengthen NATO." Jimmy Carter and Ronald Reagan were only too glad to comply!

Elbaum also cites, as one of the NCM's achievements, the intervention of competing NCM factions—in the twilight of their movement—into Jesse Jackson's two presidential primary campaigns during the 1980s. This section of the book is a case study in the behavior of small, secretive, "vanguard groups" when they seek influence within and attempted control over "mass organizations." During the grim Reagan years, Jackson's "Rainbow Coalition" initially showed much promise of becoming an ongoing mass-based, multicultural political insurgency with a progressive agenda. It quickly became a magnet for every lefty in town:

With campaign committees and Rainbow structures sprouting all over during late 1983 and 1984, and with traditional Democratic Party operatives hostile or hanging back, there was plenty of room for skilled leftists to assume leadership roles. LRS [League of Revolutionary Struggle] and Line of March cadre played the largest role, but PUL, RWH, and CLP also made their presence felt, as did a number of independent left veterans of other party-building groups.

Elbaum's Line of March, to its credit, "stressed the importance of a Rainbow structure based among grassroots activists who had a major say in decision making" and opposed "allowing the Rainbow to languish" during non-presidential campaign years. LOM's objective was to turn the Coalition "into a progressive vehicle not completely dependent on the appeal of its charismatic standard-bearer or susceptible to pressures from the Democratic Party high command." Meanwhile, the LRS—which closed up shop in 1990—proceeded to aid Jackson's project of keeping the Rainbow securely under his personal control. According to Elbaum:

> LRS emphasized what traditional communist doctrine termed a "united front from above," and worked to forge strong ties with Jackson's inner circle, local elected officials, labor and community leaders. The organization pressed for structures and tactics that would be comfortable for figures with an established base, and were reluctant to set up a bottom-up, membership-based Rainbow. . . . LRS was likewise more willing than most others on the left to subordinate building the Rainbow to the immediate needs of Jackson's campaign apparatus when these were considered by Jackson to be at least partly in conflict.

Maoist labor work in the '70s was, on the other hand, characterized by spectacular adventurism and "ultra-leftism," combined with a similar penchant for manipulation and behind-the-scenes maneuvering that hardly had a liberating effect on the working class, or even that small portion of it touched—and usually turned off—by NCM activity. As Elbaum admits, "Most of the movement gave little attention to—or actually opposed—the development of forms reflecting bottom-up initiative and working-class self-organization outside party control." Unfortunately, as Christopher Phelps points out, *Revolution in the Air* contains little detail on the trade union practice of "new communists"—i.e. what they actually did in factories, workplaces, and union halls while trying to connect "party building and mass working-class organizing."[1] We learn more about what Marxist-Leninist colonizers criticized than what they proposed as a strategy for union radicalization. For example, in the middle of Ed Sadlowski's 1976–77 "Fight-Back" campaign—the biggest challenge to the Steelworkers' leadership in that union's history—the October League denounced Sadlowski as one of "the main scabs and slickest defenders of the system." His candidacy for the USWA presidency "grew out of a militant rank-and-file movement,"as Elbaum notes. Yet, according to these Maoists, it was merely "a trick by the bourgeoisie to channel the revolutionary aspirations and strivings of the masses into reformism."

As part of its rival effort to "sink roots in the working class," Bob Avakian's Revolutionary Union (soon to become the Revolutionary Communist Party) sent some of its operatives to West Virginia to become coal miners in the early 1970s, one of the toughest assignments that any group of colonizers had anywhere. They arrived amid considerable political turmoil within the United Mine Workers and a wildcat strike movement of epic proportions. For better or worse (depending on your point of view), RCPers helped shape the latter as rank-and-file militants in the Miners' Right to Strike Committee, which sought an open-ended grievance procedure in the UMW contract with the Bituminous Coal Operators Association. Little or nothing of this experience makes it into the pages of *Revolution in the Air*—despite rich material provided by such adventures as the RCP's politically suicidal May Day marches in Beckley, West Virginia. This annual exercise in red-flag waving led one year to the near lynching of the party's small band of coalfield supporters. Fleeing a hostile crowd, they were forced to take refuge in the office of their attorney, a National Lawyers Guild member more used to fending off injunctions, damage claims, and contempt citations arising from wildcat strike activity.

Such local color rarely enlivens Elbaum's book. Instead, *Revolution in the Air* suffers from a Talmudic preoccupation with textual interpretation. Well-written and carefully researched, the book charts every ideological twist and turn of long-dead sects, as reflected in the author's voluminous collection of their now-yellowing flyers, mimeographed manifestos, newspapers, internal discussion bulletins, and "theoretical journals." As feminists have noted, "the personal" is also "political." What this history really needs is a human face. It would have benefited from personal profiles of those who once tried to change the world through NCM groups, more information about their family backgrounds and life as radical activists, and greater insight into how they feel about their political work, then and now.

Labor historians Alice and Staughton Lynd have provided a revealing retrospective look at the workplace experiences of several NCM colonizers in interviews published in *The New Rank and File* (Cornell University Press, 2000). Unfortunately, Elbaum eschews this approach—or any other involving narrative journalism—on security grounds. As he explains:

> Individual names are used sparingly in this book . . . only activists whose role was both highly public and important are mentioned by name, and even many who meet those criteria are not identified. This approach stems mainly from the power that anti-communism still exercises in U.S. society. Today, it is considered at least semi-respectable to have participated in 1960s protests and joined some kind of radical group—but to have been a member of an organization that defined itself as Marxist-Leninist is still regarded as beyond the pale. Public acknowledgment of such membership can cost a person dearly.

The possibility of creating personal embarrassment for some ex-cadre now on the capitalist road might be an additional reason for the author's reticence. According to civil rights movement historian David J. Garrow, who reviewed Elbaum's book favorably in *The Village Voice*, "Former top ideologues [of the Communist Party–Marxist Leninist successor to the October League] nowadays include a millionaire venture capitalist who worked for many years at the Blackstone Group and a management executive for a prominent Florida-based restaurant chain." According to Garrow, CP-ML chairman and founder Mike Klonsky—the toast of party circles in Beijing during the late 1970s—is currently an education professor at the University of Illinois, having taken the more usual path for "new communists" to reenter what Elbaum calls "the better-off strata from which they had once defected."[2]

Emphasizing the importance of cross-generational lesson sharing, Elbaum has promoted this book with admirable entrepreneurial zeal of his own. The website for *Revolution in the Air* (http://www.revolution-intheair.com) announces its second printing, tracks the author's extended book tour, and features both reviews and reader comments. Elbaum wants to foster a "dialogue with many talented individuals from today's new generation of activists, to gain insight into how they see things and what they have and have not learned from the past." If the book "sparks criticism and further discussion of the left's history and future, it will have met a major part of its goal," he says. He is certainly correct in concluding:

> Every new generation reinvents the Left, whether by transforming existing groups or by forming new ones of their own. This is both necessary and positive, not least because youth are far less likely than veterans to be shackled by the "tradition of all the dead generations [which] weighs like a nightmare on the brain of the living," as Marx put it. This is especially crucial today, since at no time since the birth of the modern socialist movement has the Left needed such a top-to-bottom overhaul.

One can only hope, though, that Elbaum's nostalgia for certain elements of the NCM experience is not contagious. As Garrow observes, the "movement's history is a powerful lesson in how not to pursue the progressive transformation of society." Elbaum's book illustrates how difficult it has been for radicals to build lasting and effective "intermediate organizations"—from rank-and-file caucuses to rainbow coalitions— much less left-wing political groups that have any semblance of mass appeal in American society. If current efforts at "socialist regroupment" are going to be anything more than linking together the walking wounded, what's left of the Left today must find a way to connect its anti-capitalist critique to the multiplying crises of real existing capitalism.

Corporate globalization, the post 9/11 mix of war and economic distress, the widening attacks on labor and renewed meltdown of the U.S. health care system, the mounting evidence of long-term environmental catastrophe—all these conditions and more provide openings for expanded organizing initiatives. Revolution may not be in the air, but there's more than enough human suffering and popular unrest in America today to enable radicalism to break free from the confines of narrow sectoral struggles and single-issue politics. Left-wing activists may not have Lenin, Mao, and Che as their guides this time but, based on the evidence in Elbaum's book, that may be one more factor in their favor.

LABOR'S WORST NIGHTMARE

Unlike communism and socialism, trade unionism has rarely inspired published "second thoughts" by embittered apostates. Those who turn against labor may be no less disillusioned than members of the "God that failed" generation or even our own indefatigable New Left defector, David Horowitz. But few ex-officials of an AFL-CIO affiliate end up penning renunciations over at the National Right to Work Committee. More typically, union turncoats just go to work for management and keep their mouths shut about it. Linda Chavez, a former top assistant to the now-deceased president of the American Federation of Teachers, Albert Shanker, is quite an exception to the usual rule.

Chavez parlayed her nine-year stint as an AFT staffer into an ongoing career as a syndicated columnist, Fox News commentator, and radio talk show host, after transitioning directly from Shanker's "inner circle to the upper reaches of the Reagan Administration." There, her first job was to muzzle the U.S. Civil Rights Commission, as its controversial staff director. Later, she served as White House liaison to various constituent groups then being courted by Reagan. In 1986, she ran against Barbara Mikulski for a U.S. Senate seat from Maryland, campaigning as a right-wing Republican and getting 39 percent of the vote. Her bid in 2001 to become George Bush's first Secretary of Labor also ended in defeat. Chavez neglected to disclose to the Bush transition team that she had actually done a good deed in her life—harboring an undocumented worker from Guatemala in her own home. This led to media controversy (over whether she had illegally employed her house guest) and hasty withdrawal of her nomination.

Being battered by the Washington press corps and then dropped like a hot potato by the Bush crowd was hard enough for Chavez to swallow. It must have been equally galling that the opportunity to harass her former union colleagues from a high-profile government perch went instead to a more privileged female from a different ethnic minority. Elaine Chao's elevation to Labor Secretary, as the president's second choice, was aided by her marriage to a prominent Republican senator. Chavez, in contrast, had to win Bush's initial favor through her own boot-strapping efforts in the fight against affirmative action and the minimum wage. The author's simmering resentment and desire for revenge is reflected in two related books. One is a political memoir and the other a lurid account of labor's allegedly pervasive and "corrupt" influence over American life.

An Unlikely Conservative traces Chavez's own rise from modest circumstances to Republican royalty. We learn that her mother was an Anglo divorcée from Wyoming who formed a "blended family" with Rudy Chavez, the hard-drinking, downwardly mobile descendent of wealthy Spanish merchants and landowners whose ancestral home included "much of modern-day Albuquerque." Only when Chavez moved to Denver, attending high school and college there, did she learn "that Mexicans were looked down on in Colorado—and that included me." Chavez's autobiography sheds new light on the liberal/labor gang-up that similarly surprised her in 2001, thwarting her cabinet ambitions. Initially, it turns out, there were unions (including her alma mater) willing to overlook her conversion to conservatism. After Bush nominated her, Chavez

> decided it was time to place a few calls to former colleagues and friends in the labor movement. With my name all over the papers, I had no trouble getting phone calls returned. . . . It was clear from several conversations that some officials welcomed my candidacy [and] a number of union presidents wanted to be helpful . . . none was more solicitous than Sandra Feldman, president of the American Federation of Teachers.

When Chavez soon found herself "caught in the media cross-hairs," her fair-weather friend Sandra "smelled blood in the water and decided to join the sharks." America's self-proclaimed "most-hated Hispanic" did not enjoy being shark bait. Her memoir concludes with this ominous warning: "I may not have become the AFL-CIO's worst nightmare as secretary of labor but I intend to remain a thorn in their side."

Written with Daniel Gray, former PR director for the Right to Work Committee, *Betrayal* is, as promised, a follow-up thrust at unions inside and outside the Beltway. According to the authors, the AFL-CIO has become incurably greedy, violent, radical, and a danger to the Republic because of the untold millions it spends, illegally, on Democrats. The Democratic Party, they argue, has become so indebted to "leftist labor unions" that the latter now exercise "veto power over its policy decisions and campaign strategies"—a revelation, I'm sure, to union backers of Richard Gephardt or Howard Dean during their short-lived 2004 presidential candidacies. Chavez's memoir includes a brief critique of labor's "partisan politics" but nothing quite so imaginative and wide-ranging as the indictment found in *Betrayal*. In *Unlikely Conservative*, she reveals, for example, that she once personally engaged in such "secret activities" as delivering "several boxes of union-printed leaflets to Ted Kennedy's presidential campaign headquarters in 1980"—before voting for Reagan that year. Generally, however, Chavez has nothing but fond memories of her union work in Washington, during the halcyon AFL-CIO reign of George Meany and Lane Kirkland.

According to Chavez, their ally, Shanker, "expected two things from his employees: that they be smart and that they have 'good politics,' which consisted chiefly of being pro-union, anti-communist, and opposed to racial quotas." After "Big Al" became AFT president, "almost all the leadership positions on staff" went to the Young People's Socialist League (YPSL), whose alumni also wielded influence at the AFL-CIO as members of the hawkish Social Democrats-USA. Chavez's proudest achievement was turning the *American Educator*, an AFT magazine, into "a conservative journal of ideas." "Not only did we promote Shanker's hard-line views with articles critical of China, Cuba, and the Soviet Union, but we also took on affirmative action, ethnic studies, radical feminism . . . and the 'nuclear freeze' movement." Thus, by the standards, say, of David Horowitz's youthful wanderings in the Marxist wilderness, very little of Chavez's early career was squandered on causes she regrets today. Her brief flirtation with socialism, now recalled as "liberalism," involved a political sect so anti-communist that its leaders ended up, like Chavez, on the right. After she leveraged her YPSL connections into an AFT job, she did display a certain subservience to a "union boss" herself, albeit a "true visionary" who transformed her "politically and intellectually." But even while Chavez was collecting a big salary financed by AFT members' dues, she at least tried to spread this "shakedown" money around among other neo-cons like Robert Bork, Thomas Sowell, William J. Bennett, and Jeane Kirkpatrick, all of whom wrote for her union journal!

In *Betrayal*, the "pro-union" part of Chavez's Shankerite politics is hard to detect. The book is a nonstop diatribe against all unions—clean and tarnished, militant and meek, democratic and undemocratic, liberal and conservative alike. It recycles every time-worn *Reader's Digest* exposé of labor vice—from picket line violence to project labor agreements—and depicts the labor movement as one big protection racket for criminally inclined layabouts. To put unions in their place once and for all, *Betrayal* seeks a legal crackdown that would leave workers even more defenseless than they are today. Among their "recommended reforms," the authors want to repeal the Wagner, Davis-Bacon, and Fair Labor Standards Acts, eliminate most union political activity, and expand anti-racketeering prosecutions to curb the "legalized terrorism" of strikes and contract campaigns.

The book's accuracy is best illustrated by its repeated use of the adjective "big"—as in "Big Labor," a term employed, by my count, no less than 150 times in 233 pages. Conservatives slapped this same label on their union foes in the post–World War II period when there was some basis for it because a third of the workforce was organized and nationwide strikes were common in auto, steel, coal, and other industries. Fifty years later, after the steady erosion of "union density," the AFL-CIO represents only 12 percent of all workers and barely 7 percent in the private sector. Yet somehow, in *Betrayal*, the bogeyman of "Big Labor" still stalks the land. Based on any objective measurement—membership size, strike activity, or degree of pattern bargaining—"Small Labor" is what actually exists in the United States today. Most unions lack the muscle to inflict the "economic harm" that Chavez attributes to them and fewer still have, as their goal, socializing the economy (or "choking the golden goose," as Chavez calls it).

This inconvenient reality explains why *Betrayal* dwells instead on alleged payroll padding, influence peddling, and "mediocrity protection" in labor's last redoubt, the public sector. But here too the reader enters a comic book "bizarro world," a parallel universe in which familiar people and institutions behave quite unlike their real-life counterparts. For example, politicians who've often disappointed labor by supporting "welfare reform," privatization, deregulation, or trade liberalization become, in *Betrayal*, fiery tribunes of the working class. To wit, Hillary Clinton: "Like many other leading Democrats, she has moved further to the left in her pursuit of high office, which undoubtedly pleases the labor movement's radical leadership."

Meanwhile, real left-leaning laborites are endowed with hidden influence not heretofore noticed by anyone else (except conservatives suffering from "Big Labor" phobia). In *Betrayal*'s biggest reds-under-the-bed revelation, we learn that the political clout of Democratic Socialists of America didn't peak twenty-five years ago, during the heyday of Michael Harrington. Instead, thanks to the group's closet member John Sweeney, DSA now has a stranglehold over AFL-CIO policy, far beyond any imagined by Harrington in his wildest dreams. Whether in cahoots with the

DSA, the Congressional Progressive Caucus, or "what has essentially become the U.S. Labor Party" (a.k.a the Democrats), Sweeney is portrayed as a kind of American Lenin, who "proudly preaches his socialist worldview." Even now, the book suggests, he lurks in the wings of the Kerry-for-President campaign, waiting to seize post-election power in the business union equivalent of a Bolshevik coup.

Unfortunately, *Betrayal*'s depiction of union financial shenanigans is far more accurate and not at all funny. The book condemns multiple salaries (such as Sweeney's own past double-dipping), padded expense accounts, and profiteering by union insiders at the infamous Union Labor Life Insurance Company (Ullico). Before even getting to a chapter titled "Money, Mansions, and Mobsters," Chavez and Gray flay the usual suspects—the Teamsters, Laborers, and other construction unions, whose past or present racketeering problems have been widely publicized. (According to the authors, of course, "Most newspapers bury stories about union embezzlement and fraud or don't even report them in the first place.") Ironically, the most flamboyant thievery cited in *Betrayal* involves the Teachers. Recently convicted AFT kleptomaniacs in Washington and Miami managed to make off with an astonishing haul—more than $9 million of dues money misappropriated for housing, travel, luxury hotel stays, designer clothes, jewelry, and other personal needs. Chavez implies, not implausibly, that these criminals were just emulating the lifestyles of the rich, if not famous, folks at national union headquarters. In 2000, now-retired AFT President Feldman, who was then "the most powerful woman in the labor movement," earned $354,000 as part of a perfectly legal, total compensation package worth more than $525,000. That same year, salaries for the union's three top officers alone cost the members $1.1 million.

In her fatwa against union "fat cats," Chavez barely acknowledges that others, better intentioned than her, have also inveighed against union corruption and bureaucracy—but then tried to do something constructive about it. After finishing *Betrayal*, any reader previously unaware of recent union reform activity would still never know that tens of thousands of workers struggled, for years, to challenge and change corrupt practices in the Mine Workers, Steelworkers, Teamsters, building trades, and maritime unions. (An excellent history of those efforts, *Rebels, Reformers, and Racketeers: How Insurgents Transformed the Labor Movement*, was recently published by Herman Benson, ninety-year-old founder of the Association for Union Democracy and a more helpful ex-YPSL member.)

If Chavez had hoped to become—via her latest publishing venture—"the most-hated ex-union member in America," she's going to be disappointed again. With only a book, not a cabinet post as her bully pulpit, the author is definitely not labor's "worst nightmare." There's too much corporate competition in that category, at the moment, for any right-wing scribbler to be a major contender. Among workers currently haunted by lost strikes, concession bargaining, privatization, deregulation, free trade, offshoring, outsourcing, and virulent union busting, Chavez won't even be noticed as "a thorn in their side."

WORKING-CLASS INTELLECTUALS

In recent debates about union restructuring, some successful organizers, like Bruce Raynor, president of UNITE-HERE, have argued that the United States has too many little labor organizations. According to Raynor, workers won't be able to go on the offensive again, as they did in the 1930s, until existing national unions, numbering about 60, are consolidated into 10 to 15 much larger entities, with less overlapping jurisdiction. Practicing what he preaches, Raynor arranged a 2004 merger of his own union with the hotel workers, headed by John Wilhelm (although the synergies of this marriage have not always been clear and tensions between the two partners persist to this day). In early 2009, UNITE and HERE began public feuding, and possible divorce action, featuring a messy dispute over their shared assets.

The authors of *Singlejack Solidarity* and *Punching Out* spent their entire careers challenging the assumptions implicit in Raynor's glib promotion of greater amalgamation. To Stan Weir and Marty Glaberman, meaningful change can only emerge from below in the labor movement through shop-floor struggles and "worker self-activity"; it can't be engineered from above, no matter how "progressive," dynamic, or smart the people at the top may be. At a time when union modernization efforts have a distinctly technocratic flavor, the rank-and-file perspective of Weir and Glaberman is a welcome antidote to conventional thinking. Nevertheless, *Singlejack Solidarity* editor George Lipsitz worries (in his introduction to Weir's collected works) that contemporary readers may have difficulty discerning what the author's "experiences and observations can tell us today" since "the nature of waged work in our society has changed so dramatically" since Weir last toiled as a seaman, teamster, longshoreman, house painter, or auto assembler three decades ago. Fortunately for the editors (Lipsitz and Staughton Lynd, who assembled these volumes after the deaths of their respective authors) both Weir and Glaberman have much to say that's relevant to current debates about racism, working-class consciousness, union structure and functioning, relationships between workers and intellectuals, and the role of the left in labor. Both collections also focus on important topics often neglected now, such as informal work groups, wildcat strikes, and other forms of resistance to factory automation and speed-up.

Glaberman and Weir sharply criticized the labor establishment of their day (which was not so long ago) and job conditions prevalent then, which have improved little since because of declining union power. The many like-minded essays, articles, and reviews in *Singlejack Solidarity* and *Punching Out* are rooted in the authors' socialist politics, experience as industrial workers, and in Weir's case, membership in a variety of unions. Read together, their collected works constitute a fierce, persuasive polemic against the panacea of the moment—union consolidation through a series of mega-mergers, at the local and national level. In a workers' movement top-heavy with bureaucracy and deeply enmeshed in business union practices, both authors believed that bigger was not necessarily better. U.S. labor's fulltime officials already tend to be far too removed from the day-to-day concerns of their own members and fatally entrapped in legalistic contract grievance procedures. According to Glaberman and Weir, the latter invariably give management the upper hand, particularly when linked to a no-strike clause, which pressures even well-intentioned union reps to become "cops for the boss" in wildcat strike situations. "In the 1930s and 1940s," Weir writes (in an essay touting the alternative model of Spain's Coordinadora dockers' union), "autonomy was taken from locals by the 'international' unions with the claim that this would aid the mobilization of all U.S. locals against a common corporate employer. The result has been the opposite." Too often today, "unionized employers are each free to attack a particular local union without fear that the national leaders will mobilize the other locals or work locations in defense of the attacked." Says Glaberman, in a 1992 piece, "The Labor Movement Is Not Dead": "I believe that, if one is not in a middle-class rush to reach the millennium tomorrow, worker resistance—which has never disappeared, even in the worst years—will grow and produce the kind of upsurge which helped create the CIO, the IWW, the Knights of Labor, etc." In the meantime, the authors argue, leftists should be planting the seeds for the next upsurge, not helping to erect what may become new obstacles in its path when the balance of workplace power starts to shift again in labor's favor.

Both Glaberman and Weir advocate forms of organization like the anarcho-syndicalist Coordinadora or the workers' councils of the short-lived 1956 Hungarian Revolution. They believe these models are less susceptible to bureaucratization and co-optation. Militant, member-controlled, job-based structures would enable workers to network laterally, on a nationwide and international basis, without interference from union hierarchies bent on dysfunctional domination of their local affiliates. According to Glaberman and Weir, the marginality of Marxists within U.S. unions is due, in part, to their own top-down style and "party line" mentality, a modus operandi antithetical to creative interaction between labor and the left. As Weir writes in "The Vanguard Party: An Institution Whose Time Has Expired":

> More than half a century has passed since any grouping of American radicals was a source of imaginative ideas and dialogue among indigenous working-class intellectuals. With few exceptions, radical political sects are elitist. . . . Their methodology is symptomatic of this fact. They believe that they have something to bring to workers, but not the other way around . . .

Weir himself was a genuine working-class intellectual—a rebellious college dropout from a blue-collar family in East Los Angeles. Glaberman was, in contrast, a "colonizer," an intellectual who left graduate study at Columbia to become a machinist and assembly-line worker in Detroit. Their personal and political trajectories were otherwise quite similar, although, as Lynd observes, it is "curious and sad that they did not themselves make common cause" after departing (via different routes) from the same Trotskyist "vanguard," the Workers Party (WP). Weir was recruited into the WP during World War II, while serving, due to his antiwar convictions, in the merchant marine. An offshoot of the Socialist Workers Party, the WP counted among its leading lights the noted Trinidadian Marxist and Pan-Africanist, C. L. R. James, a beloved comrade profiled in both *Punching Out* and *Singlejack Solidarity*. Many WP activists (including Glaberman) got jobs in the auto industry, where, as Weir reports, they "played a prominent role in the formation of the Rank and File Caucus, which didn't have one prominent official leader in it." Nevertheless, in 1945, this dissident group pressured the UAW into holding a nationwide referendum on whether to continue its wartime no-strike pledge. Forty percent of those voting opposed the controversial ban in an expression of sympathy for wildcatting that Glaberman says was even deeper on the shop floor in Detroit. There, a majority of UAW members defied both the government and their own union by walking out in hundreds of local disputes between 1941 and '45, a subject explored more extensively in Glaberman's 1980 book, *Wartime Strikes.*

Both Glaberman and Weir remained rank-and-file activists until the 1960s. Glaberman then went back to school, earned a Ph.D., and taught at Wayne State, where he met and influenced part-time students who worked in auto plants and belonged to the League of Revolutionary Black Workers. The author of *Punching Out* also ran a small publishing house, Bewick Editions, to distribute his own work and theoretical writing by C. L. R. James. Meanwhile, Weir made himself a major thorn in the side of ILWU president Harry Bridges, by organizing support for a seventeen-year lawsuit challenging union complicity in job-cutting containerization deals on the West Coast docks. Fired as a longshoreman in 1963, he retooled as a labor educator as well, teaching classes for workers and shop stewards at the University of Illinois. In the mid-1980s, Weir co-founded Singlejack Press in California, a publishing house devoted to "writings about work by the people who do it." Like Glaberman in Detroit, Weir was—according to labor journalist and author Kim Moody—a "mentor to many of us from the student movement of the 1960s" because he "brought a world of experience we could hardly have found elsewhere."

That experience makes for fascinating, if sometimes duplicative, reading in *Singlejack Solidarity.* Weir's collection ranges widely and includes analyses of the general strikes in San Francisco in 1934 and Oakland in 1946; the shipboard culture of work and solidarity in the Sailors Union of the Pacific (SUP); the introduction of automation in longshoring, coal mining, and other industries in the 1950s; and the development of a decade-long "labor revolt" against bad working conditions, unpopular contracts, and undemocratic union practices that began in the mid-1960s. As Weir points out in "Luddism Today," the labor unrest thirty-five years ago involved "the largest single wave of absenteeism, tardiness, and minor acts of sabotage ever experienced by American industry." This trend reflected:

> a new radical mood developing across the working class. New values were replacing old ones, a process accelerated as large numbers of young workers entered the labor force. The primary stated goal of the revolts was the improvement of working conditions. The slogan that swelled out of the auto plants in the mid-1960s—"humanize working conditions"— was not so much a call to obtain clean toilets, lunchrooms, and work areas as it was a signal that workers needed a voice in decision making about production in order to survive.

In such commentaries both Weir and Glaberman reject the usual distinctions between "business unionism" and "social unionism" (or, as the latter is known today, "social movement unionism.") Glaberman reminds us that, in the post-war era, "the classic figure of social unionism was Walter Reuther," his longtime national union president. The essence of UAW's "social contract" in auto was "the trade-off of discipline over production for financial and other benefits outside of production." As *Punching Out* notes, Reuther had

> plans at the beginning of World War II for the conversion of the automobile industry; plans at the end of the war for converting war plants to the production of housing; demands in the GM strike of 1945–46 for wage increases without price increases, opening the corporations' books; and, later on, such things as pensions, health insurance, COLA, SUB pay, etc.

Nevertheless, while the UAW founder was, for two decades, "paying lip service to social causes" and promoting "heavy involvement in Democratic politics," autoworkers faced steady "erosion of rights on the job and democracy within the union." During Reuther's widely acclaimed reign, the UAW became, according to Glaberman, "a one-party dictatorship and the totally bureaucratized institution that it is today."

Thus neither Glaberman nor Weir would have been fans of top-down reformers now. Both authors would have viewed them as Reuther's ideological heirs, union centralizers trying to consolidate power in their own hands for the greater good of dues-paying members who lack the "progressive politics" and "larger vision" of the labor officialdom. Nobody, living or dead, does a better job puncturing such self-serving rationales for autocratic rule, while also not romanticizing the rank and file (among whom Glaberman and Weir spent many years). Weir's death at eighty in 2001 and Glaberman's at eighty-three later that same year deprived the labor left of two important, if often contrarian, voices. We need more, not less, of their kind of thinking about the centrality of the workplace, the importance of rank-and-file power, and the potential of ordinary people to transform themselves and their organizations through the experience of labor solidarity and struggle.

The Man Who Hated Work

As a thirty-five-year veteran of union activity in America, I can personally attest that Tony Mazzocchi of the Oil, Chemical, and Atomic Workers (OCAW) was a rare bird, perhaps the last of his kind. In the late 1960s and early '70s, Mazzocchi's peer group—the labor officialdom—was extremely hostile to the migration of young radicals from college campuses to unionized workplaces. Organized labor had been purged of leftism during the fifties, leaving the AFL-CIO stodgy, insular, and full of foreign policy hawks. Labor's cold warriors got very upset when a new generation of "outsiders" tried to convert workers to radical politics inspired by the civil rights, antiwar, black power, environmental, and feminist movements. Only a handful of older working-class organizers welcomed New Leftists to labor. But they provided the kind of direction and encouragement that enabled some ex-students to play key roles in the much heralded, if still insufficient, "union revitalization" of recent years.

Alone among those influential mentors, Tony Mazzocchi developed a far-flung following outside his own union. As his biographer, labor educator Les Leopold, explains, "Tony was a kindhearted soul with an earthy, self-deprecating sense of humor. Unlike so many people who rise to union leadership, he did not have an ego you constantly had to tiptoe around." Those qualities alone made him the premier political *mensch* of the labor left.

Leopold's compelling new book on Mazzocchi contains many reminders of the latter's singular contribution to progressive union activism over five decades. As an OCAW local president and regional leader in New York, legislative director in Washington, and, later, national union secretary-treasurer in Colorado, Mazzocchi managed to juggle day-to-day union responsibilities with a tireless commitment to civil rights, labor-based environmentalism, job safety reform, single-payer health care, nuclear disarmament, and union democracy. He was a leading architect of the fight for a federal Occupational Safety and Health Act (OSHA) in 1972, an accomplishment warranting Leopold's description of him as "the Rachel Carson of the American workplace."

Tony's death from pancreatic cancer in 2002, at the age of seventy-six, deprived fellow activists of his catalytic role in myriad labor causes, including his last, seemingly quixotic, campaign for a U.S. Labor Party. Leopold's detailed recounting of Mazzocchi's career not only illuminates a model of "charismatic leadership" that empowered both rank-and-filers and friends of labor alike, but this important biography also addresses a question that labor leftists, young and older, still grapple with today: How can a trade unionist with strong anti-capitalist views—usually not shared by the workers he or she represents—make his or her politics relevant to workplace struggles in the absence of a mass-based left-wing party?

Unlike many of his later fans, who were middle-class baby boomers, Mazzocchi was shaped by his childhood experience during the Depression, followed by combat duty during World War II. He came from a boisterous, pro-labor Italian-American family in Bensonhurst, a section of Brooklyn later known for its working-class conservatism and/or mob connections. Mazzocchi's two sisters and a closeted gay uncle were Communists but his own radicalism never turned sectarian or contracted into a private creed. According to Leopold, "Formal Marxism and its terminology were far too doctrinaire for Tony." Instead, he was inspired by left-wingers with a popular touch, like East Harlem's Congressman Vito Marcantonio, whose American Labor Party campaign for N.Y.C. mayor Mazzocchi supported. He "watched and learned how Marc carefully serviced his base, while also staking out radical positions. Not only did he care for 'workers' as a political category—he cared for his constituents personally."

Mazzocchi took the same approach when he got a job at a Queens cosmetics factory in 1950 and became a union activist. Local 149 at Helena Rubinstein was then affiliated with the United Gas, Coke and Chemical Workers (which merged with the Oil Workers to became OCAW five years later). As a 149 shop steward, organizer, and eventually president, Mazzocchi tripled the local's size. He built a strong cadre of shop floor leaders, started a book club and credit union, and sponsored a "vast array of social activities" that "combined to create a remarkable new spirit at work." "In stark contrast with much of the labor movement in the mid-1950s, Local 149 championed the rising civil rights movement—even though its membership was 95 percent white." In 1957, Mazzocchi helped launched the Committee for a Sane Nuclear Policy (SANE) to oppose atom bomb testing. His longtime involvement with SANE put him in touch with the "leading scientists, environmentalists, and activists who would later join him building an occupational safety and health movement."

When the Rubenstein plant left the city, Mazzocchi's membership became a force in local politics and a reliable source of strike solidarity in the suburbs. By the mid-1960s, Mazzocchi was mobilizing against job cuts at military contractors on Long Island with a union-drafted plan "to use defense workers' vast skills to build public buses and subway cars." Aided by economist and fellow SANE activist Seymour Melman, this early initiative in "economic conversion" won Mazzocchi a White House audience with Lyndon Johnson in 1964. That same year, he almost ran for Congress—a move thwarted by Democratic Party bigwigs who looked askance at his peace activities and didn't want to be red-baited along with him.

Mazzocchi's aspirations for higher office were fulfilled, partially, within the 200,000-member OCAW instead. In 1965, he helped elect a new national union president, after a bitter struggle with top OCAW officials linked to the CIA's subversion of labor overseas. This victory made Tony the union's legislative/political director. In that capacity, Mazzocchi linked emerging public concern about environmental pollution to the source of the problem—workplaces in which OCAW members were exposed to toxic chemicals at much higher levels than anyone outside. In the era before OSHA and the Environmental Protection Act (EPA), as Leopold points out, "There were no effective standards. There was no enforcement. The corporations ruled as absolute monarchs over chemical production, exposure, and regulation." At Mazzocchi's initiative, labor began to shift its own focus, from a traditional emphasis on job safety (i.e., protection against injuries) to dealing with the long-term health effects of occupational hazards.

His modus operandi involved rank-and-file consciousness raising and grassroots coalition building, outside the Beltway. A high school dropout himself, Mazzocchi recruited a high-powered network of medical researchers to provide documentation for lawsuits, reports, press releases, hearing testimony, and investigative reporting. He regularly dispatched these allies to probe for the causes of job illnesses reported by his membership. At the same time, he organized nonstop "road shows" that brought workers together with friendly experts and forced lawmakers to listen to both of them. Leopold's account of the drive for passage of OSHA in 1972 is a case study in building effective labor clout, albeit in an era when legislative gains were still possible even under a Republican president.

Thanks to Hollywood, OCAW's best-known *cause célèbre* was the case of Karen Silkwood, a whistle-blower from a dangerous nuclear facility operated by Kerr-McGee in Oklahoma. As later dramatized on screen—with Meryl Streep as the star—Silkwood's story did not end happily. She died under suspicious circumstances in a 1974 car crash, while driving with a *New York Times* reporter to a meeting arranged by Mazzocchi's close associate, Steve Wodka. As an integral part of what Leopold calls "the atomic-industrial complex," OCAW nuclear workers ultimately proved to be Mazzocchi's own Achilles' heel. When he decided to run for national union president in 1979 and 1981, conservative opponents who were critical of his "anti-nuke" politics and "incessant boat-rocking" mobilized against him. In both elections, he suffered heartbreakingly narrow defeats—the second resulting from disaffiliation of OCAW members in Canada who had been strong Mazzocchi supporters.

Tony confounded his foes, as usual, by making an unexpected political comeback. In the late 1980s, he reconciled with Bob Wages, the last president of OCAW before it disappeared, via merger, into the Paper Workers and then the United Steel Workers. He returned to the OCAW leadership as national secretary-treasurer, using that post to promote the Labor Party and other worker education initiatives like the Labor Institute (which utilized the talents of radical economists and trainers like Leopold). The LP got off to a promising start with its founding convention in 1995. Since then, however, it has progressively lost much of the active support, funding, and visibility that Mazzocchi generated for the group, through years of barnstorming on its behalf. Leopold recounts the dreary sectarian squabbles that often paralyzed local chapters. A dispute about whether or not—and then how and when—to engage in electoral politics also festered unproductively. After Tony's longtime friend and ally Ralph Nader ran for president in 2000, the mainstream union backlash against third-party "spoilers" further complicated recruitment efforts. (Nader was endorsed by several key affiliates of the LP, but not the

Party itself.) Today, the LP operates on a shoestring, concentrating on a brave challenge to two-party hegemony in South Carolina, of all places.

Elsewhere, Mazzocchi's life work gets carried on in various ways. One sees his legacy in the single-payer health care campaigns of the California Nurses Association and antiwar agitation by U.S. Labor Against the War (a coalition reprising the role played, in the Vietnam era, by the Mazzocchi-backed Labor for Peace). The network of local coalitions on occupational safety and health (or COSH groups)—which Tony helped foster—continues to function in many cities, trying to fill the void left by unions that have shifted resources into organizing at the expense of job safety fights. The Steelworkers Union, now the home of former OCAW locals, has allied itself with the Sierra Club and embraced a "green unionism" of the sort promoted by Mazzocchi as long ago as the first Earth Day. Unions launching "corporate campaigns" still study the lessons of a Shell Oil strike and boycott that Mazzocchi coordinated thirty-five years ago.

In its account of Mazzocchi's personal life, *The Man Who Hated Work* doesn't ignore his less well-known shortcomings as a husband. Two wives left him, taking six kids with them—either in response to his youthful womanizing or lifelong workaholism. As a devoted friend and comrade, however, the OCAW leader never failed to inspire the author and many others by "conjuring up a labor movement that didn't really exist, but just might." As Leopold describes it:

> This movement would be militant and green. It would bring about radical changes that would stop global warming. It would give workers real control over the quality and pace of work and over corporate investment decisions. It would champion the fight against militarism and for peace and equality. It would win life-enhancing social programs such as free health care. It would dare to create a new political party to counter the corporate domination of the two major parties. In short, it would make good on its potential to transform American capitalism into something much more humane.

In a time of shrunken aspirations and dwindling membership, few union leaders today project anything like this expansive vision, which is why Tony Mazzocchi is so greatly missed.

PART TWO

RACE, CLASS, AND GENDER

The articles in Part 2 deal with the intersection of race, class, and gender in American labor, past and present. As Brandeis University historian Jacqueline Jones observes, the United States has a long suffered from "a racialized 'zero-sum game' principle of labor relations"—namely the idea that white workers have everything to lose if non-white workers are allowed to make any gains. Long before labor officially endorsed "civil rights" in the 1960s, some unions like the United Mine Workers had a better than average record of interracialism, particularly when compared to AFL craft unions. But as the work of Ruth Needleman, Judith Stepan Norris, and Maurice Zeitlin shows, even on the left wing of the labor movement, the legacy of past employer discrimination and persistent racism on the shop floor cast a dark shadow over the functioning of newer industrial unions like the United Steel Workers and Auto Workers. An equally humiliating heritage of discrimination against Chicanos in jobs, housing, schools, and public accommodations led a California community organizer named César Chávez to become a union builder as well. The work of Susan Ferriss and Ricardo Sandoval and, more recently, Randy Shaw, traces the rise and decline of the United Farm Workers. More than any other union in the past half-century, the UFW functioned (during its early years) as an inspiring social movement. It also left behind a large alumni association whose UFW-inspired activism influenced later developments in other unions, the immigrant rights movement, and campaigns for Latino political empowerment.

Several articles address the disappearance of the "working class," an ideological magic trick performed by our mainstream media and political parties, corporate propagandists, and their handmaidens in higher education. As Michael Zweig reveals, "America's best-kept secret" is that the working class still exists and, in fact, constitutes the majority of the population. Any reader seeking further confirmation that low-paid labor still abounds need look no further than *Nickel and Dimed*. In "Prole Like Me," I locate Barbara Ehrenreich's tour de force of workplace reporting in the venerable tradition of Jack London, George Orwell, and the lesser-known John Howard Griffin, who crossed the color line during the era of segregation to find out what it was like to be black in the American South. Part 2 concludes with a contemporary tale of life, work, and labor struggle in which "black and white" were able to "unite and fight" with the kind of results that unions need more often.

A Long Tradition of Bias

The civil rights movement of the 1960s and subsequent enforcement of fair employment laws have so transformed the American workplace on the surface that current generations of workers have little conception how pervasive job discrimination was in the past. For most Americans today, racial bias in hiring is an evil as remote and abstract as the black slavery that preceded it for several hundred years. We know that the old race-based division of labor was wrong and may even have a contemporary legacy (although that is now disputed in debates about affirmative action). But few of us spend much time pondering what it was like to toil under systems of job segregation or involuntary servitude that had a long-term negative impact on the economic prospects and social position of millions of people.

Jacqueline Jones's study of employment relationships in the United States from the colonial period to the modern era offers a weighty reminder that race was, until recently, a determining factor in the allocation of job opportunities. Jones, a Brandeis University historian, also reveals, in painful detail, realities about work life in pre-Revolutionary

America long ignored in our civics texts and still overlooked in their modern revisionist rewrites that emphasize, belatedly and correctly, the mistreatment of non-whites.

In the patriotic myth, yeoman farmers—free and independent all—hacked our new nation out of the wilderness, finding time to forge a uniquely egalitarian civic culture and body politic. As Jones shows, however, myriad forms of indentured labor or "white servitude" made a big contribution to colonial economic development, particularly in the South. Drawing on court records, diaries, newspaper accounts, and other contemporary sources, the early chapters of *American Work* read like a kind of "Drudgery Report." The poor whites exploited in the kitchens, fields, mines, and construction sites of Colonial America initially had much in common with the downtrodden Native Americans who were impressed into service and with Africans later imported to replace English laborers when the latter became too unreliable or hard to recruit.

All three groups did a surprising amount of fraternizing, Jones finds. And, of course, they responded to their oppressed condition with individual and collective acts of resistance, such as running away from cruel masters (Ben Franklin's route from rages to riches) or fighting back via Indian wars and slave revolts. Unfortunately, as successive waves of other European immigrants arrived on these shores, job competition entered the picture. White workers decided they had everything to lose if blacks made any kind of gains. There emerged "a racialized 'zero-sum game' principle of labor relations" that, according to Jones, has polluted the American workplace ever since.

American Work paints an unflattering portrait of unions when it comes to job bias. Until recently, Jones argues, organized labor has been part of the problem, not the solution. Before the Civil War, workingmen's organizations were invariably exclusionary. "The white working classes of the northern cities for the most part showed little sympathy for abolitionism," Jones observes. The postwar National Labor Union made some "gestures in the direction of biracial organizing," but ultimately just "reinforced antebellum forms of racial self-identification among white tradesmen."

Even a black veteran of the Civil War, like the son of the famous abolitionist Frederick Douglass, could not win access to a skilled trade such as typography. "When Lewis Douglass got a job in the Government Printing Office in Washington, the typographers barred him from union membership on the ground that he had once worked as a non-union printer for less than union-scale wages." Newspapers with union shops

had, of course, refused to hire him so he learned to set type at his father's
anti-slavery journal in Rochester, N.Y. As the senior Douglass angrily
observed, his son was then branded as "a transgressor for working at a
low rate of wages by the very men who prevented his getting a higher
rate."

The Knights of Labor and Industrial Workers of the World—active in
the late nineteenth and early twentieth centuries, respectively—get higher
marks from the author for their interracial organizing efforts. Yet both lost
out to the conservative craft unions long dominant in the American
Federation of Labor. Many of these affiliates remained hostile to non-
whites even after their restrictive practices were challenged by the
Congress of Industrial Organizations (CIO) during the Great Depression.
"What distinguished the 1930s from previous decades," says the author,
"was the (at least tentative) welcome that industrial unions offered to black
workers as members, if not as rivals for specific 'white jobs.'"

Often led by radicals, the new CIO unions tried valiantly to rally
workers with slogans such as "Black and White, unite and fight!" But
even where they succeeded in creating what were, then and now, rare integrated institutions, patterns of segregation remained embedded in the
structure of auto and steel plant jobs. There was little interracial mixing
after work outside the union hall, and white labor leaders who pushed
anti-discrimination steps too far risked a rank-and-file backlash ranging
from "hate strikes" to civil disturbances like the 1943 white-initiated
"race riot" in Detroit.

While acknowledging that passage of the 1964 Civil Rights Act and
its subsequent enforcement by the Equal Employment Opportunity
Commission were "unprecedented efforts to eradicate racial discrimination" Jones ends her book on a pessimistic note. She believes "the federally sponsored drive to ensure black people access to good jobs has
stalled" and will never succeed in the absence of large-scale job creation
in the public sector. African-Americans fought their way into better-paying, more skilled blue-collar jobs just in time to see them deindustrialized
out of existence in cities with large black populations. Many of the
"impressive gains" in workplace integration over the last forty years have
been erased as globalization of economic activity, technological change,
and the shift toward white-collar, technical, and professional work has
continued to leave black workers behind.

Blacks victimized by capital flight and corporate restructuring now
find they are not alone in their job insecurity, wage stagnation, and down-

ward mobility. These trends reflect an even bigger divide then the racial one—namely, the growing wealth and income gap between affluent Americans and middle- or lower-income workers of any color. "In the late twentieth century," Jones observes, "Americans tend to support in principle and law the ideal of equality, but they remain remarkably tolerant of the most dramatic market-based inequalities." The resulting disparities in the quality of housing, child and health care, public education, family stability, and community safety put millions of people, black and white, at a great disadvantage before they ever reach the job market. To Jones, the limits of equal-employment laws for blacks in a period when traditional manufacturing jobs are disappearing and "labor exploitation is for the most part color-blind" reveals "one of the central ironies in American law and politics: that a nation ultimately determined to eradicate legal distinctions among various groups would prove so accommodating to real distinctions between the rich and poor."

Readers looking for new political strategies to achieve greater economic justice won't find them here. *American Work* remains resolutely descriptive, rather than prescriptive—and the work of an academic, not an organizer or would-be policymaker. But perhaps Jones's book will still have the desired agitational effect. Rarely has a historian done a better job illuminating the deep roots of problems that America needs to address.

THE MOST DANGEROUS
WOMAN IN AMERICA

John Sayles's *Matewan*, a labor film classic, captured for modern audiences all the elements of pre–New Deal class warfare in America's coalfields. Melding fact with fiction, *Matewan* tells the story of a strike in southern West Virginia that ends in a shoot-out between miners and company "gun thugs" from the Baldwin-Felts Agency. The film vividly and accurately depicts violent coal operator resistance to the United Mine Workers; the squalor and hardship of life in the temporary encampments set up by strikers and their families when they were evicted from company housing; the tensions between black, Italian, and white Appalachian miners created by management's "divide and conquer" tactics; and the important role of "outside organizers"—represented in *Matewan* by a fictional former Wobbly, Joe Kenahan, who is dispatched to Mingo County by the UMW to aid the strike. Successful at defusing racial and ethnic discord, plus overcoming miners' suspicions about him, Kenahan nevertheless fails to keep their struggle on a nonviolent path. Before he is killed in the crossfire between capital and labor in the film's final scene, a local UMW activist tells him: "You expect too much of people, Joe. You're still after that One Big Union. Most of us can't see past this hollow."

Students of labor history wishing to delve deeper into the themes explored so ably in *Matewan* now have two new books to consult—Elliot Gorn's *Mother Jones: The Most Dangerous Woman in America* and Brian Kelly's *Race, Class, and Power in the Alabama Coalfields, 1908–1921*. A professor of history at Purdue, Gorn provides a rich portrait of the life and times of organized labor's leading "outside agitator" in the early twentieth century, when female union leadership was largely unknown. His book covers every miners' strike and labor *cause célèbre* that Mary Harris Jones aided anywhere in the country over three decades. Kelly's volume, on the other hand, is a much narrower but no less valuable account of UMW organizational efforts that were brutally suppressed in a single state. A lecturer in the School of Modern History at Queens University Belfast, Kelly has produced a detailed, footnote-studded academic work that is still extremely readable.

In the pre- and post-WW I strikes rescued from obscurity in *Race, Class, and Power,* UMW members provided a rare display of what Kelly calls "working-class interracialism" in the Deep South. This aroused ferocious opposition not only from local coal operators but every other defender of white supremacy, from the Birmingham business establishment to the Alabama KKK. To undermine the allegiance of African-American members, the UMW's race-baiting foes even enlisted the help of the state's "small but influential black middle class"—a coterie of ministers, minority business owners, newspaper publishers, and other community leaders "who warned black miners to steer clear of the 'white man's union.'"

Read together, Gorn and Kelly's histories explore the complexities of race, class, and gender in the coalfields, as all three came into play during early UMW attempts to challenge the economic and political power of management. Gorn's discussion of Mother Jones's unique, if contradictory, persona is particularly interesting. His biography recounts how this Irish immigrant—who was not only working class and female but poor, old, and widowed—accomplished the astonishing feat of becoming one of the best-known public figures of her era. In the process, she organized hundreds of unemployed workers to join "Coxey's Army" in its mid-1890s march on Washington; barnstormed for the Socialist Party as one of its most effective educational speakers; participated in the founding convention of the Industrial Workers of the World (IWW) in 1905; championed the Mexican Revolution in 1911; and was still rallying strikers and campaigning to free political prisoners at the age of eighty-seven in 1924!

Throughout her long career, Jones may "have clung to an antiquated nineteenth-century view of separate [male and female] spheres and virtuous republican motherhood," according to Gorn. Yet she also helped overturn prevailing "gender conventions by insisting that women speak out on public issues." "In a culture that still preferred females to be frail and ineffectual, her voice rose loud and clear" on countless picket lines and at hundreds of union meetings. In her nonstop "hell raising" among UMW members in Colorado, Illinois, Pennsylvania, and West Virginia, Jones rallied both strikers and their wives, often under the most desperate conditions. Her message was always the same: "We will express our opinions, powerful men will not intimidate us, even from jail we will be heard."

Among those who responded to Mother Jones's call for working-class solidarity were African-American miners, for whom she had nothing but the highest praise, declaring them to be "among the staunchest unionists in West Virginia." (Her views on Asians were far less enlightened and she long supported mainstream labor's racist opposition to Chinese immigration.) The first miners' strike she supported was a nationwide UMW walkout in 1894. According to Gorn, that struggle was "especially militant" in Alabama where 5,000 strikers marched through Birmingham in a "monster parade" against the use of prison labor in the mines. "For the first time in this district," one newspaper reported, "no distinction as to color was made. Negroes marched in companies sandwiched between the white men. A negro and a white miner carried a banner on which was inscribed, 'The Convicts Must Go'!

The UMW failed to win recognition and collective bargaining in Alabama in the 1890, or as a result of the later strikes chronicled by Kelly. (Coalfield unionization finally succeeded in the state only in the 1930s as part of broader CIO organizing involving the steel industry as well.) To defeat the miners' periodic rebellions against the misery of their existence, Alabama coal operators played the race card in sophisticated fashion. At the nadir of UMW influence in the years following its 1908 strike, they patched together a system of labor relations that grafted the most advanced model of labor management in the world onto more traditional methods rooted in the region's slave past. In the coal camps and mine villages throughout the Birmingham district, an ambitious reform program inspired by northern-based welfare capitalism coexisted with convict labor, the company "shack rouster,"and the whip. The centerpiece of the operators' project was a system of racial paternalism that aimed to take advantage of existing racial divisions and the relative vulnerability of black workers under Jim Crow to erect a permanent barrier against unionization.

In analyzing how this system worked to pit black against white miners, Kelly rejects the school of labor history associated with former NAACP staffer Herbert Hill, a well-known critic of "the myth of the UMW's benevolence to the black worker." According to Kelly, Hill's "positing of a fixed overriding attachment to racial supremacy on the part of white workers" fails to take into account "the obvious fact that coal operators themselves exercised far more control over the racial division of labor than the UMW ever did." In Alabama, where the UMW fought against the convict lease and exploitative subcontracting systems (both of which weighed heaviest upon black miners), the elusiveness of equal treatment for blacks had less to do with white miners' racism than the union's inability to match the operators' overwhelming power.

Kelly shows how tens of thousands of miners struck and stuck together for extended periods in walkouts ultimately crushed by the intervention of the state militia in both 1908 and 1920–21. This "pragmatic interracial collaboration" may not have always reflected "full equality" between blacks and whites in the Alabama UMW, but it does, Kelly argues, demonstrate "the singular potential for joint struggles around material interests to break down racial divisions." White miners do not emerge from *Race, Class, and Power* as "egalitarian knights" but rather as "a more complicated and varied mass." Although "deeply inscribed by the pathological culture in which they developed, their ideas on race were subject to change in the protracted social crisis that industrial confrontation" produced in the Alabama coalfields.

LEFT OUT:
BLACK FREEDOM FIGHTERS IN STEEL

In the mid-1970s, when midwestern cities were still ringed by the glowing hearths of steel mills instead of their post-industrial rubble, dissident steel workers were on the march. Their champion then was Ed Sadlowski, a critic of the union establishment who was campaigning, unsuccessfully, for president of the United Steel Workers of America (USWA). "Oil Can Eddie" was a product of the union's Chicago-Gary district, where blacks and whites united to build the Congress of Industrial Organizations (CIO) in the "old left" working-class milieu vividly described in Ruth Needleman's *Black Freedom Fighters in Steel*.

Long before bumper stickers appeared on Volvos urging us to "Celebrate Diversity," Sadlowski tried to do just that when he assembled his "Steelworkers Fightback" slate. In addition to himself, a Polish-American, it included a Serbo-Croatian, an African-American, a Chicano, and a Jew. This rainbow coalition covered all the political bases in USWA except Canada, a fatal omission in an "international union" that has since elected two Canadians as president!

In 1976, however, the emergence of a black candidate for the USWA executive board, Oliver Montgomery,was big news indeed. In the four decades since the USWA's founding, no African-American had ever made it to the top ranks of America's second largest industrial union. By the 1960s, continued discrimination in the mills and exclusion of blacks from the union leadership and staff triggered a rank-and-file revolt, led by Montgomery and others. To undercut Sadlowski's appeal to minority workers, based on his alliance with this well-known civil rights veteran, incumbent officials quickly created a new USWA vice presidency for "human rights." They then found a safer African-American candidate for the job—a union headquarters loyalist who was "not part of the black protest movement." Such partial victories are a reoccurring feature of the anti-discrimination fights recounted in Needleman's steel union history. On a broader canvas in *Left Out*, sociologists Maurice Zeitlin and Judith Stepan-Norris trace the rise and fall of radical influence within the CIO generally and its impact on race relations, workplace militancy, and union democracy. Both books are very relevant to current efforts to revive the labor movement, particularly through recruitment of more women, immigrants, and other "minorities" who together constitute a new majority in many workplaces.

Workers being wooed by "progressive unions" now are already learning the truth of Frederick Douglass's famous nineteenth-century axiom—"power concedes nothing without a demand" (which applies equally to industrial relations and internal union politics). In today's AFL-CIO, grassroots participation in the pageantry of Justice for Janitors campaigns or the Immigrant Workers Freedom Ride is highly prized, just as the CIO once put a top priority on African-American support for unionization in steel. Worker involvement can be more problematic, however, when initial organizing or contract fights are over, labor-management relationships have become institutionalized, and union bureaucracy is far more entrenched than rank-and-file power. As Needleman observes, "without membership initiative and organization, without debate and opposition, unions lose the spirit and substance that makes them work."

Left Out tracks the ebb and flow of CIO insurgency with charts, statistical data, and a critical review of past academic literature. Needleman anchors her analysis in oral history, focusing on the moving personal stories of five steelworkers whose union involvement spanned more than sixty years. The overlapping careers of George Kimbley, William Young, John Howard, Curtis Strong, and Jonathan Comer add up to a collective profile in courage. Although differing in their handling of "racial conflicts and individual prejudice," all played "instrumental roles in establishing a union in steel, implementing fairer workplace standards, and forging alliances with community, civil rights, and women's organizations."

Behind labor's official support for "civil rights," there has always been a more complex reality, even in left-led unions. CIO organizing in the 1930s broke with the AFL's tradition of craft union bias, creating integrated working-class organizations that had little precedent in a society long segregated, at all levels, in its housing, education, and employment. Citing no less an authority than W. E. B. Du Bois, *Left Out* argues that the CIO became "a major racially egalitarian force in American life." Needleman likewise notes that CIO leaders backed "anti-lynching and anti-poll tax legislation, fair employment practices, fair housing, and voting rights." Yet the legacy of past employer discrimination—and persistent racism on the shop floor—cast a dark shadow over the functioning of individual unions like the United Steel Workers.

Using collective action and the threat of workplace disruption, black USWA pioneers helped curb many of the worst abuses by lower-level management. Unfortunately, inequality on the job had a structural dimension. As Needleman explains, "The steel companies established segregation through their industry-wide pattern of hiring; blacks and Mexicans were channeled into the worst jobs in the coke plant, open hearth, and blast furnace, or into the labor gangs in predominantly white departments." Even within departments, jobs were arranged in white-dominated promotional "sequences" or groups, "segregating the better jobs from the worst ones." When minorities challenged this system, the resistance was greatest where white workers saw their higher-paying positions—and seniority—being threatened. Of course, the "seniority rights" they defended, with union backing, were neither plant-wide nor departmental but rather "seniority within sequences"—not exactly a color-blind application of the principle.

In the 1940s, black USWA members themselves, with assistance from white leftists, began to chip to away at this edifice of injustice. How much help they got from their local unions—and how much of a "melting pot" the USWA actually became—usually depended on the success of joint campaigns with fellow activists who were Communists. For conservative defenders of the status quo, in the plant or at the union hall, the political equation was clear: "Black plus white equals red."

The subsequent elimination of many Communist Party members from positions of local union influence after passage of the Taft-Hartley Act—and the ferocious attacks on left-led unions expelled from the CIO in 1949—undermined antidiscrimination initiatives in the steel industry and elsewhere. In the midst of the great purge, a columnist for the *Washington Afro-American* lamented the CIO's retreat toward "America's traditional policy of segregation and Jim Crowism." As *Left Out* reports, even Willard Townsend, a leading anti-communist and black railway union official, was forced to admit in 1955 that CPers "did keep the civil rights question alive." During the McCarthy era, two of Needleman's subjects, Young and Strong, took brave stands in defense of white radicals facing persecution within the USWA. In the interests of their own survival, other African-Americans distanced themselves from onetime political comrades and causes.

The civil rights revolution of the 1960s spawned a new alliance within the Steel Workers, among black activists themselves. They formed a rank-and-file caucus called the National Ad Hoc Committee, which launched a renewed legal, political, and public relations assault on discriminatory practices. Aided by NAACP Labor Secretary Herbert Hill, Ad Hoc members ultimately used the battering ram of Title 7 of the Civil Rights Act of 1964 to overcome promotional barriers. Nearly a decade of litigation involving major steel makers and the USWA resulted in a controversial industry-wide "consent decree." It provided little back-pay but did "open up jobs and apprenticeship programs previously off limits to African-Americans" and increased the number of women and minorities hired into the industry.

Unfortunately, black steelworkers gained access to better-paying, higher-skilled jobs just in time to see much steel making work deindustrialized out of existence. By the mid-1980s, half the workforce in East Chicago and Gary had been eliminated, due to mill closings, new technology, foreign imports, and corporate restructuring. The legacy of equal opportunity that Needleman's "freedom fighters" hoped to "pass down to the next generation" vanished. Now stranded in devastated urban communities, their "children and grandchildren would not even have access to low-paid, dirty jobs in the mills."

Despite this tragic denouement, *Black Freedom Fighters* contains important lessons for workers trying to rebuild multiracial unions, inside or outside the Rust Belt. As the basis for a concluding chapter, Needleman assembled a group of past and present USWA activists, male and female, for a freewheeling discussion of their experiences. The participants noted that blacks were not drawn to the union simply to gain rights on the job but also as an "organization that would protect their social and political rights." As one former Ad Hoc member observed, when organized labor put "social justice concerns aside in the name of business unionism, many black activists lost interest" and "black participation started its downward slide."

To make membership voices heard again and promote social movement unionism, the book's "freedom fighters" agree that workers need "self-organization"—independent clubs, caucuses, and networks that can raise issues, stimulate debate, and hold labor leadership accountable. As *Left Out* suggests, such a culture of grassroots democracy might be stronger today if the CIO had not, fifty years ago, cast out and then largely demolished those unions "that were most dynamic, egalitarian, democratic, class conscious, and advanced on issues of women's rights and interracial solidarity." Nevertheless, the example of black activists in steel—who soldiered on, even when shorn of many left allies—demonstrates the power and potential of rank-and-file initiative in a labor move-ment still top-heavy with staff and officials wedded to the status quo.

FIGHT IN THE FIELDS—AND BEYOND

Thanks to their persistent poverty and exploitation, farmworkers in the United States periodically find themselves back in the news. Labor econ-omists report that, with inflation factored in, the average hourly wage for agricultural laborers—never very high to begin with—is down 20 percent from what it was several decades ago. Following the election of new, more energetic leadership at the AFL-CIO in 1995, there was a brief spate of publicity about thousands of trade unionists coming to Watsonville, California, to support United Farm Workers (UFW) organizing among strawberry pickers. At the same time, PBS aired a two-hour documentary about UFW founder César Chávez, who died in 1993, leaving the union in the hands of his son-in-law Arturo Rodriguez. Susan Ferriss and Ricardo Sandoval, two California journalists with extensive experience covering farm labor issues, produced a very readable companion volume to this PBS film. Their biography of Chávez, *Fight in the Fields,* provides important historical background on the UFW's continuing, if much smaller scale, skirmishes with California growers.

In *Beyond the Fields,* Bay Area community organizer and journalist Randy Shaw also focuses on the union during its 1965 to 1980 heyday. Back then, the charismatic Chávez commanded the loyalty of hundreds of thousands of strike and boycott supporters around the country. But Shaw's incisive study also "connects the history of the UFW to an analy-sis of post-1980 and 21st century social movements." In particular, he describes the "role of UFW alumni, ideas, and strategies" in reshaping other unions, building the immigrant rights movement, expanding Latino voting, and forging ongoing alliances between labor and religious groups. Shaw's account picks up where Ferriss and Ricardo Sandoval leave off, tracing the influential post-UFW careers of rank-and-file organ-izers and staff members who were recruited and trained in this "incuba-tor of activist talent." Shaw contends that the spirit of "Si se puede" has never been stronger, as evidenced by the fact that the union's rallying cry (or, at least an anglicized version of it—"Yes, we can!") still "reverberates across the nation's political landscape" at campaign rallies for Barack Obama.

The UFW attracted similar enthusiasm forty years ago because its membership was fighting for dignity and respect on the job and in the community. Before his thirty-year career as a trade unionist, the UFW leader spent almost a decade working as a community organizer in Mexican-American barrios throughout California. In the 1940s and 1950s, as Ferriss and Sandoval reveal, the condition of Chicanos there was not unlike that of African-Americans in the rural South. *Fight in the Fields* describes an equally humiliating system of segregation and discrimination in jobs, schools, housing, and public accommodations.

Chávez was a rebellious teenager who had worked in the fields alongside his family and chafed at the "Whites Only" signs in restaurants and the "colored" sections set aside in movie theaters for African-Americans, Chicanos, and Filipinos. He responded by becoming a voting rights activist. Under the tutelage of Fred Ross, an apostle of Saul Alinksy–style community organizing, he succeeded in mobilizing tens of thousands of Mexican-Americans to register to vote and use their newly acquired political clout to "fight city hall on everything from potholes to police brutality." In 1962, Ferriss and Sandoval report, Chavez set aside political activism "to devote himself full-time to an improbable dream that was rooted in his migrant childhood—the creation of an independent farmworkers union that would force growers to sit at a bargaining table face-to-face with the people who helped make them rich." Agribusiness did not come to the table quickly, however. In fact, growers had every reason to believe they would never have to negotiate with Chávez's fledgling union because farmworkers lacked any rights under the National Labor Relations Act. Prior to 1974, this left UFW supporters in California with no way of securing union representation votes and no legal protection against being dismissed, which, in the case of those who lived in grower-owned migrant labor camps, meant being evicted as well. When grape or lettuce pickers walked off the job to join UFW picket lines, they faced injunctions, damage suits, mass arrests, deadly physical attacks by hired guards, and the hostility of local police.

Both *Fight in the Fields* and *Beyond the Fields* recount how Chávez and his union overcame such formidable obstacles. The authors describe in dramatic detail the late-1960s marches, rallies, recognition strikes, and consumer boycotts that produced the first UFW contracts. More than any other American union in the past half century, the UFW functioned as a social movement. It became a *cause celebre* that attracted college students, civil rights activists, liberal clergy, and national political figures like Robert Kennedy, who conducted Senate hearings on conditions in the vineyards of Delano. Chávez's own persona contributed a great deal to the union's appeal. Deeply religious, the UFW president was, like the Rev. Dr. Martin Luther King Jr., a home-grown Ghandian. In 1968, as strike-related confrontations swirled around him, Chávez embarked on the first of many fasts to help regain the moral high ground. His widely publicized 25-day ordeal became what Ferriss and Sandoval call "a defining moment for the union, one that renewed its sense of hope and unity and restored the power of nonviolence."

But attacks on the union were relentless. The UFW's initial gains were nearly swept away in the early 1970s when growers signed sweetheart contracts with the Teamsters to avoid dealing with the dreaded "Chavistas." The resulting mayhem finally forced California legislators to act. After Democrat Jerry Brown became governor in 1974, the state created an Agricultural Labor Relations Board to referee farm labor disputes. Before the board's operations were eventually subverted by Brown's Republican successors, UFW victories in government-run elections routed the Teamsters and boosted the union's membership to a reported 1980 peak of 100,000. At long last, some farmworkers were finally getting a living wage, health benefits, better housing, and protection against dangerous pesticide use. Unfortunately, the UFW fared worse than most unions during the Reagan-Bush-Clinton-Bush era. As factors in UFW's long slide toward a 2007 membership of only 6,000, Ferriss and Sandoval cite continued grower opposition; the massive influx of undocumented workers from Mexico; the union's overreliance on boycott activity and failure to back it up with ongoing organizing in the fields; and, finally, Chávez's own increasingly autocratic style.

Shaw devotes an entire sad chapter, "The Decline of the UFW," to "Chávez's shortcomings and his role in the union's post-1981 problems" that "have been minimized or ignored" as he was transformed, posthumously, into "a national icon." Shaw describes how Chávez, in his later years, brooked little internal dissent and was not accountable to any democratic structures within the union. As a result, rank-and-file critics were purged and independent thinkers on the UFW staff became so disaffected that they quit, after years of dedicated, low-paid service to the membership. One who left was former southern civil rights worker Marshall

Ganz (active in 2008 as a presidential campaign advisor and organizer trainer for Obama). As Shaw writes:

> Ganz felt that the UFW was not giving workers any real power or responsibilities in setting the union's direction. . . . Chávez's decision that the UFW would not have geographically distinct "locals" left the union without the vehicles traditionally used by organized labor to obtain worker input. [As early as 1978] the UFW's executive board had no farmworker representation, leaving those working in the fields with no way to influence the UFW's direction.

The UFW's loss was others' gain, as its political disapora ended up in new organizational roles. Some of its most talented alums were women like the late Jessica Govea, who took full advantage of the fact that the union provided what Shaw calls "an otherwise unavailable entry point for female organizers." Govea picked cotton and prunes with her parents when she was four years old. In 1967, she began developing her "extraordinary organizing and leadership skills" as a nineteen-year-old caseworker in the union's Farm Worker Service Center. Soon she was aiding the UFW legal department's occupational health and safety campaigning against pesticide hazards.

Several years later, she was coordinating grape boycott activity throughout Canada and, when she returned the United States, became a key UFW operative in California senatorial and gubernatorial campaigns. In her post-UFW career and prior to her death in 2005, she was a labor educator and Central America solidarity activist for Neighbor to Neighbor.

Shaw's book is filled with many such case studies in rank-and-file initiative, courage, and perseverance. Others can be found at LeRoy Chatfield's website, www.farmworkermovement.org, which is, as Shaw notes, an invaluable online archive of personal essays, movement memoirs, rare photographs, videos, and even music posted by past supporters of the UFW. When he first started work on *Beyond the Fields*, Shaw was concerned that "the UFW's role as a training ground for idealistic young activists had not been sufficiently explored." Thanks to his own book, Chatfield's unusual collection, and a forthcoming monumental history of the union by ex-UFW organizer Frank Bardacke, any such deficiencies in past research and writing are now being corrected.

AMERICA'S BEST-KEPT SECRET

In recent years, the AFL-CIO has spent millions of dollars highlighting the concerns of what it calls "working families." The working families mantra has now become a staple of speeches by politicians trying to appear responsive to these concerns. (Usually they're Democrats, but even George Bush had a rally for "working families" when he ran for president in 2000.) In New York, there's even a Working Families Party, which provides an additional ballot line for labor-backed candidates.

To the extent the phrase acknowledges the existence of a constituency broader than just union members, its expanded usage represents a commendable effort to project organized labor as the voice of unorganized workers as well. "Working Families" rhetoric also seems to be a response to the Right's claim to be the main defender of "family values" and, by extension, of families themselves. But one thing that talking about "working families" does not do is lift the fog of confusion that has long obscured the existence and condition of a working class in the United States. "Class," explains economist Michael Zweig, "is one of America's best-kept secrets. Any serious discussion of it has been banished from polite company. Yet the sooner we realize that classes exist and understand the power relations that are driving the economic and political changes swirling around us, the sooner we will be able to build an openly working-class politics."

Zweig's highly readable and useful new book, *The Working-Class Majority*, strips away the usual misconceptions about this topic. Employing down-to-earth examples and a writing style remarkably free of academic jargon, the author places current trends like wage stagnation, privatization, de-unionization, and the erosion of social programs within the broader context of class structure and conflict. "We often think of class in terms of different status, income or lifestyles," he says, "and it is true that these differences exist. But the real basis of social class lies in the varying amounts of power people have at work and in the larger society." Using U.S. Department of Labor data, Zweig effectively rebuts the myth "that a vast middle class contains the overwhelming majority of Americans." In fact, more than 82 million people—or 62 percent of the total labor force—do the direct work of production, typically have little control over their jobs, and have no supervisory authority over others.

Zweig's book examines the ways in which upward mobility, Cold War ideology, consumerism, and racial divisions have inhibited the political mobilization of this majority on behalf of greater economic justice. The resulting "increase in inequality is not just a case of the rich getting richer and the poor getting poorer," even though many workers have in fact experienced a steady decline in their living standards and quality of life. Rather, Zweig argues, growing inequality of wealth masks a growing inequality of power. "One of the great weaknesses of the standard view of class is that it confuses the target of political conflict," he contends. When the working class disappears into the middle class—or into amorphous PR formulations like "working families"—"the capitalist class disappears into 'the rich.' And when the capitalist class disappears from view, it cannot be a target."

Striking Steel, by labor educator Jack Metzger, makes Zweig's point about the damaging political and even psychological effects of the "everyday theory of social class"—i.e. the three-class model of rich, poor, and middle class that leaves the working class out of the picture. But Metzger does so in a much more personal way. The son of a steelworker, he has written both a moving family memoir and a detailed history of postwar labor relations in the steel industry, with a particular focus on the United Steelworkers four-month national strike in 1959. In Metzger's view, the fifties were "the golden age of the American working class," an era when shop-floor power and pride, steadily rising living standards, and solidaristic blue-collar communities—like his hometown of Johnstown, Pennsylvania—provided a bulwark against such hostile cultural values as competitive individualism. "It was a time," he writes, "when the working-class sense of possibility was large, and there was a unity and coherence to working-class life that is not there today."

Many social and economic forces over the past forty years have eroded that collective identity. Metzger lays particularly blame on the "cultural hegemony" of the professional middle class, both its conservative "managerial-technical wing" and its more liberal "cultural-communications" segment. Operating within a framework established by "the power of the market and Big Money," middle-class professionals dominate politics, the mass media, entertainment, higher education, and the arts. Through their control over "what to remember and what to forget," they have shaped an "official memory" of life in postwar America that renders the working class invisible and depicts union influence as negative and negligible.

"Now that the American labor movement is indeed small and weak, it has begun to dawn on some of us within the liberal wing of the professional middle class how important labor was when it was large and strong," Metzger notes. "But the telling of history hasn't caught up with that perception yet." As both Metzger and Zweig suggest, unions can help rebuild their strength by reclaiming the idea of class from the dustbin to which it has been consigned. Their books should be widely read as part of that process.

PROLE LIKE ME

About every thirty years for the last one hundred, a crusading journalist somewhere has gotten the same idea: Abandon the middle-class literary life (for a brief period), get a real job, gain firsthand experience in the underclass, go home and write it up. Not surprisingly, most practitioners of the genre have been left-wing whistle-blowers—notably, Jack London and George Orwell. London's 1902 book *People of the Abyss* chronicled the misery of urban and agricultural workers, plus the unemployed, in turn-of-the-century England. "Work as they will," he discovered, "wage-earners cannot make their future secure. It is all a matter of chance. Everything depends upon the thing happening, the thing about which they can do nothing. Precaution cannot fend it off, nor can wiles evade it."

Already a renowned writer, London entered this new world of poverty and insecurity "with an attitude of mind which I may best liken to that of an explorer." Orwell's expedition, at the time of the Great Depression, followed in London's footsteps in the same East End neighborhoods, later ending up in Paris. Published in 1933 as an autobiographical novel, *Down and Out in Paris and London* records the author's experiences toiling under terrible conditions as a *plongeur*, or restaurant dishwasher, in the bowels of a great Paris hotel. In both cities, Orwell's narrator struggles to make ends meet—just like his co-workers and fellow tenement dwellers.

> A plongeur is better off than many manual workers, but still, he is no freer than if he were bought and sold. His work is servile and without art; he is paid just enough to keep him alive; his only holiday is the sack. Except

by a lucky chance, he has no escape from this life, save into prison. If plongeurs thought at all, they would strike for better treatment. But they do not think; they have no leisure for it.

Three decades later, on the eve of the civil rights revolution in the United States, journalist John Howard Griffin was down and out in Dixie. His book, *Black Like Me*, featured the additional twist of an author trying to cross both class and racial lines. To find out, as a white, what it was like for African-Americans to live and work in the segregated South, the author darkened his skin and traveled about in the guise of what was then called (appropriately enough for Griffin) a "colored" person. *Black Like Me* had a great impact at the time because of the novelty of the author's assumed identity and the book's shocking (for many whites) account of the routine indignities and monstrous injustice of apartheid in America.

It took far less makeup for Barbara Ehrenreich, the well-known social-ist and feminist author and columnist, to "pass" among the mainly white working-class people she met while researching *Nickel and Dimed*. Between 1998 and 2000, she took jobs as a waitress and hotel maid in Florida, a nursing-home aide and a house cleaner in Maine, and a retail clerk in Minnesota. Her trip across the class divide did require that she temporarily leave behind most of the accoutrements of her normal exis-tence—home ownership, social connections, professional status, "the variety and drama of my real Barbara Ehrenreich-life."

Retaining, as her private safety net, credit cards (to be used only in emergencies) and a series of "rent-a-wrecks" to make job-hunting easier, she set out to determine how a person with every advantage of "ethnicity and education, health and motivation" might fare in the "economy's lower depths" in "a time of exuberant prosperity." Not surprisingly, her attempt to "match income to expenses" on the $6–$8 an hour wages of the working poor succeeds only briefly—and just barely—in Portland, Maine, where she is able to juggle two jobs at once. Like Orwell living in Left Bank penury in Paris, she quickly becomes obsessed with counting her pennies and staying within a daily budget that does not allow for any splurges or unexpected financial adversity. Unlike the hundreds of thou-sands of single mothers with children who have been dumped into the job market by "welfare reform," she doesn't have to worry about finding and paying for child care while holding down a draining, low-income job (or two). Nevertheless, she ends up being defeated by the same fundamental obstacle they face: despite much hard work, "many people earn far less than they need to live on."

"How much is that?" she asks. "The Economic Policy Institute recently reviewed dozens of studies of what constitutes a 'living wage' and came up with the figure of $30,000 a year for a family of one adult and two children, which amounts to a wage of $14 an hour." The problem is that "the majority of American workers—about 60 percent—earn less than $14 an hour," while 30 percent, according to the EPI, made $8 an hour or less when Ehrenreich joined their ranks in 1998. At each stop on her low-wage tour, the author tests out local support services for the working poor. Not surprisingly, the things that people need most to make their lives better—health coverage, affordable housing and access to mass transit—aren't available at the agencies she visits. (Instead, she gets the occasional bag of free groceries, plus referrals for apartment rentals she can't afford.) She finds that many of her co-workers, particularly those without family support networks, lack sufficient funds for the rental deposits and one month's advance rent needed to acquire an apartment. As a result, they are forced into overcrowded, rip-off lodging arrangements at seedy residential motels, which charge by the day or week. Even trailer-park living, which Ehrenreich tried in Key West, is now prohibitively expensive in tighter local housing markets. The nation's widespread deficiencies in public transportation also limit workers' options about where they can live—and work—if they don't own a car.

Many low-end employers don't offer health insurance, of course. Even when they do, workers in places like Wal-Mart often can't afford the payroll deductions required for family or even individual coverage when their starting pay is only $7.10 an hour (rising to $7.75 after two years in the Minneapolis store where Ehrenreich worked). The resulting lack of preventive medical and dental care leads to a cycle of daily discomfort and, sometimes, life-threatening deprivation. The work that Ehrenreich describes in painful detail—scrubbing floors, waiting on tables, lifting Alzheimer's patients—is hard on the body. Years of it breeds myriad aches and pains, injuries, and allergic reactions, which, left untreated, become a never-ending source of misery, not to mention missed work, lost income, and potentially ruinous bills. As Ehrenreich notes, she held up as well as she did in several of her jobs only because she hadn't been doing them for long; without her personal history of regular exercise, proper diet, and medical care, a woman her age (late fifties) would have been struggling to stay on her feet all day as a Merry Maid or Wal-Mart salesclerk.

What makes *Nickel and Dimed* so engaging, however, is not its tutorial on the economics and ergonomics of low-wage life and work. Rather, it is the author's insights into the labor process in the retail and service sectors, and into workplace power relationships. If Wal-Mart had been around in Orwell's era and he, rather than Ehrenreich, had worked there, he would have written *1984* much sooner. The private empire created by Arkansas billionaire Sam Walton boasts both a Big Brother figure—the late "Mr. Sam" himself—and a workforce of "proles" (now 825,000 strong) whose docility, devotion, and non-union status are major corporate preoccupations. Entering this "closed system," replete with its own "newspeak" and "doublethink," Ehrenreich discovers that all the workers, like herself, are "associates," all the customers "guests," and the store supervisors "servant leaders."

One of management's top priorities, she learns, is eradicating "time-theft," a crime most often committed by associates who violate Wal-Mart's strictly enforced "no-talk" rule, linger on their smoke breaks, or otherwise dally in the never-ending task of stocking, straightening, and re-stocking shelves. Potential malingerers (and others with rebel tendencies) are ferreted out during the pre-hire process of personality screening and drug testing. Once you're on the job, close surveillance by "servant leaders" and continuing "education"—via taped messages and training videos featuring Mr. Sam—are a constant feature of company life. To leaven this atmosphere of brainwashing and intimidation, "team meetings" for associates often end with a special "Wal-Mart cheer"—a morale-boosting device personally imported from Japan by the founder himself.

Given the widespread existence of such demeaning conditions and "the dominant corporate miserliness," why don't the wretched of this low-wage world revolt? What's holding them back? *Nickel and Dimed* offers several explanations for the absence of collective action: high job turnover among the unskilled, their low self-esteem, the universal fear of being fired for speaking out or challenging management authority, and, in some cases, actual worker identification with corporate values or individual bosses. Even with a background quite different from that of her fellow restaurant workers, Ehrenreich finds herself being affected by the culture of low-wage work in ways that she doesn't like:

> Something new—something loathsome and servile—had infected me,
> along with the kitchen odors that I could still sniff on my bra when I final-

ly undressed at night. In real life, I am moderately brave, but plenty of brave people shed their courage in POW camps, and maybe something similar goes on in the infinitely more congenial milieu of the American workplace.

In the course of the book, after much buffeting by rude customers, abusive supervisors, and unreliable co-workers, a kind of working-class alter ego of the author emerges—the "Barb" of her Wal-Mart ID who "is not exactly the same person as Barbara" (nor as sympathetic):

> Barb is what I was called as a child, and still by my siblings, and I sense that at some level I'm regressing. Take away the career and the higher education, and maybe what you're left with is this original Barb, the one who might have ended up working at Wal-Mart for real, if my father hadn't managed to climb out of the mines. So it's interesting, and more than a little disturbing, to see how Barb turned out—that she's meaner and slyer than I am, more cherishing of grudges, and not quite as smart as I'd hoped.

The author sounds more like her usual self when, as a house cleaner for Merry Maids—the McDonald's of its industry—she is forced "to meet the aesthetic standards of the New England bourgeoisie" down on her hands and knees, with a scrub brush. A particularly obnoxious client, the owner of a million-dollar condo on the coast of Maine, takes Ehrenreich into the master bathroom whose marble walls have been "bleeding" onto the brass fixtures, a problem she wants Ehrenreich to address by scrubbing the grouting "extra hard."

> That's not your marble bleeding, I want to tell her, it's the worldwide working class: the people who quarried the marble, wove your Persian rugs until they went blind, harvested the apples in your lovely fall-themed dining room centerpiece, smelted the steel for the nails, drove the trucks, put up this building, and now bend and squat to clean.

Unable to deliver this political tirade—lest she blow her cover—Ehrenreich instead fantasizes about exacting revenge similar to that witnessed by Orwell and described so memorably in *Down and Out* (i.e., the disgruntled cook who spat in the soup, the waiters who put their dirty fingers in the gravy, etc.). "All I would have to do," she muses angrily in a gorgeous country house, "is take one of the E. coli–rich rags that had been used on the toilets and use it to 'clean' the kitchen counters." No one, she concludes, should be asked to wipe out someone else's "shit-stained" bathroom bowl or gather up the pubic hairs found in their "shower stalls, bathtubs, Jacuzzis, drains, and, even, unaccountably, in sinks."

Ehrenreich has long been a rarity on the left—a radical writer with great wit and a highly accessible style. While often sad and grim, *Nickel and Dimed* is nevertheless sprinkled with the author's trademark humor. She is, for example, frequently struck by the oddity of her circumstances. Sitting alone in a cheap motel, eating takeout food after a hard day at Wal-Mart, she watches an episode of *Survivor*. "Who are these nut-cases who would volunteer for an artificially daunting situation in order to entertain millions of strangers with their half-assed efforts to survive? Then I remember where I am and why I am here."

Half-assed as her attempts to learn unfamiliar jobs may have been—and as funny as she sometimes makes the experience seem—Ehrenreich is still engaged in a serious project. *Nickel and Dimed* may not be prime-time fare for millions. Yet, one hopes that it will still reach enough readers to expand public awareness of the real-world survival struggles that many Americans faced even before the current economic downturn. If anything, this book should command greater attention now because the life of the working poor—never easy in good times—is about to get harder in ways we'll never see on "reality TV."

On the Waterfront

In 2001, when the "Charleston 5" case became a well-known labor *cause celebre*, I was part of a group in Boston that invited a South Carolina longshoreman to speak about the criminal prosecution of his co-workers. The sponsoring committee wanted to broaden the turnout beyond the usual suspects on the labor left (us) and the kind of "friends of labor" who would gather in a fashionable Cambridge living room to give generously to any left-initiated "defense fund." So we also contacted the Boston-area affiliate of the International Longshoremen's Association (ILA) to see if they wanted to meet our guest as well.

The ILA's local headquarters is in "Southie," the Irish-American neighborhood where public school desegregation and busing was violently contested in the mid-1970s. Both locally and nationally, the scandal-scarred ILA had little past connection to progressive trade unionism. Its rather insular Massachusetts membership was rarely seen on the picket lines of other unions. But when the South Boston ILA official who answered the phone was informed that a union brother named Ken Riley was coming to town, arrangements for a meeting were quickly made. To the surprise of some who attended, the main speaker turned out not be a fellow son of "the auld sod," but rather a brother from another planet indeed—a black longshoreman from a local union in the Deep South whose picket-line militancy had triggered a worldwide solidarity campaign.

Suzan Erem and E. Paul Durrenberger's *On The Global Waterfront* is an engaging study of the fight to save five ILA members from politically motivated felony charges that threatened them with many years in jail. The prosecution of the Charleston 5—four blacks and one white accused of rioting—could easily have remained an obscure local problem. Instead, as the authors note, their far-flung supporters "created a blueprint for a future where commerce—having torn down national boundaries in its neoliberal, greed-driven gallop across the globe—is forced to stop and negotiate not with statesmen and diplomats, but with the lowest members in the hierarchy: the workers who move its goods and the local communities in which they live."

The main character in this unusual story is Ken Riley, our visitor to Boston in 2001, president of ILA Local 1422, the public face of the Charleston 5 campaign and a leading African-American trade unionist. With crucial backing from then-AFL-CIO headquarters staffer Bill Fletcher and North Carolina labor federation president Donna DeWitt, Riley built a defense campaign with considerable interracial and cross-border appeal. Among those it brought together were labor and civil rights groups in South Carolina (and elsewhere), longshoremen on the East and West Coasts (who belong to two different unions), and dockworkers around the world.

Such solidarity did not come naturally. It took a lot of hard work, organizational arm twisting, and bottom-up pressure generated by member-to-member networking that often flouted the official protocol of labor bureaucracies, here and abroad. As Fletcher told the authors, even some of his fellow activists in the Black Radical Congress "didn't quite see the relevance" of the case initially because "people looked at it as a 'labor struggle'" lacking sufficient "crossover with the black community." Meanwhile, DeWitt, a retired telephone operator presiding over one of the smallest AFL-CIO state bodies in the country, faced similar resistance. As she recalls:

> Before we even tried to do defense committees, we were trying to make South Carolina members understand. A lot saw it as a racial issue, not something labor should be involved in…. I had to do a lot of convincing that this is about keeping union jobs in the port and that we're all about civil rights. It became real contentious—conservatives were saying this is a bunch of renegade members that got out of hand and we shouldn't support them.

The "renegade" label applied in several ways, and was used by Local 1422's political foes in their attempt to isolate and discredit "a small union in a rabidly anti-union state" with an organized workforce of less than 5 percent. Although almost entirely African-American, Charleston longshoremen did not fit the usual profile of southern workers under siege. The latter, more often than not, are low-wage blacks or immigrants picking vegetables, plucking chickens, slaughtering hogs, or tending to farm-raised catfish, under conditions of extreme exploitation. Riley's members who worked full-time earned $1,350 a week, "performing what many perceived to be unskilled if dangerous work in a state with an average wage of $8 per hour." In the immediate aftermath of the waterfront encounter that led to charges of a felonious "conspiracy to riot," the Charleston dockers were widely denounced by the state's political establishment. According to the authors, even the city's community-oriented police chief (an African-American Jew named Reuben Greenberg) regarded them as "rough, drunken, and violent"—an image unfairly reinforced by media coverage of the picket-line battle.

The political and economic context of that showdown on January 19, 2000, made it no ordinary dust-up. In Columbia, South Carolina, more than 45,000 people had just spent Martin Luther King Day marching on the state capitol building to protest the Confederate flag that had flown over it for three decades. The event highlighted a controversial NAACP-backed boycott of tourism in the state, aimed at removing the rebel banner. Among the marchers were members of Local 1422 and their newly elected president, Ken Riley, a college-educated second-generation longshoreman. Several days later, all the law enforcement agencies mobilized to keep order in Columbia shifted their forces to the Charleston docks. There, 1422 was vigorously challenging Nordana Lines, a Danish shipping company, which had, after twenty-seven years of bargaining with the ILA, decided to cut costs by using a non-union stevedoring firm to handle its cargo.

In the four-month run-up to January 19, Nordana ships faced growing interference with their unloading in Charleston. This disruption at South Carolina's main port, like the NAACP boycott, posed a "distinct economic threat with the added insult of being orchestrated by blacks." The local power structure responded by marshalling "six hundred police in riot gear who shot at longshoremen with beanbag bullets and concussion grenades." They clubbed or arrested more than a dozen ILA members, sending Riley (who was singled out for assault) to the hospital to get twelve stitches in his head. In addition to the heavy cost of defending against the resulting criminal charges, Local 1422 and various individual members soon faced a $2.5 million damage suit filed by the scab stevedoring outfit. If the plaintiff won and some "longshoremen lost their homes and savings accounts for picketing and protesting . . . other shipping companies would be free to go non-union without risk."

What turned the tide against these multiple threats—and beat Nordana in the process—was a creative, wide-ranging effort to invest 1422's fight with national and international significance. Not surprisingly, the initiative did not come from the top of organized labor, which, as the authors note, is "often long on threat and short on action." Early on (and for too much of the campaign), Riley's own national union "was useless." Internationally, Local 1422 "couldn't budge" the International Transport Workers' Federation (ITF) without a much-delayed official request for assistance from ILA president John Bowers, who abhorred Riley's ties to the Longshore Workers Coalition, an ILA reform caucus. Even the AFL-CIO, under the new leadership of John Sweeney, "was asleep" until Fletcher and other allies of Riley prodded the federation to put resources into the campaign and sanction direct fund-raising for Local 1422. (True to form, some labor officials continued to red-bait Charleston 5 backers; to his credit, "Riley refused to distance himself from the leftists who had helped out in his union's time of need.")

Among the activists best positioned to help get the criminal charges dropped were those in the International Longshore and Warehouse Union (ILWU), based in California, and the International Dockworkers

Council (IDC), whose solidarity-minded affiliates threatened disruption of Nordana cargo handling across Europe. The cause of the Charleston 5 was quickly adopted by radicals in the ILWU, which made large financial contributions to Local 1422 and resolved to hold "stop-work meetings" in West Coast ports on the first day of any trial. By the fall of 2001, ILA supporters within the state, throughout the U.S., and around the globe had combined to make such a big ruckus about the case that everyone—except South Carolina's right-wing attorney general, Charlie Condon—just wanted it to go away. Over Condon's objections, the defendants were allowed to pay $100 fines and plead "no contest" to misdemeanors, thereby averting a worldwide day of "industrial action" planned by the IDC (and even the ITF) if the prosecution proceeded. (Once an up-and-coming GOP candidate, Condon lost bids to become governor and U.S. senator, in part because his personal crusade against "mob violence" ended up backfiring so badly.)

For labor, the main lesson of the Charleston 5 campaign is as follows: American unions need all the help they can get from wherever they can get it. The example of ILA Local 1422—which gave to and received from the black community, and then made new friends and allies throughout the United States and the world—needs to be widely emulated. In today's increasingly hostile political and economic climate, no union is an island. Any that tries to be one won't survive for long.

PART THREE

VOICES OF DISSENT AND REFORM

This third section of the book covers the period of hope, opportunity, and, later, disappointment following the election of John Sweeney as president of the AFL-CIO. Sweeney's 1995 "New Voice" victory over incumbent Tom Donahue led to a change in organized labor's relationship with academia. Students and professors who had previously viewed labor as hopelessly pale, male, and stale suddenly began hailing the possibility of a new progressive, multicultural unionism emerging from the AFL-CIO leadership shake-up. As indicated in the title of one upbeat account of Sweeney's first term, this was not going to be "your father's union movement" anymore. Meanwhile, some labor historians and activists remained doubtful that real transformation was possible without far more "rank-and-file pressure from below." In a similar vein, Part 3 argues that labor's mid-1990s makeover was the product of many years of grassroots organizing by indigenous militants and their left-wing helpers. Several chapters note, for example, that the AFL-CIO "palace coup" that made Sweeney president would not have occurred without a prior shift in power within the International Brotherhood of Teamsters. The election of TDU-backed Ron Carey as Teamster president in 1991 represented a genuine grassroots upheaval, much like the coal miners' revolt twenty years before. (On loan from CWA, as a member of Carey's Teamster headquarters "transition team" and supporter of TDU, I witnessed the reclaiming of the IBT's "Marble Palace" by the rank and file, in a raucus Washington, D.C., inaugural ceremony that many Teamster reformers thought they would never live to see.) Three years later, within the AFL-CIO, Carey's support enabled Sweeney to win his bid for the presidency.

In Part 3 we also see that new federation leadership emerged in reaction to lost strikes, concession bargaining, and the breakdown of solidarity during the 1980s. Unfortunately, labor's "heartland losses," analyzed at length herein, did not end in the '90s (as airline, newspaper, and manufacturing workers in the Midwest all learned the hard way). To overcome the union-busting strategies that still weaken private-sector organizing and bargaining today, workers need stronger internal mobilization, plus effective community-labor coalitions and "cross-class" alliances like those on display during the World Trade Organization protests in Seattle in 1999. This section concludes with a consideration of various scenarios for labor renewal, including those favored by Bill Fletcher and Fernando Gapasin. Both served as staff members or consultants to the "new" AFL-CIO during its heyday (and became more critical of Sweeney after leaving his employ). If, as sociologist Dan Clawson argues, labor's current decline is just a prelude to its "next upsurge," the eventual reassertion of workers' power—on the job and in politics—will not be purely spontaneous. It will depend, in part, on prior infrastructure building. That's why many of the case studies discussed in this section highlight the importance of rank-and-file education and action, nurturing relationships between labor and community groups, and union recruitment of younger workers and the foreign-born.

NOT YOUR FATHER'S UNION MOVEMENT

The election of new AFL-CIO leadership in 1995 ushered in an era of *glasnost*. Where open discussion and criticism of union problems was once *verboten* under the regime of George Meany and Lane Kirkland, current labor federation president John Sweeney has, to his credit, let a hundred flowers bloom. As a result, some union activists and officials have joined academics who write and consult on workplace issues in a wide-ranging dialogue about what must be done to revive the labor movement. Jo-Ann Mort's *Not Your Father's Union Movement* and the Ray Tillman-Michael Cummings collection, *The Transformation of U.S. Unions*, are useful additions to this literature of change. They offer different but complementary perspectives on the challenges facing labor today. Both address many of the same topics: how and why Sweeney's reform administration came to power, what it's doing to promote new organizing and political initiatives, the importance of community-labor alliances, the challenge of globalization, and the role of women and immigrants in unions.

As Mort's subtitle suggests, her contributors are mainly "insiders"— new AFL-CIO department chiefs, other union headquarters staffers or their pollsters, consultants, speechwriters, and journalistic admirers. In contrast, the Tillman-Cummings book draws more on the workplace and organizing experience of union rank-and-filers, past and present. Its nineteen contributors include two subway motormen, several auto workers, a letter carrier, a machinist, a former Teamster and a onetime telephone installer.

The authors rounded up by Mort, communications director for UNITE, give Sweeney's "New Voice" team high marks for its media savvy, campus outreach, liberal pronouncements, sensitivity to diversity issues, and purge of cold warriors. Some who aided in the production of the book are, in effect, grading their own papers or something close to that. For example, the editor thanks "Denise Mitchell and her entire AFL-CIO public affairs staff . . . for assistance in making sure that the articles got written." Three chapters later, there's a laudatory account by Mort of the $10 million "repositioning" ad campaign engineered by Mitchell to enhance labor's public image. The overall tone of the book is often more self-congratulatory than self-critical. (One writer, an outside-the-Beltway contributor, warns his colleagues that "we must be careful that our public relations initiatives don't outweigh the substance of our accomplishments.") There is heavy emphasis on technocratic solutions to labor's problems (i.e., more sophisticated use of paid media, opinion surveys, union pension funds, and new policy ideas) and not as much focus on membership empowerment.

The Tillman-Cummings crowd acknowledges the differences between Sweeney and his conservative predecessors, but they are more apt to find gaps between the new AFL's upbeat rhetoric and the grim reality of continuing union decline. They express concern about the degree to which implementation of the federation's programs is still top-down and staff-driven. They believe there's a crucial link between union strength and internal democracy (a subject rarely mentioned in Mort's book) and that organized labor's failure to permit a greater rank-and-file role in decision making will prevent it from becoming an instrument of fundamental social change. Says Herman Benson, elder statesman of the group and defender of union dissidents for the past forty years: "Before the labor movement can effectively spread the message of freedom and social justice to the nation, it must renew that same spirit within its own ranks and convince its own members that this great movement belongs to them and not to its officials."

Contributors to both books agree that Sweeney's ascension to power was, as Benson notes, more in the nature of a "palace revolt" than a rank-and-file rebellion like the one that made Ron Carey the first member-elected president of the Teamsters in 1991. Yet Los Angeles journalist Harold Meyerson, author of the lead essay in *Not Your Father's Union Movement*, takes a particularly narrow view of the historical context of the first AFL-CIO leadership fight in more than a century, while other contributors to the Mort book and *Transformation* see a connection between mounting local unrest and the 1995 leadership coup.

To Meyerson, the deciding factor in Sweeney's challenge to Kirkland and later his successor, Tom Donahue, was the AFL-CIO's "dismal performance" in the 1994 midterm congressional elections, which elevated Newt Gingrich to the House speakership. Neither Sweeney, then president of the Service Employees International Union, nor Gerald McEntee, president of the American Federation of State, County and Municipal Employees, could imagine battling Gingrich's Contract with America without progressive "alliances with community, civil rights, and feminist groups" and "large-scale and highly effective political action programs" like the ones their own unions had developed. So they organized an Executive Council majority to oust the old leadership and overhaul AFL-CIO departments along the lines of SEIU and AFSCME headquarters operations. "This insurgency was not ideologically based," contends Meyerson. "The revolt would not have broken out even among the most diehard anti-Kirkland unions had the Democrats maintained their hold on Congress."

In contrast, Chicago UNITE leader Noel Beasley views Sweeney's victory as the product of discontent with the outcome of union organizing, bargaining, and strikes in the 1980s and early '90s. "The new AFL-CIO is," he argues, "the accomplishment of thousands of union activists who pushed and shoved and argued against stagnation, who shook off the status quo." Those helping to lay the groundwork for change at the top in the '90s included reformers in the Mine Workers, Steelworkers, and Teamsters whose grassroots organizing in the 1970s and '80s was aided by Benson's Association for Union Democracy.

Benson traces the development of these and other less well-known union reform movements in his essay, "A Rising Tide of Union Democracy in the American Labor Movement." He recounts how New Voice slate member and now AFL-CIO secretary-treasurer Rich Trumka got his chance to become president of the United Mine Workers because of the miners' decade-long struggle against authoritarian practices left behind by John L. Lewis. The even longer (and ongoing) rank-and-file fight for Teamsters reform contributed directly to the success of Sweeney, Trumka, and their running mate, Linda Chavez-Thompson, now executive vice president of the AFL-CIO. Carey's election as Teamsters president in 1991 put 1.4 million votes in the New Voice column four years later, providing most of Sweeney's margin of victory. Furthermore, according to Benson, the reformers' "successful insurgency in the Teamsters gave moral legitimacy to insurgency throughout the labor movement and demonstrated that such a revolt could refurbish labor's public image."

Since taking office, however, the main priority of the Sweeney administration has been external rather than internal organizing. The latter obviously remains the province of individual reform caucuses—where they exist—within the local, regional, or national bureaucracies they seek to transform. What Sweeney and his staff have done is challenge AFL-CIO unions to "change to organize." To "make itself a living example of the organizing model," the federation has shifted millions of dollars of its own resources into campaigns to recruit nonunion workers. It has also aided the training and deployment of new organizers by expanding the activities of the Organizing Institute, brainchild of Richard Bensinger, a contributor to Mort's collection and, until recently, Sweeney's organizing director.

Bensinger's chapter highlights the gains made through efforts backed by his department, like the Las Vegas hotel and casino drives conducted by the Hotel and Restaurant Employees. He calls for more coordinated, multi-union campaigns aimed at strategic targets. He also wants greater member involvement in organizing (although one-third of all OI graduates are still recent college graduates rather than union rank-and-filers).

Labor's attempt to increase its "organizing capacity" will not succeed, Bensinger predicts, without "a cultural transformation of our institutions," "a fundamental, even radical, urgent institutional shift" in the way unions operate.

Since writing for Mort's book, Bensinger's own boat-rocking in this area has earned him an early retirement from the higher echelons of the AFL-CIO. He was suddenly sacked in June 1998 and replaced by an ex-SEIU staffer described by *Fortune* as "a career bureaucrat and former political campaign manager with close ties to Sweeney." This controversial move was protested to no avail by organizing directors from the AFL-CIO affiliates most actively involved in membership recruitment. In *Fortune*'s account, Bensinger fell out of favor because he questioned the cost and effectiveness of the federation's ad blitz and the "large-scale staff buildup . . . in departments like field mobilization, which some on Bensinger's team derisively nicknamed the 'Department of Buzzwords.'"

Such criticisms, needless to say, don't appear in the pages of *Not Your Father's Union Movement*. But numerous contributors to the Tillman-Cummings reader—all activists far removed from Washington headquarters squabbles—echo Bensinger's concerns in their critiques of mainstream organizing and contract campaign strategies. In six different essays or case studies, researcher Jane Williams, former organizer Michael Eisenscher, labor educators Staughton Lynd and Pete Rachleff, and longtime *Labor Notes* contributors Jane Slaughter and Kim Moody all make the point that, in Rachleff's words, these strategies "do *not* begin by empowering rank-and-file workers to fight their own battles directly, but rather are premised on taking such power out of the workplace as quickly as possible and putting it at a bargaining table where full-time union officials can wield it 'responsibly' in the interests of a 'larger agenda.'"

In Williams's chapter on SEIU's creative, high-profile Justice for Janitors campaign, she praises its tactical militance and strategic breakthroughs in overcoming contracting-out schemes designed to keep low-wage workers from unionizing anywhere in their industry. However, in both of the locals she mentions—in Washington and Los Angeles—tensions and divisions quickly developed because of the clash between the high expectations of newly organized workers and the "hierarchical power relations" of existing union structures. "We built this union," she quotes Local 399 member Cesar Oliva Sanchez as saying. "We want to be able to make the decisions. . . . We must be respected as much by the companies we work for as by the union we pay dues to." What Slaughter calls a "militancy-without-democracy" approach to organizing can boost union membership, plus add to bargaining clout, but, as Eisenscher points out, the ultimate source of any union's power is the members, and that power can be fully realized only if they—not just full-time staff and officials—are engaged in all aspects of union building, including key decisions about leadership, tactics, strategies, and goals.

Current attempts at "rebuilding the labor movement . . . by hiring and training more staff" will, according to Eisenscher, provide only "a patina of activism" and lead ultimately to "staff-dependent unions" not much different from the old "service model" variety. Nevertheless, one hallmark of the new AFL's organizational style is "staffing up" rather than tapping the skills and abilities of rank-and-file volunteers. Not just any staff will do, either. When Amy Dean, a Mort contributor and Central Labor Council leader, was profiled recently in a San Jose newspaper, she boasted to the reporter: "I have the brightest staff in the county! We have a joke that the first week you come to work at the [100,000-member South Bay] Labor Council, you have a nervous breakdown, because you're used to being the youngest and smartest, and here are all these other people who are also used to being the youngest and smartest. You have to figure out who you are and what you're about."

When going to work for a workers' organization has become an experience akin to being a freshman at Harvard, there's definitely something wrong with the "new" organizational culture that's being created to replace the old one. Labor's old guard may have been eased out in some places and its new faces may be more energetic, racially diverse, and gender mixed. But if the main movers and shakers are appointed hotshots instead of the people who punch a clock and pay dues, not enough has really changed.

That's why, to a degree greatly downplayed in Mort's book, it is still their "father's union movement" that workers must try to change. In fact, some sections of organized labor are in such bad shape under today's leaders that an earlier generation of leadership—whatever its shortcomings—looks good in comparison. One striking example of this is the recently trusteed AFSCME District Council 37, one of the union's largest local bodies. Its mounting corruption scandals have generated almost daily bad ink in the *New York Times* for months. How many millions of dollars in "repositioning" ads will it take to repair labor's image in New York City, thanks to the ratification-vote fraud and massive dues ripoffs perpetrated under executive director Stanley Hill's reign? In addition to damage control on the PR front, shouldn't some of labor's "best and brightest" be grappling with the question of how large union structures like DC 37 can be made more accountable to the workers they are supposed to serve?

Under former director Victor Gotbaum, DC 37 was once a beehive of activity, with progressive staffers and policy experts like those Dean has recruited, who belonged, as Mort does, to the Democratic Socialists of America. They went to work for the labor movement to do good, did some of that and did well for themselves in the process. But what did they and the elected officials who hired them bequeath to the members? Several decades later in DC 37, it's not a pretty sight. No matter how liberal-minded a union may be in its political endorsements, coalition partners, or policy statements, if the members don't have any effective control over the functioning of the organization, particularly its finances, that's a formula for decay and decline—sooner or later.

The contributors to *Transformation* have, for the most part, been active participants in union cleanup efforts. So they understand this iron law of union organization (and how hard it is "organizing to change" or "changing to organize" within the DC 37s of the world). With a few notable exceptions—newspaper-union activist and columnist Juan Gonzalez among them—Mort's contributors have not had the same personal exposure to the underside of business unionism. Or perhaps their reform impulses have been directed elsewhere. That's why *Not Your Father's Union Movement* needs to be read together with *The Transformation of U.S. Unions* to get a more accurate picture of life "inside the AFL-CIO."

FROM THE ASHES OF THE OLD

In the 1970s and '80s, Stanley Aronowitz was one of organized labor's most incisive and scathing critics. In books like *False Promises* and *Working-Class Hero*, the former organizer turned sociology professor regularly chided American unions for their lack of militancy, diversity, internal democracy, and progressive politics. While influential on the left, Aronowitz's published views were not popular in mainstream union circles during the era of George Meany and Lane Kirkland. In the 1990s, however, we find Aronowitz in a more conciliatory mood about the labor establishment. His latest work, *From the Ashes of the Old*, offers a kinder, gentler critique of the AFL-CIO and concludes that its prospects have greatly improved since the election of John Sweeney as federation president in 1995. According to the author, Sweeney's "insurgent leadership" has "infused new hope among working people, their unions, and those sympathetic intellectuals who have been alienated from organized labor."

Among the positive developments cited by Aronowitz is the reestablishment of closer ties between unions and academia—a trend promoted by his editor at Houghton Mifflin, labor historian Steve Fraser, and others in Scholars, Artists, and Writers for Social Justice (SAWSJ). Of course, easing the alienation of labor-oriented intellectuals with opportunities for speaking, consulting, research projects, and graduate student job placements is much easier than rebuilding the collective power of workers. *From the Ashes* is most effective when it exposes the unfortunate gap between the new AFL's upbeat rhetoric and the grim reality of continued union decline.

As Aronowitz notes, labor's weakness is now evident in the public sector, as well as private industry, despite the fact that the only significant growth in union membership in the last thirty-five years has been among government workers. America's public employees barely had time to enjoy the fruits of their recently won collective bargaining rights (in those states that have granted them) before the right wing launched "a campaign to turn back the clock" through privatization. While some transit, teacher, and social service unions have resisted contracting out, the author reports that "public union leaders in the largest cities have tended to adopt policies like those of industrial unions confronted by concession demands: retreat to protect the core of long-term employees, even if it means sacrificing the bottom."

At the bottom layer of public sector employment today are hundreds of thousands of "workfare" participants. They now toil for big city agencies in near-minimum wage jobs but without the right to organize or bargain and as replacements for union-represented civil service employees. This central feature of Clinton administration "welfare reform" obviously undercuts labor's own public sector membership base. Yet, as Aronowitz argues, the AFL-CIO's capitulation to workfare schemes is symptomatic of a failed political strategy "tragically tied to the past" and the Democratic Party.

For the past quarter-century, unions have operated on the "outmoded assumption" that the Democrats are still interested in meeting workers' needs. This position "ultimately undermines the union movement's most urgent tasks"—organizing the unorganized, defending what's left of the welfare state, and developing new labor-based alternatives to market domination of economic and social life. Aronowitz believes that labor could better accomplish such goals by "focusing on the vigorous promotion of legislation with direct consequences to working people, running its own candidates in selected races, and allying itself with independent political formations and social movements."

The "social movement unionism" the author favors looks quite different from the "business unionism" that still prevails, requiring a lot more rank-and-file involvement in policymaking and strategizing. As the book's union-organizing case studies show, non-union employees—whether white- or blue-collar—respond far more favorably to overtures from fellow workers than they do to the appeals of "professional organizers." To grow, as they did in the 1930s, unions must also become more of a force for broader social change. According to Aronowitz, they must "reach beyond the specific interests of their members and speak boldly to the interests of all working people" by allying with citizen action, religious, civil rights, environmental, and women's groups. He shows how community-labor coalitions have in the past and are today aiding union building among African-Americans and immigrant workers.

To make his case, Aronowitz draws effectively, if selectively, on labor history and his own experience as a New York union activist. *From the Ashes* would be a stronger book if the author had rooted more of his sweeping proposals in current examples of successful workplace organizing. If, for example, "self-perpetuating bureaucracy" is still a big problem in unions, what lessons can we learn from Teamsters for a Democratic Union (TDU) or other reform groups that have struggled for years to make leaders more accountable to the rank and file? If labor needs more lively internal debate about new ideas and strategies—Aronowitz's or anyone else's—where and how should this debate be conducted so that workers themselves can participate, rather than just academics, union staffers, and elected officials? The Aronowitz of old would have addressed such questions, but today's milder and mellower commentator on union affairs fails to grapple with them.

THE NEW RANK AND FILE

If nothing else, the early years of John Sweeney's AFL-CIO presidency have been a public relations success. Sweeney's "New Voice" administration has generated lots of favorable media coverage so far—a welcome change from the long decades when crusty conservatives ruled the roost. In labor's not-so-distant "era of stagnation," unions were not a hot topic in part because the face of American labor was so unappealing to the public, the press, and the intelligentsia. Today, daily newspapers, from the *New York Times* on down, are quick to publish personality profiles of rising stars in the new AFL firmament. There is often long-overdue ethnic, racial, or gender diversity in such portraits, plus more than a little "movement history" since local union leadership bodies, central labor councils, national executive boards, and headquarters staffs now include veterans of the civil rights, antiwar, and feminist movements.

What's unfortunately missing from mainstream media coverage is any sense that there ever was a grassroots movement, within labor, that might have contributed to the upward mobility of Brother Sweeney, his "New Voice" running mates, and the sizable crowd of former student radicals now working at AFL-CIO headquarters. In *The New Rank and File*, Staughton and Alice Lynd provide a timely reminder that recent changes in labor did not just originate at the top. Their book reveals that labor's current revival is, in fact, the product of little-heralded workplace organizing that began long before Sweeney's election in 1995. Among the eloquent voices heard in this oral history collection are those of Rust Belt resisters Ed Mann, Charlie McCollester, and Mike Stout, who tried to make "community-worker ownership" a viable alternative to steel mill shutdowns in Pennsylvania and Ohio; Mia Giunta, Jim Ong, Wing Lam, and others involved in immigrant worker organizing in New York and Connecticut; Margaret Keith and Jim Brophy, two pioneers of union campaigning for occupational health and safety in Canada; Marshall Ganz, a onetime field organizer for the Student Non-Violent Coordinating Committee, who moved to California to help build the United Farm Workers; and Marty Glaberman, a Detroit autoworker, author, and C. L. R. James associate whose courses on Marxism influenced wildcat strikers in the League of Revolutionary Black Workers.

In a labor movement still top-heavy with full-time staff (many of them highly paid), the book highlights a different model of labor activism—namely, that of "the permanent rank-and-filer." That's exactly how

Service Employees dissident Kay Eisenhower describes herself in an impressive account of twenty-five years of work as a Bay Area socialist, feminist, and public sector union steward. She and Andrea Carney, another SEIUer interviewed by the authors, have both repeatedly spurned opportunities to join the union staff or even run for higher-level elected office because they believe in rising, as Debs said, "with the ranks, rather than from them."

This is not the first time that the Lynds have saluted such unsung heroes and heroines of labor. Their widely read 1973 book, *Rank and File: Personal Histories by Working-Class Organizers* (which is still in print today, thanks to Monthly Review Press), highlighted the role of local activists in the great industrial union drives of the 1930s and '40s. The additional personal histories they have collected here number more than two dozen and are heavily weighted toward people they've met in their travels or during their own quarter-century of work as labor lawyers in Youngstown, Ohio. Prior to becoming active in that field, the Lynds were in the forefront of civil rights and anti-war activity in the 1960s, political commitments that ultimately derailed Staughton's career as an academic historian. Given their own activist backgrounds, the Lynds are well positioned to illuminate the contributions that have been made to labor's current renaissance by those, like themselves, toiling far outside the Beltway and often at odds with both employers and union officials.

Several of the most interesting interview subjects in *New Rank and File* are "colonizers"—"individuals from middle-class backgrounds who decided that change had to come, or was most likely to come from the working class" and, therefore, "sought employment in a union of farmworkers, an industrial plant, or a hospital in order to do political organizing." Colonizing was how many former New Leftists migrated from campuses to the ranks of labor. It was not an easy transition because most, but not all, took blue-collar jobs that were hard enough to do without the additional task of proselytizing for revolutionary sects or Third World causes. Lynd interviewee Rich Feldman, for example, hired on in the paint shop at a Ford truck factory in Wayne, Michigan, in 1971. As Feldman recalls:

> I had the dream and the commitment to bring the student movement of the 1960s into the plant. . . . Whatever I believed politically I put on the table. . . . I had no problems defending Cuba, defending the National Liberation Front in Vietnam. . . . From the very beginning, I was totally

honest with people. I couldn't deal with the hypocrisy of radicals who were hiding newspapers, and hiding what organization they belong to, and hiding who they were.

At a GM assembly plant near Boston, where Wellesley graduate Elly Leary spent twelve years building cars, such brashness was more likely to get you punched in the nose than elected shop steward. The workforce in Framingham "never [had] any CIO history to draw on or any union activists who were former Reds." When Leary arrived in 1977, members of her United Auto Workers local commuted long distances to work from all directions, had "no natural community," and were saddled with corrupt, do-nothing leadership. Newcomers in the plant tried to rally the rank and file against the incumbents. But, according to Leary, sectarian shenanigans by the October League triggered such a labor-management backlash—replete with spying, blacklisting, and plant-gate beatings—that "it set back any radical work in the plant for ten years." The fallout for "other political people" was "scary." As Leary tells the Lynds:

> Two of us had guns drawn on us. People got spit at too. Verbal abuse was constant. People would scream "Communist bastard" at you. My husband used to get phone calls all the time threatening our kids and me.

Along with their counterparts elsewhere, Framingham colonizers were forced to reassess their approach to co-workers. Leary and others decided they had "to develop roots in the working class and just become regular people . . . be part of everyday life and talk about everyday things" rather than the latest exciting developments in Mao's China. The more patient, persistent, and people-oriented left-wingers succeeded, as Leary did, in building close personal relationships with indigenous militants. ("I had to have 'body guards' in the plant for years because it was too dangerous to walk around alone. I had to have protection. And the only way I could get protection was to be someone people wanted to protect.")

Eventually, Framingham radicals and their allies created an opposition caucus called the Standup Coalition, which published a widely read shop newsletter. The coalition campaigned for greater democracy in the UAW, opposed contract concessions, and challenged race and sex discrimination in the plant. It might well have gone on to take over the local if GM hadn't closed the place in 1989. Like many other colonizers in basic industry, Leary found herself "de-industrialized" out of a job. The

limits of what the Left had been able to accomplish prior to the shutdown, plus the irony of its timing was not lost on her:

> We built a fabulous caucus but erred on the side of getting caught up in
> the trade union crap. Everybody knew that we were socialists and com-
> munists. The red-baiting was so intense you couldn't hide who you were.
> But we spent so much time trying to defend ourselves and trying to build
> a power base and a democratic union that we really neglected the long-
> run vision of a different kind of society. We need to talk about that vision.
> Ironically, just as the plant was closing we began to talk much more polit-
> ically.

Meanwhile, back in Michigan, Rich Feldman was having second
thoughts of his own. He wondered why he shouldn't just quit and
become a lawyer if all that his ten-hour days in the paint shop enabled him
to do was "be six months ahead of what the corrupt plant chairman [was]
saying" about health and safety, contracting out, or bosses doing bargaining unit work.

With the encouragement of two formidable mentors, Detroit
Marxists James and Grace Boggs, Feldman decided to stick it out. His
factory managed to stay open and, lo and behold—after some tough
shop-floor campaigning in the late 1990s—he became the plant chairman. Did his election, after twenty-six years as a UAW member, require
any political compromises? Feldman's interview ends somewhat sheep-
ishly on a subdued note, with fewer trumpets blaring for the NLF or
Fidel. "My role is not as revolutionary as the concept I began with in
1971," he admits. "I remember consciously deciding to stop talking
about Cuba. That was the price of deciding to run for union office. But
that's where it's at for me."

And that's where it's ended up for many others who've struggled in
similar circumstances, over the past three decades, to find the right balance between an exclusive focus on grievances, contract negotiations, or
union democracy and efforts to engage workers around issues related to
societal transformation. Radicals' effective handling of "trade union crap"
has clearly been the key to their winning acceptance among co-workers
and gaining positions of influence in unions. Yet Leary is hardly alone in
wondering how, at the end of the day (or a lifetime on the line), this often
mundane work connects to a "long-run vision" of a different kind of society. "If we want workers to take control and be empowered," she

observes, "then we have to begin to create those situations in small ways while still thinking about the larger questions."

Meeting this challenge can be even more difficult when left-wing activists raise the banner of union reform on the national level (as many, including Leary, have tried to do), with varying degrees of success. In the early 1970s, for example, insurgent UMW members—aided by progressives inside and outside the mines—took on and toppled W. A. "Tony" Boyle, a murderous union dictator. Later that same decade, thousands of steelworkers—colonizers of almost every stripe among them—rallied behind dissident regional director Ed Sadlowski when he ran a strong but losing race for USWA president. Critics of the UAW leadership formed the "New Directions" caucus during the 1980s to unite local opposition groups behind a common anti-concessions agenda. And, in 1991, the most durable rank-and-file movement of all, Teamsters for a Democratic Union, spearheaded the election victory of Teamster president Ron Carey—just sixteen years after TDU was formed by a group of truck drivers that included key cadre of the International Socialists. (The latter proved to be among the best organizers of all the colonizers from the Sixties generation.)

Regardless of how these efforts fared, the Lynds take a dim view of them—to such a degree that the book's IBT-related material never once mentions TDU, its role in the union upheaval that enabled both Teamster interviewees to work effectively as organizers at Overnite, or the fact that one of them was also a TDU member. The editors erroneously claim that campaigns for "top union offices" have resulted only in "modest improvements in several labor organizations." In their introductory essay for *New Rank-and-File*, the Lynds also fault all the best-known national union reformers and reform organizations for being unwilling "to challenge the fundamentals of capitalism" and failing to break out of the confines of "business unionism," with its no-strike agreements, "management rights" clauses, and automatic dues deduction devices.

The problem with this critique is that many of the book's own contributors have done no better making opposition to capitalism the centerpiece of their workplace organizing, no matter how locally focused it was. The Lynds basically disdain all bids for organizational power above the local union (or even steward) level and favor concentrating instead on building "horizontal networks for mutual support." Yet their preferred approach doesn't seem to produce a "solidarity unionism" any more radical and certainly not more widespread than the version fostered by TDU in the Teamsters for twenty-five years or by New Directions activists like Leary in the UAW as well.

Similarly, building entirely new unions outside tainted old mainstream bureaucracies—another Lynd enthusiasm—is no guarantee of lasting political purity or "participatory democracy" either. As Marshall Ganz acknowledges in his interview about the United Farm Workers, the organization launched by César Chávez in the 1960s went from being a vibrant example of "social movement unionism" to a cult-like shell of its former self, with few members and even less membership control, all within a generation. (Even in its recently revived mode, the UFW is still headed by Chávez's son-in-law, an arrangement reflecting one of business unionism's hoariest traditions, nepotism!)

What went wrong at the Farm Workers? Its staff and support network was swarming with anglo Lefties in its early years; some of its key field organizers (like Eliseo Medina, now a national officer of SEIU) went on to work for other unions after being driven away by Chavez. In the Lynd's book, we never find out, in any detail, how power in the union became so centralized or why "no tradition of legitimate opposition" ever developed. (Gans reports that he's working on a doctoral dissertation on the UFW so maybe that's where we'll discover the answers.) This gap in information and analysis is a real shortcoming of the Lynds' oral history approach to illuminating the victories and defeats of the past. Personal anecdotes and rambling old war stories—no matter how vivid—don't necessarily provide a coherent guide for the future. And some contributors to the book still need one.

Among those are rank-and-file supporters of the Coalition of University Employees (CUE), some of whom are interviewed in a concluding chapter. In 1998, they threw out the increasingly dysfunctional American Federation of State County and Municipal Employees (AFSCME) in a representation vote that made CUE—an independent union—the new bargaining agent for 19,000 University of California clerical employees. Before rebelling against their old union at the University of California, CUE's founders tried to work within it. But when they approached AFSCME organizing director (and former SDS leader) Paul Booth to obtain national union backing for their attempt to rebuild their weak and ineffective locals from the bottom up, they were rebuffed.

So, they created a new union instead, on a shoe-string budget with the kind of volunteerism that once made CIO organizing in the 1930s so exciting. Recalls CUE member Margy Wilkinson:

It was incredibly liberating. We had been in a situation of working for a terribly nasty employer. Our principal objection was to the employer. But we were also constantly in battle with our union over resources, over how the union should present itself, over what role the paid staff should play. . . . It was so much easier when all we had to do was build the union and fight the employer. It was like, wow! This is fun.

Now that the "fun" part is over, CUE members must figure out how to institutionalize their grassroots approach without it calcifying into some new form of the bureaucratic unionism they experienced within AFSCME.

There's much in the Lynds' book of an inspirational nature to help CUE activists and others similarly situated remain on a different course. *The New Rank and File* offers role models far more complex and compelling than some that are showcased in the AFL-CIO's new "change to organize/organize to change" program. But many readers will notice that the book lacks any detailed road map for large-scale movement building. In part, that's because organizational alternatives to mainstream unionism are still being developed "in the field" but also because the Lynds mistakenly undervalue some of the most important union reform efforts that have emerged so far.

LABOR'S HEARTLAND LOSSES

American unions are not known for their penetrating postmortems on strikes, won or lost. Even when these fights cost millions of dollars and the workers involved make enormous sacrifices over many months or years, union reps rarely file what the military calls an "after-action report." There are, therefore, few labor equivalents of the Pentagon scribes who meticulously compile official military histories based on voluminous battlefield records. Particularly during the 1980s and early '90s—when the landscape of labor was littered with the wreckage of lost strikes—the dominant tendency was to bury the dead and move on, quickly, to the next disaster.

Strikes are, of course, still celebrated as part of a more heroic working-class past. Authors of books like *Three Strikes: Miners, Musicians, Salesgirls, and the Fighting Spirit of Labor's Last Century*, a collection of essays by Howard Zinn, Dana Frank, and Robin D. G. Kelley, strive to "capture the fighting spirit of labor's last century" and preserve the lessons of labor history "for the struggles yet to come." Unfortunately, the great worker upsurges of yore—the sit-downs and general strikes of the 1930s, the industry-wide walkouts for union recognition earlier in the twentieth century, and the political strikes of the late 1900s—are little more than museum curios in the new millennium, not part of the living history of the labor movement. Their scope and intensity is far removed from the day-to-day experience of most organized workers now. In fact, few trade union-ists—other than labor history buffs and ever-hopeful lefties (often one and the same)—can even imagine how such a "fighting spirit" could manifest itself again on such a wide scale in the United States.

There is, however, a growing body of literature on more recent strikes that, regardless of their outcome, contained within them the seeds of change. These books were produced by journalists, law professors, labor educators, and even a novelist. Their work is essential reading for anyone trying to revive the strike weapon as an instrument of union building, eco-nomic advancement, political consciousness-raising, and rank-and-file leadership development. Among these books are Barbara Kingsolver's tribute to women's role in the Phelps-Dodge walkout, *Holding the Line: The Great Arizona Mine Strike of 1983,* and Jonathan Rosenblum's legal analysis of the same struggle, *Cooper Crucible;* Peter Rachleff's *Hard-Pressed in the Heartland* and Hardy Green's *On Strike at Hormel,* two insider accounts of the mid-1980s fight by UFCW Local P-9 in Austin, Minnesota; Julius Getman's incisive study of the 1987–88 campaign against International Paper, *The Betrayal of Local 14: Paperworkers, Politics, and Permanent Replacements;* and *Ravenswood,* Tom Juravich and Kate Bronfenbrenner's 1999 report on the USWA's successful corpo-rate campaign over a lockout at an aluminum mill in West Virginia.

The latest addition to this genre is *Chicago Tribune* reporter Stephen Franklin's vivid account of the overlapping industrial conflicts that gripped Decatur, Illinois, in the mid-1990s. Franklin's book describes all the key players—in labor, management, and the community—who helped create or were caught up in the resulting maelstrom. The author is partic-ularly adept at recounting the human cost of worker resistance to corpo-rate greed—the anger and disillusionment, lost jobs, homes, and savings, the broken marriages, divided families, and tragic deaths from suicide. Amid all this, *Three Strikes* also offers inspiring stories of personal trans-formation and selfless devotion to labor's cause.

The cast of characters includes workers at A.E. Staley Co., who belonged to the Allied Industrial Workers (later to join the United Paperworkers, now known as PACE); members of the United Auto Workers Local 75 at Caterpillar; and United Rubber Workers Local 713 at Decatur's now closed Bridgestone/Firestone plant (which, in the course of the struggle, became part of the Steel Workers). The lockout at Staley's corn-processing facility was a one-plant affair; the Cat and B/F strikes affected thousands of tractor and tire builders throughout the Midwest. The longest of these disputes—the UAW's ordeal at Cat—lasted 6 1/2 years. By late summer 1994, the existence of three simultaneous high-profile work stoppages in a single factory town had created what union supporters called a "war zone" in central Illinois.

As Franklin shows, the conflicts had more in common than geography. All involved better-off members of the working class. Although good-paying manufacturing jobs were getting harder to find anywhere by 1990, Decatur's unionists had ample seniority and, so it seemed, job security.

> They earned a decent salary and more. They received a raise every year, several weeks of vacation, generous benefits, and completely company-paid health care—all the fruits of union bargaining. In good years, which were many, ample overtime helped them buy bigger houses, newer cars, newer pickup trucks, vacations, and other blue collar dreams.

Prior to Staley's takeover by UK-based Tate & Lyle, AIW members had few labor relations problems other than a 1970 strike against the then-family-owned firm. At Cat, the UAW had staged a 205-day walkout in 1982–83. But, following that fight, Local 75 and others signed on to "company-wide agreements calling for more cooperation between the company and the union." Likewise, the URW had welcomed the change in management style that initially accompanied the 1988 acquisition of Firestone Tire & Rubber by Japanese-owned Bridgestone Corp. B/F briefly became "a 'poster child' for American firms, which had yet to learn how to trust and empower their workers," Franklin reports. "The Federal Mediation and Conciliation Service even gave the company and the union its partnership award."

Soon B/F became a lot less labor-friendly. New CEO Yoichiro Kaizaki informed the URW in 1992 that he wanted major alterations in the master contract covering 4,200 former Firestone workers. Meanwhile, over at Cat, a formidable new UAW foe, Donald Fites, began flexing his muscles.

Before becoming CEO in 1990, Fites had spent most of his management career overseas. His "years in Japan had made him admire that nation's dominant companies and docile unions." It was time, Fites decided, for Cat "to cut itself loose from the pattern bargaining that the UAW had historically used to link it to other major manufacturers."

In short, none of the employers in *Three Strikes* acted, in the early 1990s, as if the era of give-backs ended in the'80s. They demanded—and eventually got—health care concessions; radical changes in scheduling (by introducing, at Staley and B/F, 12-hour shifts); the elimination or reduction of extra pay for overtime, weekend, or night work; second-tier pay rates for newly hired employees; and/or greater flexibility in job classifications and assignments. The new, more aggressive owners or managers of each firm believed that union members had gained too much shop-floor power and that previous bosses had "pampered" them. "It was," observes Franklin, "simply a matter of rules and control. Who ran the place?"

Decatur workers tried to defend their contracts in many of the same and different ways. Realizing their isolation as a small local affiliated with a 50,000-member national union "barely capable of supporting its members," Staley workers voted to quadruple their dues. Then they hired two outside consultants, Ray Rogers of Corporate Campaign, Inc., and Jerry Tucker, the former UAW regional director, Solidarity House critic, and "in-plant campaign" strategist. Tucker persuaded Local 837 to stay on the job when its contract with Staley expired. Rogers's contribution—like his controversial role in the Hormel and IP strikes—was to publicize the Staley fight, raise several million dollars for it, and "devise an attack on the company's financial network." The carefully planned in-plant phase of the struggle ended after nine months, when shop-floor resistance to management's imposed conditions led to a spontaneous walkout. Several weeks later, Tate & Lyle locked the whole group out. Within several months, the company was, according to Franklin, able to resume full production, using managers, temps, white-collar, and clerical workers.

From mid-1993 until early 1996, when Local 837 finally capitulated under newly elected leadership, its then-president Dave Watts, Rogers, Tucker, and their allies, inside and outside the local, succeeded in putting Decatur on the map as a "key battlefront for American labor in the 1990s." Up to 5,000 people participated in "war zone" marches and rallies, while the Staley workers endured mass arrests and police misconduct on the picket line. Along with two other pro-labor candidates, Watts ran for the Decatur city council, helping to elect the first Democrat as mayor in fifty years. The local dispatched teams of "road warriors" to cities around the country, where more than eighty support committees were created. In February 1995, they descended on the "labor mandarins" of the AFL-CIO in Bal Harbour, Florida—providing a timely reminder of why the palace coup then brewing against Lane Kirkland was so necessary. Afterward, when Kirkland held an abortive series of reelection pep rallies in cities like Boston, he was dogged by Decaturites demanding greater strike support. Meanwhile, back home, Staley activist Dan Lane embarked on a 64-day protest fast, which landed him a starring role at the AFL-CIO convention that chose John Sweeney to be Kirkland's successor.

The trajectory of the UAW's fight against Caterpillar was more complicated and less colorful. First the union struck in some plants and was locked out in others. Then it returned to work without a contract and worked to rule. Then it struck again, in all nine plants. The overall campaign was marked by impressive grassroots militancy but, in Franklin's recounting, considerable ambivalence at higher levels of the union. *Three Strikes* contains sympathetic portraits of strike leaders at the bottom and top of the UAW hierarchy: New Directions activist Larry Solomon, who was elected president of Local 75 as a critic of "jointness," and Detroit-based UAW Secretary-Treasurer Bill Casstevens, who spent the last four years of his career locked in reluctant combat with Fites.

It was Casstevens, a Solidarity House alumnus of "the old school," who dismissed the idea of transforming the union's Cat fight into any kind of labor *cause célèbre*. "It would be a battle the UAW would take on by itself. . . . There would be no fancy public relations war. No corporate strategies," Franklin writes. When the union's first walkout buckled under the pressure of Cat's threat to hire permanent replacements, there was, the author contends, "no plan, no escape route, no comeback. No one was riding to the UAW's rescue. Organized labor watched from the sidelines."

In the seventeen-month second Caterpillar strike—which followed two years of in-plant guerrilla warfare, with many disciplinary casualties—the national UAW again opted "to go it alone." Strike benefits were boosted to $300 a week, and the union "was paying about $600 a month per member for health benefits." Nevertheless, before Round Two was over in December 1995, somewhere between 1,000 and 5,000 members had deserted the strike. The plants were operating profitably and smoothly with scabs, temps, supervisors, and office help. New UAW President Steve Yokich "ordered an end to public hostility toward the company" and held a contract vote in which remaining strikers overwhelmingly opposed the company's offer. Solidarity House then sent them back to work anyway. (After another rejection vote in 1998, a settlement was finally negotiated and approved—because it included amnesty for 150 fired strikers.)

The Decatur Rubber Workers' new national union, the USWA, ends up looking much better in comparison. Unfortunately, then-Steel Worker president George Becker, the hero of Juravich and Bronfenbrenner's *Ravenswood*, arrived on the scene rather late in the game. By the time the USWA began aiding the B/F strike, it had already been undermined by 1,000 line crossers and the hiring of 2,300 permanent replacements. Steel Worker staffers ramped up an international campaign to get all union members—including fired strikers—back in the plants after the URW's 1996 surrender. The USWA stirred up trouble for the company with the help of union allies in Japan, Argentina, Turkey, and Brazil. It put sixty workers on the payroll full-time to demonstrate at tire dealers, company meetings, and industry conventions; eventually, more than thirty city governments joined a union-initiated boycott of B/F products. Borrowing on the UMWA's "Camp Solidarity" experience during the Pittston strike, the USWA also rented a vacant lot next to B/F headquarters in Nashville and set up "Camp Justice" as a staging area for protests by workers from all the struck plants. Finally, the 27-month dispute was settled—but on terms far from "the pattern agreement the rubber workers still had in mind in 1994." (In June 2001, following the safety-related recall of 6.5 million Firestone tires and Ford's cancellation of its contract with B/F, former strikers and scabs in Local 713 suffered a final blow when management decided to close the 59-year-old Decatur plant.)

Ultimately, labor was defeated in Decatur because it lacked strike leverage, a problem that remains widespread in a U.S. manufacturing sector with fragmented and eroding unionization. Even though the UAW and URW had members in multiple work locations and a "company-wide" bargaining relationship, none of the workers in *Three Strikes* were able to curtail enough of their employer's production. Nor were they able to interfere with the worldwide operations of Tate & Lyle, Cat, or B/F in any other way that was sufficiently disruptive to bring about a favorable settlement. The unions were, after all, up against "three global giants—the reigning powers in their industries." Tate & Lyle operates in fifty countries. In the United States alone, it had twenty-three other plants similar to the one in Decatur that were either non-union or covered by local agreements with other unions, with different expiration dates and no bargaining coordination. At twenty of them, management had already introduced the rotating twelve-hour shifts so bitterly opposed by Local 837.

Long before the showdown described by Franklin, Cat began "to spread out its production, beyond its UAW plants in the United States to smaller, non-union contractors, and beyond the U.S. to other plants worldwide." By the mid-1990s, a significant share of its manufacturing was overseas—ranging up to 60 percent for some product lines. When the Cat workers walked out for the second time in June 1994, only 25 percent of the company's 54,000 workers were UAW-represented. Management had more than thirty unorganized plants, where production could be shifted. To defeat the URW, B/F management in the U.S. made similar contingency plans with the company's Japanese parent to provide millions of tires during the strike.

Union weakness was exacerbated by the usual dreary internal divisions. Building tradesmen scabbed on each of the locked-out or striking Decatur locals because—their CLC president claimed—"autoworkers and rubber workers had, in earlier years, ignored picket lines put up by the trades." After the AIW merged with UPIU during the Staley dispute, top Paperworker officials in Nashville began lobbying for the removal of Local 837's outside helpers. Staley workers were told that Tucker and Rogers "had too many enemies within the AFL-CIO" and the federation "would not budge" on Local 837's behalf as long as they were involved. Of course, even after both had departed and Kirkland was replaced by Sweeney, the "war zone" received no great infusion of resources or reinforcements from the "new" AFL-CIO.

By then, a few Decatur workers had strong premonitions about their fate—not the least because they had begun to study history to find out "how their situation fit into the bigger picture of organized labor." If the other *Three Strikes*—the one by Zinn, Frank, and Kelley—had been available then, it would have been just the kind of book that strike activists were searching out. Zinn's contribution describes the violent 1913–14 Colorado coal strike that resulted in the Ludlow massacre. In those days, a "war" between labor and management wasn't figurative, it was literal—in this case, claiming sixty-six lives. Frank's account of how female retail workers occupied a Woolworth store in Detroit at the peak of sit-down activity during the 1930s highlights the role of creative new tactics and favorable media coverage in strikes. Robin D. G. Kelley's sad tale of a movie theater musician's protest against canned music traces the impact of new technology and craft union competition on worker solidarity.

In their own quest to understand the changes occurring in their workplace world, key Decatur activists turned to "leftist, alternative magazines, books not easily found locally, anything that explained labor history to them." According to Franklin, strikers and their wives also signed up for a course taught by local labor historian Bob Sampson.

> As the classes progressed, Sampson was struck by how much the workers tied into the disputes seemed to have changed, how much more radical their words and arguments had become. They were unlike the Reagan Democrats he had met over the years in town. They were not complacent. They were angry. . . . They had a feeling about class differences he had not encountered before.

As the disputes dragged on, however, some students "stopped coming to Sampson's classes and soon he understood why." For them, labor's terrible setbacks in the mine, mill, and railroad strikes of the late nineteenth and early twentieth century were no longer an abstraction. From the perspective of the "war zone," this history was now too personal, too painful, and immediate. The knowledge that workers might rise again someday—as they had so many times in the past—was small comfort on the picket lines of Decatur, circa 1994. Instead, the strikers "identified with labor's past defeats as if they were their very own and they were reliving them," as indeed they did.

SOLIDARITY SOMETIMES

In May of 1970, hundreds of flag-waving New York City construction workers—egged on by labor officials linked to the Nixon administration—attacked a crowd of antiwar demonstrators on Wall Street. As played up by the media, it became an encounter emblematic of the Vietnam era—a battle of political stereotypes in which hard hats showed their hatred of long-hairs, "patriots" were provoked by "kooks," and real-life Archie

Bunkers railed against a whole generation of spoiled "meathead" college kids. In some middle-class circles, the incident tarnished the image of unions for a long time afterward.

Nearly thirty years later, news reports from Seattle presented a different picture of organized labor. In the fall of 1999, Teamsters and sea turtle lovers, steelworkers and radical students were seen marching side by side (or at least on the same side) in street protests against the World Trade Organization (WTO). There was no blue-collar cheering squad for the cops or the establishment this time; instead, top officials of the AFL-CIO proclaimed their support for alliances with feminist, environmental, consumer, and Third World groups. Even the '60s-like atmosphere— street theater, body paint, tear gas barrages, and a few broken windows— didn't seem to bother the union participants.

The contrast between these two scenes raises some questions: What has happened in the intervening decades to produce such an apparent "greening" of the labor movement? Has Seattle solidarity really replaced the brawls and catcalls of yesteryear? *Coalitions across the Class Divide* and *Taking History to Heart* will interest readers who believe, as Fred Rose does, that "the success of progressive politics in the U.S. depends on reconciling the immediate needs of working people with the social, environmental, and peace-related goals often raised by middle-class movements." The authors offer varying assessments of how much potential for conflict still exists between "middle-class movements" and organized labor. Now a research professor at Tufts University, Rose was an organizer for an economic conversion project at a shipyard in Tacoma, Washington. His case studies on relations between labor and non-labor groups involve industries such as logging, construction, or defense-related metalworking in Maine, Minnesota, and the Pacific Northwest. In such settings, local campaigns for forest conservation, limits on development, or a shift in investment from military to civilian production frequently encounter blue-collar resistance because of the perceived threat to jobs. To defuse such opposition or, better yet, to turn unions into coalition partners, peace and environmental groups must modify their organizational style, broaden their agenda to include workers' rights issues, and address the question of employment.

James Green has tried to find common ground with workers by way of labor history. A coordinator of labor studies at the University of Massachusetts, Green draws on twenty-five years of experience with a wider range of private and public sector employees who have participated in adult education programs designed to help them "discover and record" their own history as workers and union members. Around Boston such efforts have been aided by the area's high concentration of labor activists formerly involved in the civil rights, women's, and antiwar movements of the 1960s. Initially scorned and distrusted by AFL-CIO officials, these ex-New Leftists—along with their local working-class allies—have, over three decades, moved into positions of greater influence in organized labor. Along the way, they've played what Rose calls a "bridge-building" role—helping to link unions to broader causes like the nuclear freeze, the anti-apartheid movement, and campaigns against U.S. intervention in Central America.

As Rose acknowledges, workers without an ideological predisposition toward coalition politics are more open to alliances when they're engaged in a high-stakes strike or lockout. For example, prior to their 1987–88 dispute with International Paper, members of the United Paperworkers Union in Jay, Maine, "had long accepted polluted rivers, a high cancer rate, overwhelming smells, and toxic waste" as the price of full employment at the Androscoggin Mill. IP's attempt to bust the union in Jay and elsewhere made workers and their families considerably less tolerant of the company's environmental record. Meanwhile, IP's hiring of inexperienced, poorly trained "scabs" put the health of the community at risk.

Aroused by such incidents as a chlorine dioxide leak and a waste treatment plant malfunction that dumped 16 million gallons of waste into the river, the strikers joined forces with Ralph Nader, Greenpeace, and other environmentalists in Maine to get the town of Jay to adopt an unprecedented local ordinance empowering it to monitor and enforce state and federal environmental standards. According to Rose, this labor and environmental alliance remains intact, aided no doubt by IP's continued nonunion operation of the plant.

A more recent lockout of 3,000 steelworkers at Kaiser Aluminum in Spokane, Washington, propelled their union into a united front with Earth First. The resulting Alliance for Sustainable Jobs and the Environment has gotten wide publicity for its activities directed at a common enemy, financier Charles Hurwitz. His Texas-based Maxxam Corp. owns both Kaiser and Pacific Lumber, a firm that harvests large tracts of Northern California redwoods. As part of the Alliance, United Steelworkers of America has filed suit to challenge Pacific Lumber's logging. Meanwhile, environmentalists have backed initiatives to aid workers at Kaiser. Members of both groups played a prominent role in the anti-WTO protests in Seattle.

Still, there's no guarantee that making new friends during a strike produces lasting changes in a union's political orientation once its hour of need has passed. Green provides a stirring account of the United Mine Workers (UMW) strike against Pittston Coal Group in 1989. He describes how the union mobilized its own members, linked arms with Jesse Jackson, used civil rights movement tactics like nonviolent civil disobedience, staged the first plant occupation since the 1930s, and created an encampment in southwest Virginia (Camp Solidarity) that became a magnet for thousands of supporters from around the country. According to Green, UMW leaders, including current president Cecil Roberts, won the strike because of their willingness to take risks. "They promoted and supported a local culture of solidarity and consciously transformed a strike into a people's resistance movement against corporate greed," Green writes.

Today, this same union's position on what might be seen as another manifestation of "corporate greed"—global warming—is not so inspiring. Fearing job losses due to legally mandated reduction of carbon emissions, the UMW has played a lead role in an industry-backed group called Unions for Jobs and the Environment (UJAE). As labor journalist David Moberg reported recently in *The Nation,* UJAE "was launched with a grant and loan from a consortium of coal, railroad, and related businesses that promote coal use." Its membership includes AFL-CIO affiliates in the cement, utility, construction, retail, and trucking industries. The group "accepts the most exaggerated forecasts of job loss while disputing predictions of climate change and its adverse effects" and "has thus far driven labor policy on climate change." In attacking the admittedly flawed Kyoto Protocol on global warming, the UMW and its new friends have, according to Moberg, taken positions even "less protective of the environment than those of big companies like BP Amoco."

In 1996, two other Pittston strike leaders lauded by Green—Rich Trumka and Eddie Burke—teamed up with some of the key figures in the fund-raising scandal that toppled Teamster reformer Ron Carey, dealing a major setback to the "social movement unionism" that the author advocates. *Taking History to Heart* describes Carey's 1991 election to the Teamsters presidency as "the single most important political event in the revival of the labor movement." The product of twenty years of rank-and-file organizing by Teamsters for a Democratic Union (TDU), it tilted the balance of power within the AFL-CIO in John Sweeney's favor, enabling him to unseat the incumbent leadership and begin to overhaul labor's creaky central bureaucracy. But Carey's own reelection effort in 1996 was hijacked by inside-the-Beltway types. A group of lobbyists, consultants, political operatives, liberal donors, and union headquarters staffers tried to convert more than $800,000 in Teamsters dues money into Carey campaign revenue. As a result, a union just beginning to shed the taint of past mob ties was corrupted again by alumni of Students for a Democratic Society, the Midwest Academy, Common Cause, Planned Parenthood, and the Democratic National Committee. (Central to their scheme was laundering money through Citizen Action, a now-defunct "good government" group.)

This criminal conspiracy ultimately led to the very result that the liberal activists were trying to avoid: election of Jimmy Hoffa as union president. Carey was barred from the union, TDUers were purged from the staff by Hoffa, and six upper-middle-class professionals have pleaded guilty or been convicted of illegally diverting money into Carey's reelection campaign (including one who received a three-year jail term). Not surprisingly, Teamsters reformers have concluded that, with "progressive" friends like these, their movement doesn't need enemies.[1]

Most outsiders who seek to work with unions or rank-and-file groups are more principled than the crew that sunk Carey. As Green's book shows, interaction between workers and intellectuals at the grassroots level is critically important because it can help counteract union parochialism—the tendency of labor organizations to focus on day-to-day workplace problems to the exclusion of the big picture. On the other side of "the class divide," members of Scholars, Artists, and Writers for Social Justice (which Green helped launch) have found that engagement with actual workers' struggles, on campus or off, can be a welcome relief from the arcane discourse and hermetic politics of academia. For community-based organizations trying to challenge corporate power or make government more responsive, support from labor increases the chances of success. Despite their latter-day shortcomings, many unions can still deliver money, manpower, and, in some situations, much-needed political clout.

The political synergy on display in the streets of Seattle will be hard to duplicate in other locales and even in future national mobilizations related to globalization (although subsequent protests in Washington against the World Bank and International Monetary Fund drew a similar eclectic mix of labor and nonlabor participants). The emergence of a post–Cold War debate about the merits of corporate-dominated trade deals creates a political opening for the left. This did not exist when protests against U.S. foreign policy had to contend with patriotic fervor, from the flag waving of the Vietnam era to the yellow-ribbon fever of the Gulf War. Participation in popular resistance to unfettered global capitalism has been a learning experience for many trade unionists. It has enabled more than a few to move beyond nativist responses to a new understanding of the need for worker solidarity on an international scale.

When Pat Buchanan's Reform Party candidacy looked to be the only likely electoral challenge to the Bush-Gore consensus on trade issues in 2000, many labor leftists were worried that disaffected industrial workers would gravitate back toward foreigner-bashing and "America First" politics for lack of a progressive alternative. The surprising emergence of Ralph Nader as an active Green candidate—and his displacement of Buchanan in third place in the polls—does address that concern. In the wake of congressional approval of President Clinton's China trade bill, the United Auto Workers (UAW) and even Hoffa's Teamsters have announced they will explore, in the UAW's words, "alternatives to the two major political parties, including possibly supporting Ralph Nader." But so far, Nader's only major labor backing is from the California Nurses Association, a militant 30,000-member independent union that has long cooperated with him on health care reform issues.

For the rest of the AFL-CIO—despite whatever "blue-green" alliances with Naderites may have been blooming at or since Seattle—general elections are a time when the pressure of political pragmatism and the lure of lesser-evilism is great. In the 1980s, when Jesse Jackson was the great hope of progressive coalitionists, unions could repay Jesse for past picket line support in places like Jay, Maine, by backing his insurgent races in Democratic primaries; by November of 1984 and 1988, most labor activists were back in the mainstream fold, toiling for Mondale or Dukakis respectively. Nader's campaign offers a different and more threatening form of political competition that is already being denounced for its "spoiler role" by union leaders genuinely fearful of the fallout from a second Bush administration. In the short term, familiar old tensions between the "practical politics" of trade unionists and the more idealistic, radical agenda of their Green-oriented allies in the anti-globalization movement are sure to reassert themselves. No one's likely to get beaten up over electoral differences now, however, and that's still an improvement from thirty years ago. Regardless of whether Bush or Gore wins this November, efforts to bridge "the class divide" will continue to be necessary if labor, environmental, and consumer groups hope to achieve common goals.

THE NEXT UPSURGE?

As the Ronald Reagan–George H. W. Bush era began to wane, Hollywood released a film called *Flashback*, which illustrates the uncertainty of "upsurge" prognostication. In this movie, an Abbie Hoffman–style Sixties radical, now a fugitive from old criminal charges, is being pursued by a much younger, yuppie-ish FBI agent. A cross-generation political dialogue (of sorts) ensues between the two. At one point in their exchange, the ever-optimistic Hoffman character (played by Dennis Hopper) warns the smug, conservative G-man (Keifer Sutherland) that America's next big social and political upheaval is just around the corner. "Once we get out of the '80s," he boasts, "the '90s are going to make the '60s look like the '50s!"

For American labor—and the Left as well—this prediction didn't quite pan out. Despite Bill Clinton's election to the presidency, a mid-decade shake-up at the AFL-CIO, and some inspiring global justice mobilizations in Seattle and Quebec City, the 1990s were a period of continued decline in union membership, political influence, strike activity, and negotiating clout. To make matters worse, the first few years of the new millennium have been a flashback to two decades ago. As the *New York Times* reported in mid-2003, workers are "seeing a return to the bargaining climate of the 1980's"—with private sector employers demanding contract concessions and the second Bush administration engaging in federal employee union busting reminiscent of Ronald Reagan's war on PATCO.

The sense that we're moving backward instead of forward—or, at best, just treading water—should be particularly troubling for social movement veterans who went into labor thirty or more year ago. A product of the postwar baby boom, this now-graying (or balding) group of activists had both the 1960s and the 1930s as political reference points. After participating directly in dramatic, high-profile struggles around civil rights, antiwar, and women's issues, they migrated from campuses to workplaces and union halls in the 1970s. There, they hoped to play a catalytic role similar to that of the Communists, Socialists, Trotskyists, and anarcho-syndicalists who helped build city-wide general strikes and powerful new unions during the period of the great Depression and Roosevelt's New Deal.

Unfortunately, the New Left's "long march" through the existing institutions of American labor has slowed to a crawl. "Participatory democracy" is still not a strong feature of most unions and no great transformative moment appears to be on the horizon. There have been existential crises, dropouts, and defections, accompanied by a healthy decline in political sectarianism but also a less helpful tendency among some labor leftists to become so absorbed in day-to-day trade union work that, over time, they've ceased to be agents of radical change. Patient "boring from within" has nevertheless elevated progressives to positions of influence in a few union bureaucracies and the "new" AFL-CIO. It's often debatable whether this now makes them part of the problem or the solution.

Dan Clawson, author of *The Next Upsurge*, is a '68er in good standing, a sociology professor, and leader of the University of Massachusetts-Amherst faculty union. His new book ponders when, if, and how the ship will finally come in for the Class of '68 in labor—and for the millions of workers it once hoped to rally around slogans more stirring than "America Needs a Raise!" (which it does). Clawson believes that a "new upsurge is by no means inevitable" but is more likely than slow and incremental union growth, which has never been the pattern of American working-class resurgence in the past. "Historically, labor has not grown a little bit each year," he observes. "Most of the time unions are losing ground; once in a while labor takes off." During these "defining bursts"—in the 1880s, between 1898 to 1904, during the 1930s, and (in the public sector) the 1960s and '70s—mass activity by workers changed "cultural expectations, the form that unions take, laws, structure, and accepted forms of behavior. . . . What yesterday seemed impossible suddenly became commonplace."

According to Clawson, the next great burst will not occur until three contemporary trends are reversed:

First and foremost, the relentless employer assault, backed by government policies that support employers and attack workers; second, the

drastic decline in labor's willingness and ability to mobilize; and third, a
decline in rank-and-file involvement and an increasing reliance on staff
and other substitutes for worker power and solidarity.

The author believes that labor can revive and win "improved conditions for American workers" *if* it forms "alliances with other social movements"; *if* "those groups, not employers, have greater cultural and political momentum"; and *if* "a mass movement, not staff, take leadership."
That's a lot of *ifs*. Taking them one at a time, Clawson makes a convincing case for building union coalitions with social movement allies.
"Perhaps the single greatest failure of the U.S. left in the past fifty years,"
he argues, "is the lack of connection between labor and the movements of
the 1960s," a division that weakened both and contributes to the current
"failure of assorted social movements to connect with each other." Since
John Sweeney's "New Voice" team came to power at the AFL-CIO, labor
outreach to students, immigrants, anti-globalization activists, and community groups involved in local "living wage" agitation has greatly
increased. *The Next Upsurge* examines some of the "innovative campaigns in the area of major social change" that prefigured or flowed from
Sweeney's overhaul of federation programs, recruitment of new personnel, and promotion of organizing.

The book's case studies are an eclectic mix. They range from examples of successful "cross-border" solidarity and global justice activity to
campus and community-based efforts to improve pay and benefits for
low-income workers employed by university-linked apparel manufacturers or contractors. Clawson applauds the integration of feminist concerns
and "gender styles" in the white-collar organizing of AFSCME's Harvard
Union of Clerical and Technical Workers (HUCTW). At the same time,
he finds much to admire in the far more militant alliance between white-
and blue-collar workers that's developed at Yale over the past twenty
years under the banner of HERE. On the West Coast, the author revisits
SEIU's seminal "Justice for Janitors" campaign, which employed an
organizing model "based on the civil rights movement and its tactics,
rather than on a conventional [NLRB representation] election campaign." He reports on another, less well-known strike in Southern
California by Latino drywall construction workers, which had a more
ambiguous ending in the early 1990s (and didn't become the subject of a
laudatory Ken Loach film). Next, the author examines the strengths and
weaknesses of "workers' centers" that have tried, in various cities, to deal

with job problems, develop workplace leaders, and sustain rank-and-file networks, largely outside official union structures.

Finally, Clawson lands back in Connecticut, where he finds that the AFL-CIO's multi-union Stamford Organizing Project "combines many of the advantages of workers' centers with those of unions." In Stamford,

> the union is the community and the community is the union. The coordinated group of unions involved [UAW, HERE, and SEIU janitors and health care locals] identifies and takes leadership on the issues of concern to the working poor—that is, to actual and prospective union members. In turn, the community relies on unions to fight hard on issues of importance to people of color and the economically marginal.

According to the author, this cooperative effort to organize service sector workers—who would otherwise be powerless and ignored in affluent Fairfield County—has made impressive membership gains. It has signed up 4,700 workers and won "strong contracts" while "defending public housing and building an impressive reputation among both friends and foes, drawing in pastors and political leaders."

Most of these organizational experiences have been summed up before, in other books and articles, by publicity-minded participants or admiring journalists and academics. What's different is Clawson's warning that some "organizing unions" may be putting a higher priority on forming alliances with other social movements than mobilizing their own members. As the author notes, "using militant tactics, publicity, and community alliances to protect workers' rights" is no guarantee that union functioning will be "democratic and worker controlled." The original Justice for Janitors contract struggle in Los Angeles was followed, for example, by an immigrant worker challenge to the leadership of the local involved. No sooner was SEIU Local 399 taken over by an opposition caucus than it was trusteed by the International and later merged into a larger entity. (SEIU has since used trusteeships and mergers elsewhere to install non-janitor staff members as new building service union leaders in ever-expanding statewide and multi-state mega-locals, where incumbents will be well insulated from similar reelection threats.) As Clawson observes, "There's something wrong when the labor movement's model campaign results in the national union not being willing to accept the election results in a local that's just been revitalized." If labor's "central premise" really is "that workers should have the right, the ability, and the power to at least participate in, and possibly to control decisions about their work and their lives," why, Clawson asks, is the role of union members so circumscribed within their own organizations?

His book offers an interesting explanation of this phenomenon. *Next Upsurge* notes that one of the political legacies of the 1960s was on the proliferation of "public interest" and "citizen action" groups with "a strongly middle-class character." These outfits rely on a youthful, low-paid (and high-turnover) staff of recent college graduates, on social change foundation grants, and mailing lists that are utilized for "legislative alerts" and fund-raising. The typical member relates to such organizations mainly through direct mail and phone solicitation of donations or, less frequently, door-to-door canvassing. But "members neither hold office nor vote for the leaders" and most never even attend a meeting of the group. "For many years," Clawson observes, "the distinction was sharp and clear between the style and character of unions and citizen/public interest groups." Recently, the modus operandi of the latter seems to have been adopted by several unions in which former student activists play a key role. These New Unity Partnership (NUP) affiliates are not fully developing and deploying labor's "greatest source of power—the participation and solidarity of millions of members able to disrupt the economic functioning of the system," according to Clawson. Instead, they are focusing more on "corporate campaign" research, lawsuits and symbolic protests, paid media, and other staff-directed efforts to "take battles to a wider public."

Although this approach may add to an individual union's "market share" or "density" in a particular industry, it doesn't do much to lay the groundwork for a future labor upsurge rooted, as in the past, in bottom-up mobilization and "workers' self-activity." As Clawson argues, labor needs both additional members and more effective, workplace-based unions. Member-led "internal transformation would improve organizing, and organizing victories would make it more possible to develop union power." Union staff, he acknowledges, "can play a crucial role in building workers' self-confidence, abilities, power, and leadership," but "only if they organize, not lead; help workers realize their full human potential, not become the person who does everything for workers." Likewise, the integration of labor and non-labor activism—promoted throughout Clawson's book—will not move us forward either, if such fusion merely takes the form of a face-lift (or, more appropriately in unions, a tummy tuck!):

[It] might combine the best of both worlds—the energy, imagination, media savvy, and militant symbolic actions of the new social movements with the broad outreach, local chapters, face-to-face majoritarian mobilization, deep commitment and staying power of the labor movement. Or it might combine the worst of both—the thin, direct-mail and phone solicitation based "membership" of some public interest movements with the social worker inside-the-box passivity of some bureaucratic unions.

At such a fork in the road, Clawson's book is an invaluable guide to right and wrong turns. It contains many important insights into the dynamics of labor-based movement-building, past, present, and future. It is readable, accessible, and should be studied closely by activists still seeking a favorable resolution of "the tension/contradiction between the radical democratic potential" of organized labor and the less-inspiring reality of our existing unions.

AFTERTHOUGHTS ON SWEENEY

Although he looks old and tired today, AFL-CIO president John Sweeney was once hailed as a dynamic reformer, with a sharp eye for new talent. One of the first things he did, after getting elected in 1995, was appoint former Sixties radicals to be federation field reps and department heads. In Washington and around the country, Sweeney's "New Voice" administration quickly filled up with energetic ex-staffers of the Service Employees International Union (SEIU), his own union. Among them were veterans of campus and community organizing, the civil rights and black power movements, feminism, and Vietnam-era antiwar activity. On the labor left, no single personnel decision by Sweeney raised higher hopes and expectations than Bill Fletcher being named education director (a job he had held, under Sweeney, at SEIU previously).

Bay Area labor journalist David Bacon was still in awe of Fletcher's "key decision maker" role as Sweeney's assistant when he interviewed him for *The Progressive* in 2000. Bacon recounted Fletcher's background as an African-American activist and "self-described socialist," with ties to the Black Radical Congress and Marxist journal *Monthly Review*.

Drawing on his own history as "a left-wing organizer," Bacon recalled the political hostility of AFL-CIO operatives during the era of Sweeney's conservative predecessors. "With Fletcher," he wrote, "I felt as though I was talking to someone from the same movement and history I've lived myself." Concluded Bacon: "Times have changed."[1]

Not long after this interview appeared, times changed again. Fletcher was purged from his post and exiled to Silver Spring, Maryland, where he toiled briefly at the AFL's George Meany Center. Then, he left organized labor altogether, for half a decade, to replace anti-apartheid campaigner Randall Robinson as president of TransAfrica Forum. After that, Fletcher taught labor studies in New York City and began work with co-author Fernando Gapasin, a well-known West Coast labor activist, on a critique of organized labor during the Sweeney era and earlier periods, which has now been published by University of California Press. Their collaborative effort, *Solidarity Divided,* is quite unlike the usual "tell-all" tome by a presidential appointee who has quit the White House staff or been dropped from the cabinet. In fact, we never do learn what personal falling-out with Sweeney or political conflicts with his real inner circle led Fletcher to be pushed out the door of the "House of Labor." (In 2007, he was finally able to return, as a headquarters staffer for the American Federation of Government Employees.) Instead, we get a thoughtful, analytical overview of recent developments in American labor, and much of its earlier history as well. But, as a practical "guide for those seeking to reconstitute [a labor-based] Left and build a globally conscious social justice unionism in the U.S.," the book contains many curious omissions. *Solidarity Divided* is far more detached (and lacking in specificity) than one might expect from authors long engaged in day-to-day trade union work and left-wing politics.

The book's report card on Sweeney is, in contrast, quite detailed and displays little of Fletcher's previous bullishness about his boss (before he left his employ). In a *Monthly Review* article published in the summer of 2000, while Fletcher was still at the AFL, he chided other labor radicals for their skepticism about "New Voice reforms." He accused "this grousing element" of being deficient in both theory and practice because they were prone to "simply criticizing whatever initiatives come from labor's leadership." Instead, Fletcher argued, the labor Left should "examine and organize around the inner dynamics of the trade union movement." He urged leftists to "interact with the New Voice leadership . . . on the basis of a united front," offering "critical support" for Sweeney and guarding against the AFL-CIO's "staunchly right-wing elements who would like nothing better than to regain their power."[2]

Nearly a decade later, those "staunchly right-wing elements" no longer seem to be lurking in the wings, plotting a comeback. Rather, it's Sweeney himself, now in his mid-seventies, who has become part of the problem. By hanging on to his job long past his once promised retirement age—surrounded by the same tight-knit circle of former SEIU staffers who gave Fletcher the heave-ho—Sweeney helped create a new status quo at the AFL-CIO, which led some unions to question why they still needed to be part of it. In 2005, the frustration and/or complaints of seven disgruntled affiliates reached the boiling point. The result was Change To Win (CTW), a rival labor federation spearheaded by Sweeney's own alma mater, SEIU.

In *Solidarity Divided*, Fletcher and Gapasin express equal dissatisfaction with "the inner dynamics" of both CTW and the AFL-CIO. The authors first compile a stinging critique of the latter under Sweeney. We learn now, for example, that his "reform efforts seemed to be running out of steam" as early as 1998. The AFL-CIO president was already unable or unwilling to "replicate the exciting first months of his tenure" and "fell back into the consensus-building mode with which he seemed most comfortable." What Fletcher and Gapasin describe as "the essential conservatism of the Sweeney approach toward change" had negative consequences in a number of areas. Even in the early days of his presidency—when Sweeney inherited the challenge of providing stronger strike support—the "new" AFL-CIO reneged on commitments made to locked-out members of United Paper Workers Union Local 837 at A.E. Staley Co., in Decatur, Illinois, scene of a long-running community-wide conflict.

As the authors note, the Decatur workers and their supporters "expected the New Voice team to champion their cause," but "they were to be disappointed" instead. Due to UPIU leadership pressure for a contract settlement on almost any terms, "no significant support came from the national AFL-CIO, despite promises, implied and explicit." The Staley dispute "ended in defeat," as did the Detroit newspaper strike, a multi-union fight that also "overlapped Sweeney's assumption of office" and became another "missed opportunity" for "mobilizing the union movement" around key "mass struggles."

Even in the areas of education and organizing, where Sweeney received much initial praise, the authors find deeper commitment lacking.

One of Fletcher's first projects was creating "a member-focused economics education program."

> Common Sense Economics . . . was conceived as a means of speaking about
> capitalism, class, and ultimately, the importance of new organizing and new
> trade unionism. Piloted in 1997, it received rave reviews; since then, insuf-
> ficient usage and engagement by the national AFL-CIO and its affiliates have
> undermined the achievement of the [program's]original objectives.

On the organizing front, Fletcher and Gapasin recount the AFL's
short-lived rallying of its staff on behalf of the United Farm Workers. By
1997, this once vibrant union "was a shadow of what it had been in the
1970s." Its weak infrastructure was, according to the authors, a legacy of
internal purges conducted when union founder César Chávez turned dictatorial and "eliminated many of his left-leaning supporters, leaders, and
staff, including numerous veterans who had led previous UFW campaigns."

Nevertheless, Sweeney's Washington brain trust decided that "mobilizing major support" for California strawberry worker organizing would
demonstrate the AFL-CIO's commitment to low-wage immigrant workers and serve as a much-publicized "coming-out party" for its revived
Organizing and Field Mobilization Departments. Despite initial enthusiasm, this heavily funded effort "unraveled" within a few months, as the
UFW drive "seemed to disintegrate." According to the authors, the cause
of farm workers—as re-marketed by New Voicers in the late 1990s—"did
not gel as a social movement." Lacking an effective strategy and "the long-
term commitment necessary to organize strawberry workers. . . . in a campaign that was essentially a major rebuilding effort," AFL staffers soon
moved on to other projects. (In 2005, an ungrateful and/or resentful
UFW quit the federation to join Change To Win.)

Reflecting their own political orientation (and organizational ties), the
authors fault the AFL for not tackling the larger challenge of organizing
the Sun Belt. They note that "during its first five years in office, the
Sweeney administration put forth rhetoric about organizing the South,
but it accomplished little overall." Even an effort to just study the problem
and begin outreach to potentially supportive "community-based organizations . . . failed and simply disappeared into the wind." Meanwhile, on
another issue of related concern, racism, *Solidarity Divided* accuses
Sweeney of dropping the ball when the federation was asked to partici-

pate in a Clinton administration Commission on Race. "The AFL-CIO took no initiative to support the Commission," created in 1997 to promote a "national dialogue" about race relations. The authors argue that the panel could have "advanced working people's interests" by holding "hearings around the U.S. in union halls and community centers" about discrimination in jobs, housing, and health care.

Solidarity Divided also describes, in some detail, how the "new" AFL-CIO maintained "a nearly uncritical relationship with the Democratic Party." Bill Clinton's 1996 repeal of welfare was, the authors say, "a de facto Republican initiative and should have been attacked for what it represents." Instead, "the AFL-CIO took a pass" and did nothing to defend "the poorest sections of the working class." Two years later, "in keeping with its alliance with Clinton, the AFL-CIO took the position that the World Trade Organization (WTO) could and should be reformed"—on the eve of anti-globalization protests in Seattle where demonstrators were seeking to "sink or shrink" the WTO. Across the board, Fletcher and Gapasin find, the federation failed "to offer badly needed criticisms of the economic policies of the [Clinton] administration."

In 2000, lack of popular enthusiasm for Clinton heir Al Gore—as evidenced by some small labor defections to the Nader camp—led to the disastrous reign of George W. Bush. Further union woes ensued after 9/11. Soon, "the strategic and policy paralysis of the AFL-CIO had become so clear that the ties binding the union movement started to unravel." Writing two years after the 2005 organizational split that followed, Fletcher and Gapasin "can identify very little significant change in organized labor"—notwithstanding the many PR claims of CTW (which lead some to call it "Change To Spin"). Initially, one of the biggest fears of the authors (and others) was that feuding national federations might disrupt promising new work by the CLCs—state and local central labor councils. *Solidarity Divided* cites "research by Gapasin for the AFL-CIO" showing that some CLCs "have transformed the labor movement in their communities" (while others have just displayed continuing "lethargy"). Never very excited about any Sweeney-era initiatives—as they view them today—the authors argue that "most ideas for reforming these central bodies" didn't "stray far from the existing paradigm of U.S. trade unionism" (with the exception of Gapasin's own proposals for the AFL's Union Cities program).

Solidarity Divided is much preoccupied with the labor Left's failure to "analyze" and "debate" this old "paradigm" properly or wage "com-

prehensive struggle" against it. That's an understandable complaint
from activist/intellectuals who find themselves stranded in a labor
movement without the organized radical presence it had in the 1970s.
Back then, many unionized workplaces were flush with Sixties-inspired
agitators who devoted almost as much time to Marxist "study groups"
(and related political sects) as they did to shop-floor militancy. In contrast, most surviving members of this same generational cohort function
today merely as trade unionists—whose politics long ago contracted
into a semi-private creed. Their day-to-day work is very competent,
even creative, but it lacks the collectivity and broader agenda of thirty
years ago. Meanwhile, the frenetic activity of younger activists—who
missed out on the big radicalizing upsurges of the 1960s or '70s, on
campus or off—suffers from the same absence of a shared political
framework. Many former New Leftists, as well as more recent recruits to
the cause, realize they'd have greater impact if they were acting together on a cross-union basis regardless of what "business union" they're
stuck in and still trying to change. Most labor leftists favor a stronger
voice for workers on the job and in their unions. They also want to unite
workers and community activists in common struggles because these, in
turn, create expanded opportunities for rank-and-file education and
leadership development.

Reform movements like Teamsters for a Democratic Union (TDU)
and the fledgling SMART—SEIU Member Activists for Reform Today—
remain a fertile ground for left-wing labor work. (See www.reformSEIU.
org or www.seiuvoice.org for more information on long-overdue, TDU-
style activity within SEIU.) Other radicals continue to function in less
oppositional fashion, by building the durable, twenty-year-old network of
community-labor coalitions known as Jobs with Justice (JWJ). They also
devote themselves to the scores of immigrant "workers' centers" that
fight for the foreign-born and immigration reform. Some lefties wield
influence in fighting unions like the California Nurses Associations
(CNA), recently affiliated with the AFL-CIO, and the still independent
United Electrical Workers (UE), always a beacon of rank and file unionism. Veterans of "anti-imperialist" organizing during the Vietnam era
launched U.S. Labor Against the War to rally workers against the U.S.
invasion of Iraq in 2003. USLAW has steadily gained official backing,
while labor radicals active on other foreign policy fronts have developed
strong cross-border ties with union organizers and free trade foes in
South and Central America.

Last but not least, indigenous militants and leftists of varying hues have kept *Labor Notes* afloat for nearly three decades. The Detroit-based monthly newsletter (and related labor education project) has been a vital source of alternative union news and views, plus a key catalyst for rank-and-file organizing and strike support. In April of 2008, 1,100 *Labor Notes* backers had one of their largest, liveliest, and most diverse gatherings ever. This two-day solidarity conference in Dearborn, Michigan, attracted hundreds of local officers or stewards from SEIU, CNA, AFSCME, the Teamsters, CWA, IBEW, UAW, ILA, and other unions, here and abroad. Many left the meeting with a copy of *Troublemaker's Handbook*, a thick *Labor Notes* guide to workplace activism and "social movement unionism" that (in two editions) has sold more than 32,000 copies to an audience of working-class readers far larger than Fletcher and Gapasin are likely to reach with a university press book like *Solidarity Divided*.

Strangely enough, their book fails to acknowledge the existence of *Labor Notes* anywhere in its 288 pages even though they favor a "more open approach to [union] education." In the authors' account of events in the 1990s, TDU gets a passing pat on the head (for being a surviving '70s "caucus"), but its central role in making Ron Carey president of the Teamsters in 1991—and Carey's subsequent critical support for Sweeney's election in 1995—is barely noted. Despite very successful political work in California and a distinctive critique of labor-management partnerships, CNA gets no mention in a chapter titled "Putting the Left Foot Forward." Also missing from the book is any sense of the rank-and-file backlash that's been developing within SEIU against its top-down, anti-democratic methods. (The authors do agree that "the SEIU model" of forced membership consolidation into locals with little opportunity for "worker control" is "not the only solution to problems of competitive markets and aggressive employers.") While touting "internal democracy" and "membership votes" throughout labor, Fletcher and Gapasin manage to ignore the singular contribution of the Association for Union Democracy (AUD), another left-initiated project which has, for forty years, fostered a more "democratic union culture." Even the huge immigrant work stoppages that occurred during the spring of 2006 get less attention, in the book's concluding chapter (on "Strategies for Transformation"), than "central labor councils" and "non-majority unionism."

Jobs with Justice does get the F & G seal of approval (sort of). But, at the same time, *Solidarity Divided* makes the factually challenged assertion that JWJ is not really a "union-community coalition" after all—at least compared to the authors' preferred model, which is the Black Workers For Justice (BWFJ) in North Carolina. According to Fletcher and Gapasin, BWFJ "is open to both union and non-union workers [and] plays an active role in both workplace-based and community-based struggles." (It's also small and limited to one state.) Meanwhile, JWJ—with active multiracial affiliates in 40 cities and 25 states—doesn't fit this description? In reality, it does, in far more places and on a much larger scale.

To add insult to injury, the authors have the chutzpah to highlight, in my own state of Massachusetts, a recently launched competitor to JWJ known as Community Labor United (CLU). With little supporting evidence—because not much is available—Fletcher and Gapasin theorize that the CLU could become a "working people's assembly" in Boston, "a joint concentration of progressive forces" based on "real (rather than symbolic) solidarity." Such a development would certainly surprise Massachusetts JWJ supporters since that's exactly the kind of solidarity that JWJ has long promoted by working in feisty and independent fashion, with or without the cooperation of the Boston Central Labor Council or state AFL-CIO. In contrast, the CLU has been, from birth, an appendage of the CLC—even housed in its offices—and far more under the thumb of Massachusetts labor officials. As such, it's far less likely to become a local reincarnation of the Knights of Labor!

To this reader, therefore, the Fletcher-Gapasin road map to "social justice unionism" seems sketchy and incomplete. It doesn't do justice to some of the most valiant efforts to move the ball down the field in the direction of that goal. And it's little consolation to learn that "no existing union or formal labor body" anywhere in the country "is practicing social justice unionism" or "social justice solidarity," as the authors define and describe these organizational holy grails. Appended to the book, we do find a 20-page account of "local union transformation" written by Gapasin and focusing, in the authors' approved fashion, on the intersection of race, class, and gender. Unfortunately, this takes the form of an academic-style "blind study," in which Gapasin disguises the name, location, and other details about the local involved. As such, his case study lacks the follow-up contact information that's helpfully provided in every section of *Troublemaker's Handbook,* the "how-to" guide published by *Labor Notes.*

The authors conclude with an indisputable point: "If the union movement is to shift further left, the left-wing forces within it must achieve organizational coherence." But here again, *Solidarity Divided* is strangely silent about the efforts made, just several years ago, to hold a series of "Labor Left Meetings" at which, it was hoped, radical trade unionists would finally cohere into a more formalized network. Various groups on the left—Solidarity, the Committees of Correspondence for Democracy and Socialism (CCDS), the Freedom Road Socialist Organization (FRSO), Democratic Socialists of America (DSA), and other "political tendencies"—were represented in that process. (FRSO later came to a fork in the "road"—and split, so there are now two of them.) This reviewer was one of the meeting participants; Gapasin and Fletcher were among the original convenors or organizers. Yet, in *Solidarity Divided*, the whole two-year labor Left "regroupment" attempt, involving several hundred people, has disappeared down the Orwellian "memory hole," along with any useful lessons to be derived from it. In addition, none of the "real existing" socialist groups involved are even mentioned in the book, nor do we learn anything about their respective "trade union practice."

Perhaps such blind spots are inevitable in any work of history produced by participant/observers writing about recent events or institutions in which they are still involved. But *Solidarity Divided* would have been a stronger, more useful guide to labor Left activism—now and in the future—if it was less theoretical and generally prescriptive and, instead, more accurately described the actual struggles, setbacks, and accomplishments of union radicals.

PART FOUR

WORKERS' RIGHTS AND WRONGS

In the absence of any imminent 1930s-style labor upsurge, one necessary ingredient for incremental growth is better protection of the "right to organize." As this book was going to press, American unions had helped to elect a new, more labor-friendly president and, hopefully, enough additional Senate Democrats to permit passage of the Employee Free Choice Act (EFCA) in 2009. EFCA would require private sector employers to recognize unions based on signed authorization cards, rather than allowing management to insist on a contested representation election run by the National Labor Relations Board (NLRB). Under the Obama administration, unions are also looking forward to stronger NLRB enforcement as Bush appointees to the Board get replaced by more union-friendly members. Section IV injects a cautionary note into this hopeful scenario, reminding readers of the troubled history of labor law reform and NLRB enforcement since the Wagner (or National Labor Relations) Act was passed in 1935.

The Pickett's charge of NLRA reformers since then was the failed effort to overcome a Senate filibuster in 1978, which blocked passage of a reform bill tepidly supported by President Jimmy Carter. Fourteen years later, Bill Clinton made an even less halfhearted attempt at a Wagner Act overhaul by creating a White House task force to study the problem. Headed by a Harvard professor and former secretary of labor John

Dunlop, the "Commission on the Future of Worker-Management Relations" became a political fiasco for labor, as recounted herein by a still disgruntled Dunlop panel witness (me). The two years (1993–94) that Dunlop and his colleagues spent collecting testimony and developing recommendations turned out to be the only period during Clinton's presidency when the Democrats had House and Senate majorities. Dunlop's proposals, not all of them even helpful to unions, ended up being dead on arrival due to mid-term election victories in 1994, which gave Republicans control of Congress. The articles in this section assess the state of labor law—and union efforts to use or change it—via an examination of books by Tom Geoghegan, Lance Compa, Bob Schwartz, and William Gould, a controversial former chairman of the NLRB under Clinton. This section also reviews *State of the Union,* Nelson Lichtenstein's sweeping account of how "the labor question" as a whole has fared in twentieth-century America, particularly since the development of a 1960s-inspired "rights consciousness." As Lichtenstein shows, this has led more workers to seek individual or "class action" legal remedies for their workplace problems, rather than embrace collective bargaining. Like Geoghegan's *Which Side Are You On?* Lichtenstein's intellectual history of the "union idea" contains useful insights and lessons for would-be labor law reformers today who are still trying to rally broader public support for making "union organizing rights as unassailable as basic civil rights."

WHICH SIDE ARE YOU ON?

In its heyday in the 1930s, labor's cause attracted many talented outsiders, and for good reason: they wanted to be on the side that was winning. Playwrights, novelists, professors, artists, civil libertarians, and New Deal Democrats actively supported the great industrial union organizing drives and strikes of that era. Workers' demands for justice on the job were perceived to be part of a larger fight for social and economic justice for all Americans. Many labor struggles were suffused with radicalism and romanticism that appealed to middle-class sympathizers.

However, by the time Harvard-educated lawyer Tom Geoghegan offered his services to the workers thirty-five years later, organized labor had become much less of a movement. During the extended period of relative industrial peace that followed World War II and coincided with the postwar economic boom, union militancy and membership participation waned and union structures became even more bureaucratized.

In the early 1970s and '80s, many employers sensed labor's new weakness and returned to the class warfare approach that was more common prior to the New Deal. Unions were woefully unprepared for the sustained assault that followed and continues to this day. Plant shutdowns, contract concessions, failed strikes and organizing defeats soon produced what Geoghegan calls "an Italian army in retreat [with] cars breaking down, baggage getting lost, officers getting fired on by their own troops."

This unhappy but largely accurate portrait of labor's troubles is embellished in *Which Side Are You On?* by the author's often amusing personal ruminations about his life as a labor lawyer in Chicago, "the last union town" in America. Geoghegan is at his best describing the social and economic devastation wrought by deindustrialization in the Midwest. Once vibrant labor strongholds have become "Rust Belt" ghost towns filled with depressed, jobless people. The book's analysis of the political, legal, and economic developments contributing to the accompanying union decline is interwoven with colorful portraits of his various labor clients. They range from embattled Teamster dissidents to steelworkers left without pensions or severance pay when well-heeled corporate con artists took over their mill, shut it down, and then used bankruptcy proceedings to shed "legacy benefit" obligations.

For Geoghegan, the eight-year court battle required to settle his retired steelworkers' case reflects the general breakdown of workers' rights protections in every area—collective bargaining, strikes, organizing, and even the grievance arbitration procedures of so many union contracts. As labor's labor law problems deepen, so has the involvement of union activists in the law, an unhealthy and unhelpful development all by itself. "The entire labor movement has become a giant bar association of non-licensed attorneys," Geoghegan observes. Union business agents, staff reps, local officers, and even shop stewards now spend more time "shuffling papers" and "marking exhibits" than mobilizing members on the job or in the community.

At the level of his individual cases, the author feels there should be little ambivalence about which side one is on nevertheless. The American workplace remains employer-dominated terrain with few of the substantive legal entitlements or procedural rights that workers enjoy in other industrial nations whether or not they're union members. In the United States, only a union contract, however weak, can begin to provide equivalent protection. But, as Geoghegan points out, the labor movement as a whole suffers from the perception that it's no longer an effective guarantor of workplace fairness or a vehicle for progressive social change. Particularly to the author's peers in liberal circles and the professional classes, unions look like hopeless losers—tacky, blue-collar institutions that are irrelevant at best, reactionary at worst.

While often dispirited itself about labor's future, *Which Side Are You On?* mounts a strong challenge to such attitudes. It pleads for greater public understanding of what unions do on behalf of their members and millions of unrepresented workers. And it suggests that even people with a pronounced yuppie-ish distaste for collective bargaining—or collective action in any form—would gain from the national health insurance, paid parental leave, and guaranteed annual vacation time that a stronger labor movement would be able to win for everyone.

In the course of delivering this useful message, Geoghegan himself displays quirky flashes of elitism, disdain, and personal detachment—all seemingly at odds with his professed support for "the hard-line rank-and-file party" in labor that's agitating for change. At one point, for example, he belittles the current level of grassroots union activity in crude, stereotypical fashion: "Out there in suburbia . . . the rank and file sit in front of the TV, corrupt, stupefied, like the rest of the country." According to the author, figuring out how unions can fight back more effectively (and, where necessary, overcome membership apathy or defeatism) is not his job. Says Geoghegan, "My job, as a lawyer, is to hold the client's coat." But if things are as bad for unions as this book suggests—and they are—somebody needs to provide a few pointers about standing up and throwing better punches or labor will be "flat on its back" for years to come.

WITH FRIENDS LIKE THESE

Can a presidential commission dominated by Cambridge academics rescue organized labor from increasing marginalization? The answer to that question was still in doubt after the Clinton administration's Commission on the Future of Worker-Management Relations released its preliminary findings. Chaired by seventy-nine-year-old John Dunlop, a Harvard professor and former secretary of labor, the ten-member commission spent all of 1993-4 pondering what forms of employee participation, collective bargaining, or dispute resolution might boost U.S. productivity and competitiveness and, not incidentally, improve working conditions.

Many trade unionists had hoped this process would aid labor's long-thwarted campaign to strengthen workers' rights under the National Labor Relations Act (NLRA) before upcoming mid-term elections produce a Congress more hostile to new Clinton initiatives. Unfortunately, Dunlop's panel is neither moving that fast nor in the right direction. In fact, its final proposals may not be all that helpful to employees trying to overcome fierce management resistance to unionization. At commission hearings around the country, workers reported that organizing efforts are routinely crushed by management harassment, threats, intimidation, anti-union propaganda, legal delays, and the firing of thousands of union activists. Despite such evidence of corporate America's continuing dedication to the cause of "de-unionization," one of the commission's "principal findings" is that labor, employers, and the general public all agree on "the principle that workers have the right to join a union and engage in collective bargaining if a majority so desires." Key members of the commission believe that instances of employer anti-union behavior can be reduced if labor just makes itself more flexible and compliant, and management finally realizes the benefits of employee representation. According to the commission, any recommended changes in federal labor law should reflect both "consensus" and a commitment to "labor-management partnership."

This quixotic endeavor owes much to Dunlop's own half-century career as a top-level broker of labor-management deals in heavily unionized industries. But the Clinton administration and his younger commission colleagues, such as Richard Freeman from Harvard and Tom Kochan from MIT, are far less interested in promoting collective bargaining as an instrument of workplace democracy, economic justice, or labor peace. Some, like Freeman, have devoted themselves to justifying organized labor in terms of its contribution to productivity or have dabbled with the idea that "employee committees" can fill the "representation gap" that exists in non-union workplaces.

In *What Do Unions Do?* (Basic Books, 1984), Freeman and his Harvard co-author James Medoff argued that giving workers a union voice can actually make workplaces more efficient by allaying shop-floor discontent, reducing turnover and raising skill levels through union-negotiated job-training programs. But this useful study apparently failed to convince even their fellow Kennedy School faculty member, Robert Reich, who served as President Clinton's labor secretary. He asked the Dunlop Commission to conduct further research on the link between employee organization and competitiveness because, in his view, "The jury is still out on whether the traditional union is necessary for the new workplace."

For most employers, no further study is necessary—the verdict is already in. They're convinced that a union doesn't "add value" to a company, regardless of how "non-adversarial" it is. They prefer to run their businesses themselves, without the collective intervention of their workers. Dealing with a bona fide labor organization that has independence from management, its own outside resources, and the legal right to bargain involves too much sharing of power and loss of control. According to the commission's own findings, companies employing up to one-third of the workforce have already introduced ways of soliciting employee input to increase output. They simply consult the vast array of shop-floor committees, advisory councils, quality circles, and production "teams" that operate securely under management's thumb. The commission, not surprisingly, is quite bullish about these "employee participation" programs. It concludes that they "generally improve economic performance" of individual firms and, if expanded properly, "may contribute to the nation's competitiveness and living standards."

Downplayed in the commission's initial report is the fact that company-controlled employee participation schemes are central to the strategy of "union avoidance." When management's modern-day version of a "company union" fails to satisfy demands for fair treatment, decent compensation, or involvement in decision making, workers sometimes try to form a genuine union to achieve these goals. Then we see what the commission gingerly calls the "dark side" of labor relations in the United States. Even the most benevolent boss turns to "Plan B" in the union avoidance handbook, often unleashing a consultant-orchestrated campaign of coercive persuasion that results in damaged careers, lost jobs, and terrible workplace tension.

Only a small minority of private sector unionization drives ever survive Plan B, regardless of how much support they have initially. Most don't even reach the stage of a representation election; National Labor Relations Board statistics compiled by the commission show that employers have won more than half of the NLRB votes held since 1980. Even more revealing is the commission's finding that "roughly 40 percent of workplaces that vote to be represented by a union do not obtain a contract with their employer" because so many companies "engage in bad faith bargaining with newly certified unions." During the many months or years that recalcitrant employers drag out negotiations on a first contract with no intention of reaching agreement, they also keep Plan B in effect. This means that workers who have already endured a union-busting campaign before an NLRB election are then subjected to one after it as well.

Continuing management pressure on union supporters, combined with frustration over the lack of a contract settlement, invariably leads to turmoil, turnover in the workforce, recriminations about unionization, and a company-inspired decertification effort. If the union is voted out, the employer's obligation to engage in any further sham bargaining ceases and everything can be returned to "normal" within a year or two of the original majority decision in favor of representation. All that remains to be done at this point is to weed out any surviving "union troublemakers," who can expect even less help from the NLRB than was provided earlier. In a typical understatement, the Dunlop Commission confirms that "the probability that a worker will be discharged or otherwise unfairly discriminated against for exercising legal rights under the NLRA has increased over time."

The grim scenario above—or elements of it—is what scores of workers and union organizers described in their testimony before the commission. Labor witnesses pointed out that in the public sector, where management interference with workers' choice of a union is the exception rather than the rule, union membership has grown nationally (even though twenty states don't have public employee bargaining laws). So unions today are proposing some of the same remedies they sought from the Carter administration sixteen years ago when private sector labor law reform was last on the agenda of Congress: quicker procedures for union recognition and reinstatement of fired workers; tougher penalties for employers' unfair labor practices; and a Canadian-style mechanism for imposing first-contract terms through arbitration when a deadlock develops.

Needless to say, business remains dead set against such changes. Worse yet for labor, the Dunlop Commission seems persuaded that the non-union employee participation plans so valued by the Clinton administration require an amendment to the NLRA that would weaken, rather than strengthen it, by removing its fifty-nine-year-old restrictions on company unionism. As Kochan told a union official at one commission-related forum last year, "My fundamental concern is effective representation . . . not to rebuild or increase the size of the labor movement. If other forms come along, so be it." With "friends" like this on Clinton's Dunlop Commission, workers seeking to unionize have a long fight ahead for new legal protection.

UNFAIR ADVANTAGE

In every presidential election campaign, the major-party candidates—even the one backed by labor—spend little time debating labor-law reform. Al Gore's bid for the White House in 2000 was no different. Nevertheless, the AFL-CIO had hoped that a Gore victory and Democratic gains in Congress would lead to strengthening of the National Labor Relations Act (NLRA) or, at least, more union-friendly appointments to the National Labor Relations Board (NLRB). Continued Republican control of Congress now eliminates the possibility of the former, while Bush's Supreme Court–assisted Electoral College victory makes the latter highly unlikely. In fact, when our new president gets through filling three vacancies on the NLRB early in his administration, those appointees will ensure that the failure of labor law—a scandal exposed in different ways by former NLRB chairman William Gould in *Labored Relations* and by lawyer Lance Compa in *Unfair Advantage*—will continue to stymie union organizing for the next four years.

Since the AFL-CIO began putting greater emphasis on membership recruitment in 1995, there have, of course, been important new gains. But some of the most significant victories involved organizing campaigns in which unions used their bargaining or political clout—where they still have it—to secure recognition in new units without using Labor Board certification procedures. For tens of millions of workers in the private sector, bypassing the law is not an option, however. For better or worse, the sixty-five-year-old NLRA continues to shape organizing strategies in many key industries.

Long hailed as the "Magna Carta of American labor," the NLRA (or Wagner Act) is definitely showing signs of age. The act was designed in 1935 to promote collective bargaining as a peaceful alternative to the many violent, Depression-era battles over union recognition. Its New Deal sponsors viewed unionization as a necessary corrective to the "inequality of bargaining power" between individual workers and management. To referee workplace disputes, Congress created the NLRB, which conducts representation elections, awards bargaining rights based on them, and investigates "unfair labor practices" by employers that might discourage organizing or prevent workers from negotiating a union contract. The limited remedies, light penalties, and secret-ballot elections available under the NLRA are meaningful only if its administration is swift and efficient. Yet, in few other areas of the law is there greater truth to the axiom that "justice delayed is justice denied." When union votes are stalled for months, union victories tied up in litigation for years, bad-faith bargaining goes unpunished, and fired union supporters only get reinstated (if at all) long after an organizing campaign has ended, management wins even if the NLRB ultimately rules otherwise.

The selection of board members and the agency's influential general counsel is determined by who controls the White House and what kind of nomination deals are brokered with the Senate. (Functioning at full strength, the board consists of three appointees, including the chairman, from the president's own party, and two from the opposition party.) However, as the AFL-CIO argued in its last major campaign for labor-law reform in the late 1970s, unfair-labor-practice victims need more than a sympathetic NLRB majority or efficient functioning by the agency's 2,000 career employees around the country. The law itself must be repaired.

The enormous gap between workers' legal rights on paper and the reality of NLRA enforcement under Democrats and Republicans alike is most effectively documented in *Unfair Advantage. Labored Relations* also describes how bad substantive decisions, "the creakiness of the NLRA's administrative procedures" and its "lack of effective remedies" have undermined worker organizing and strike activity in recent decades. But the bulk of Gould's memoir is devoted to refighting the personal political battles that preoccupied him during his four and a half years as a Clinton appointee on the NLRB. Gould's book thus invites comparison with *Locked in the Cabinet* (Alfred A. Knopf, 1997), Robert Reich's glibly amusing account of his stint as Clinton's secretary of labor. Both men assumed their Washington posts—Reich at the Labor Department and Gould at the board—after a career in academia. Even before Clinton nominated Gould in 1993, Reich had tapped him (based on his work as a

Stanford University law professor and respected arbitrator) to serve on the Dunlop Commission, a panel of experts convened to recommend labor-law changes.

At the time, Gould had just offered his own ideas on this subject in a book titled *Agenda for Reform*. In it, he called for many of the same corrective measures now advocated by Human Rights Watch: employer recognition of unions based on signed authorization cards rather than contested elections; imposition of first-contract terms by an arbitrator when the parties can't reach agreement by themselves; greater use of injunctive relief to secure quicker reinstatement of workers fired for union activity; a ban on permanent replacement of economic strikers; and heavier financial penalties for labor-law violators. Needless to say, Senate Republicans weren't too keen on Gould's proposals and kept his nomination to the NLRB dangling for almost a year. Even Reich's labor-law-reform panel—which Gould left prior to being confirmed as NLRB chairman—failed to promote these much-needed changes. Instead, the Dunlop Commission stressed the importance of amending the NLRA so management-dominated "employee participation" schemes could flourish even more widely as an alternative to unions. Repackaged as the Teamwork for Employees and Managers (or TEAM) Act and adopted by Congress after the GOP took over in 1994, this anti-union legislation was ultimately vetoed by Clinton, after frantic labor lobbying.

To survive his contentious confirmation process (and avoid the fate of fellow African-American Lani Guinier, whose nomination to a top Justice Department post was dropped by Clinton when her writings as a law professor were attacked by the Right), Gould played up his credentials as a "professional neutral." He proclaimed that his goal in Washington would be "to reduce polarization both at the board and also between labor and management." Equipped with what turned out to be a serious lack of diplomatic skills, Gould might have had an easier time trying to bring peace to the Middle East. During Gould's tenure, congressional Republicans sought to cripple the NLRB's operations with budget cuts, harassing oversight hearings and nonstop political sniping. Positive initiatives, like general counsel Fred Feinstein's attempt to get more federal court orders reinstating fired workers while their cases were being litigated, became a lightning rod for conservative criticism. Under these trying circumstances, Gould, Feinstein, and pro-labor board members like Sarah Fox and the late Margaret Browning needed to stick together and coordinate their strategy in the face of common adversaries. Gould, however, quickly fell out with his colleagues in a fit of pique over their failure "to accord me stature and defer to my leadership." His "leadership" soon took the form of public feuding with, and criticism of, his fellow Clinton appointees—combined with attention-getting public statements about many of the leading labor-management controversies of the day. Even when he was on the right side of these disputes, his ill-timed interventions had the effect of exacerbating the NLRB's political problems.

In 1998, for example, Gould injected himself into the debate about a state ballot initiative in California that would have required unions to obtain the individual consent of their members before using dues money for political purposes. Gould's statement of opposition to this Republican-backed "paycheck protection" scheme correctly noted that it would "cripple a major source of funding for the Democratic Party." When his testimony was briefly posted on the NLRB's website after being presented to state legislators, it created such a ruckus that even congressional Democrats generally supportive of labor and the board raised the possibility that Gould should resign to avert further Republican retribution against the agency.

Ironically, Gould's batting average at the board shows that he was not as much a union partisan as his business critics claimed. According to a recent law-review analysis by Professor Joan Flynn, Gould's "votes in disputed cases were considerably less predictable than those of his colleagues from management or union-side practice . . . [they] broke down in a much less lopsided fashion: 159 for the 'union' position and 46 for the 'management' position." In contrast, when Ronald Reagan tried to change the NLRB's alleged pro-union tilt during his administration, his chairman was a management-side lawyer, Donald Dotson, a figure no less controversial in the 1980s than Gould was in the '90s. Of course, Dotson didn't pursue Gould's stated goal of "return[ing] the Board to the center to promote balance." Despite equally hostile congressional oversight by members of the then-Democratic majority, Dotson openly promoted a Right-to-Work Committee agenda, defending management interests just as zealously as he had when he was on the corporate payroll.

Naming Gould to chair the board was thus very much an expression of Clinton's own political centrism. Unhappily for labor, Gould's unexpected personal showboating, squabbling with would-be allies, and what Flynn calls his "near-genius for irritating Congress" impeded, rather than aided, the administrative tinkering that Clinton appointees were able to do at the NLRB during his tenure. Vain, impolitic, and—in the view of some critics—hopelessly naïve, Gould often did as much harm as good. In this respect, he was not unlike the Dunlop Commission, Reich's vehicle for building a political consensus on labor-law reform that instead fed right-wing attempts to weaken the NLRA.

Gould's defense of his record seems designed to avoid the kind of flak that Reich received over his memoir's fanciful reconstruction of private and even public exchanges with various Washington notables. *Labored Relations* quotes extensively from the author's minutiae-filled daily journal, leaving the impression that no Reich-like literary license has been employed. Unfortunately, Gould lacks Reich's self-deprecatory humor and acute sense of irony. The author's tedious recitation of his speaking dates, telephone calls, case conferences, lunch and dinner conversations, etc., will be a hard slog for anyone but specialists in the field or ex-colleagues searching for critical comments about themselves (of which there are many).

Outside the Beltway and the "labor bar," settling old scores about who did what to whom as part of the "Clinton Board" is much less a preoccupation than the difficulty of defending workers' rights under any administration. *Unfair Advantage* does a much better job of keeping this big picture in focus, by documenting the rising toll of workers fired for what, in board jargon, is called "protected concerted activity." In the 1950s, author Lance Compa reports, "workers who suffered reprisals for exercising the right to freedom of association numbered in the hundreds each year. In the 1960s, the number climbed into the thousands, reaching slightly over 6,000 in 1969. By the 1990s, more than 20,000 workers each year were victims of discrimination for union activity—23,580 in 1998, the most recent year for which figures are available."

The "right to freedom of association" is, of course, enshrined in international human rights standards that the United States nominally supports and often seeks to apply to other nations. Compa, a former organizer for the United Electrical Workers who now teaches international labor law at Cornell, exposes the hypocrisy of this official stance in light of persistent NLRB enforcement problems and the structural defects of the NLRA itself. In this Human Rights Watch report (also available as a Cornell ILR Press book) he concludes that "provisions of U.S. law openly conflict with international norms . . . of freedom of association." Millions of workers, including farmworkers, household domestic workers, and low-level supervisors, are expressly barred from the law's protection of the right to organize. American law allows employers to replace permanently workers who exercise the right to strike, effectively nullifying that right. New forms of employment relationships have created millions of part-time, temporary, subcontracted, and otherwise "atypical" or "contingent" workers whose freedom of association is frustrated by the law's failure to adapt to changes in the economy.

The problem with Compa's sweeping indictment of the status quo is that it contains no strategy for change—other than elevating the debate about what should be done from the lowly sphere of labor-management relations to the higher moral plane of international human rights norms. At the local level, Jobs with Justice coalitions and some AFL-CIO central labor councils around the country are actually trying to build a long-term campaign to promote greater public support for the right to organize. Their target audience is the same elements of academia, the arts, churches, and the liberal middle class that have long displayed admirable concern about human rights violations abroad or discrimination against women, gays, and minorities at home. Public officials, university professors, the clergy, civil rights leaders, and neighborhood activists are now being encouraged to intervene in organizing situations to help neutralize illegal management resistance to unionization. Workers' rights activists will find plenty of new ammunition in *Unfair Advantage*, and even some that's buried in *Labored Relations*. Where successful, their community-based efforts can improve the climate for organizing in some parts of the country and put NLRA reform back on the national agenda of labor's putative ally, the Democratic Party. As eight years of Bill Clinton have demonstrated, having a Democrat in the White House may be a necessary condition for reform initiatives but it's hardly sufficient and no guarantee of progress. Workers who form unions will continue to be at risk until Americans elect both a Congress and a president willing to do more than just tinker with our tattered protection of the right to organize.

OUR COLLECTIVE BARGAIN

The fortunes of American labor took a turn for the worse early in the new millennium. Thanks to terrorism and recession, union members are reeling from a series of economic and political setbacks. Nearly half a million now face unemployment in the hotel and airline industries, at Boeing, Ford, major steelmakers, and other manufacturing firms. Many public employees will be clobbered next, as state and local budget crises deepen around the country. Already, teachers in New Jersey and state workers in Minnesota have been forced into controversial strikes over rising health care costs—a trend that affects millions of Americans. The accompanying loss of job-based medical coverage by many people who still have jobs should be fueling a revived movement for national health insurance, but not enough unions bother to raise that banner anymore.

Promising new AFL-CIO initiatives on immigration, like its call for legalization of undocumented workers, have been undermined by post-9/11 paranoia about Middle Easterners and federal scrutiny of thousands of them. Union organizing is stalled on many fronts and rank-and-file participation in protests against corporate globalization—on the rise in Seattle and Quebec City—has faltered amid the myriad political distractions of the "war on terrorism." While labor's nascent grassroots internationalism is now overshadowed by flag-waving displays of "national unity," trade unionists have yet to be rewarded for their patriotism, even with a modest boost in unemployment benefits. Instead, President Bush is seeking cuts in federal job training grants for laid-off workers. He's already won House approval for "fast-track" negotiating authority on future trade deals that threaten even more U.S. jobs and expects a Senate victory on that issue soon. To ensure that collective bargaining doesn't interfere with "homeland security," the White House stripped tens of thousands of new federal employees of their right to union representation. As University of Illinois labor relations professor Michael LeRoy observed in the *New York Times*, "a time of national emergency makes it more difficult for unions to engineer public support."

Into this bleak landscape arrives *State of the Union*, Nelson Lichtenstein's intellectual history of labor's past hundred years. Readers might take comfort from the fact, well documented by the author, that labor has been down before and, as in the 1930s, bounced back. Nevertheless, Lichtenstein's book raises disturbing questions about when, where, and how that's going to happen again in a period when "solidarity and unionism no longer resonate with so large a slice of the American citizenry." The author's views on this subject are informed by both scholarship and activism. A professor of history at the University of California, Santa Barbara, Lichtenstein wrote *The Most Dangerous Man in Detroit*, a definitive biography of United Auto Workers founder Walter Reuther. In 1996 Lichtenstein helped launch Scholars, Artists, and Writers for Social Justice (SAWSJ), a campus-based labor support network. Through SAWSJ, Lichtenstein has aided teach-ins and protests about workers' rights and worked with AFL-CIO president John Sweeney to reestablish links between unions and intellectuals that might help labor become a more "vital force in a democratic polity."

Consistent with this mission, Lichtenstein hopes to revive interest in what liberal reformers in politics and academia once called "the labor question." *State of the Union* is thus a history of ideas about labor that animated much of the action—all the great union-building attempts—during the last century. "Trade unionism requires a compelling set of ideas and institutions, both self-made and governmental, to give labor's cause power and legitimacy," Lichtenstein argues. "It is a political project whose success enables unions to transcend the ethnic and economic divisions always present in the working population."

He begins his survey in the Progressive Era, a period in which "democratization of the workplace, the solidarity of labor, and the social betterment of American workers all stood far closer to the center of the nation's political and moral consciousness." Politicians, jurists, academics and social activists—ranging from Woodrow Wilson to Louis Brandeis and Florence Kelley of the National Consumers League—all joined the debate about the threat to our "self-governing republic" posed by large-scale industrial capitalism. How could democracy survive when America's growing mass of factory workers were stripped of their civic rights, and often denied a living wage as well, whenever they entered the plant gate? The Progressives' response was "industrial democracy"—extending constitutional rights of free speech and association to the workplace, enacting protective labor laws, and securing other forms of the "social wage." Unfortunately, after World War I, national-level progress toward these goals foundered on the rocks of lost strikes, political repression, and Republican Party dominance in Washington. "Neither the labor movement nor the state, not to mention industrial management itself, generated the kind of relationships in law, ideology, or practice, necessary to institutionalize mass unionism and sustain working-class living standards" during the 1920s.

The years of the Roosevelt administration were a different story. *State of the Union* recounts how Depression-era unrest—plus the efforts of an uneasy alliance between industrial workers, labor radicals, dissident leaders of American Federation of Labor affiliates, pro-union legislators, and New Deal policymakers—led to passage of the Wagner Act. It created a new legal framework for mediating labor-management disputes and boosted consumer purchasing power via the wage gains of collective bar-gaining. As industrial unions experienced explosive growth before and during World War II, the previously unchecked political and economic power of the great corporations was finally tempered through the emer-gence of a more social democratic workers' movement, led by the Congress of Industrial Organizations. The CIO spoke up for the poor, the unskilled, and the unemployed, as well as more affluent members of the working class. Even the conservative craft unions of the AFL ultimate-ly grew as a result of the CIO's existence because many employers, if they had to deal with any union at all, preferred one with less ideology.

Then as now, the nation's manufacturing work force was multiethnic, which meant that hundreds of thousands of recent immigrants used CIO unionism as a vehicle for collective empowerment on the job and in work-ing-class communities. Successful organizers, according to Lichtenstein, "cloaked themselves in the expansive, culturally pluralist patriotism that the New Deal sought to propagate." "Unionism is the spirit of Americanism," proclaimed a labor newspaper directed at "immigrant workers long excluded from a full sense of citizenship." The exercise of citizenship rights in both electoral politics and National Labor Relations Board voting became, for many, a passport to "an 'American' standard of living." *State of the Union* credits some on the left for noting, then and later, that New Deal labor legislation also had its limits and trade-offs. Wagner Act critics like lawyer-historian Staughton Lynd complain that it merely directed worker militancy into narrow institutional channels. These were soon dominated by full-time union reps, attorneys for labor and management, not-so-neutral arbitrators, and various government agencies. During World War II, attempts by the labor officialdom to enforce a nationwide "no strike" pledge led to major rifts within several CIO unions and helped undermine the position of Communist Party members who tried to discourage wildcat walkouts.

The "union idea" that was so transcendent among liberals and radi-cals during the New Deal underwent considerable erosion in the 1950s. Many leading writers, professors and clergymen had signed petitions, walked picket lines, spoken at rallies, testified before congressional com-mittees and defended the cause of industrial organization in the 1930s. These ties began to fray after World War II and the onset of the Cold War, when the CIO conducted a ruthless purge of its own left wing. This made it much harder for "outsiders" with suspect views to gain access to the increasingly parochial world of the (soon to be reunited) AFL and CIO.

As Lichtenstein shows in his survey of their writings, the subsequent alienation of intellectuals like C. Wright Mills, Dwight Macdonald, Harvey Swados, and others was rooted in the perception—largely accurate—that union bureaucracy and self-interest, corruption and complacency, had replaced labor's earlier "visionary quest for solidarity and social transformation."

Lichtenstein questions whether unions were ever quite as fat, happy, and structurally secure as some economists and historians claimed (after the fact) in books and articles on the postwar "labor-management accord." If such a deal had really existed during those years, *State of the Union* argues, it was "less a mutually satisfactory concordat" than "a limited and unstable truce, largely confined to a well-defined set of regions and industries, a product of defeat, not victory." Measured by dues payers alone, "Big Labor" was certainly bigger in the 1950s, at least compared with the small percentage of the workforce represented by unions now (33 percent at midcentury versus less than 13 percent today). Unfortunately, union economic gains derived more from members-only collective bargaining than from social programs like national health insurance that would have benefited the entire working class. Labor's failure to win more universal welfare-state coverage on the European or Canadian models led to its reliance, in both craft and industrial unions, on "firm-centered" fringe-benefit negotiations. The incremental expansion of this "privatized welfare system" left a lot of people (including some union members) out of the picture. Millions of Americans in mostly non-union, lower-tier employment ended up with health care, pension coverage, and paid time off that was limited or nonexistent.

The fundamental weakness of this edifice, even for workers in long-time bastions of union strength, was not fully exposed until the concession bargaining crisis of the late 1970s and '80s. As Lichtenstein describes in painful detail, the employers launched a major offensive—first on the building trades, then on municipal labor, and then on union members in basic industry. Pattern bargaining unraveled amid a series of lost strikes and desperate give-back deals. This allowed management to introduce additional wage-and-benefit inequalities into the workforce, including two-tier pay structures within the same firm; health care cost shifting; more individualized retirement coverage; and greatly reduced job security due to widespread outsourcing and other forms of de-unionization. By then African-Americans in the South, who suffered longest and most from economic inequality, had already risen up and made a "civil rights revolution." Their struggle was one that unions in the 1960s—at least the more liberal ones—nominally supported and in which veteran black labor activists played a seminal role. Yet the civil rights movement as a whole clearly passed labor by and further diminished its already reduced stature as the champion of the underdog and leading national voice for social justice. In a key chapter, "Rights Consciousness in the Workplace," Lichtenstein explores how unions, their contracts, and negotiated grievance procedures have been further marginalized by the enduring legal and political legacy of the civil rights era. According to the author, this has created "the great contradiction at the heart of American democracy today."

In the last forty years, a transformation in law, custom, and ideology has made a once radical demand for racial and gender equality into an elemental code of employer conduct. But during that same era, the rights of workers, as workers, and especially as workers acting in an autonomous, collective fashion, have moved well into the shadows. Little in American culture, politics, or business encourages a collective employee voice. Now, every U.S. employer has to be an "equal opportunity" one or face an avalanche of negative publicity, public censure, and costly litigation. Discrimination against workers—on grounds deemed unlawful by the 1964 Civil Rights Act and subsequent legislation—has become downright un-American, with the newest frontiers being the fight against unfair treatment of workers based on their physical disabilities or sexual preference. At the same time, as *State of the Union* and other studies have documented, collective workplace rights are neither celebrated nor well enforced. What Lichtenstein calls "rights consciousness" is the product of heroic social struggle and community sacrifice but, ironically, it often reinforces a different American tradition: "rugged individualism," which finds modern expression in the oft-repeated threat to "call my lawyer" whenever disputes arise, on or off the job.

To make his point, Lichtenstein exaggerates the degree to which individual complaint-filers at the federal Equal Employment Opportunity Commission (and equally backlogged state agencies) end up on a faster or more lucrative track than workers seeking redress at the National Labor Relations Board. There is no doubt, though, that high-profile discrimination litigation has paid off in ways that unfair-labor-practice cases rarely do. Among other examples, the book contrasts the unpunished mass firing of Hispanic phone workers trying to unionize at Sprint in San Francisco—a typical modern failure of the Wagner Act—with big class-action victories like the settlement securing $132 million for thousands of minority workers victimized by racist managers at Shoney's. The restaurant case involved much public "shaming and redemption" via management shakeups at the corporate level; Sprint merely shrugged off NLRB allegations of union busting, until a federal court finally ruled in its favor.

Lichtenstein's solution is for labor today to find ways to "capitalize on the nation's well-established rights culture of the last 40 years," just as the CIO "made the quest for industrial democracy a powerful theme that legitimized its strikes and organizing campaigns in the 1930s." He looks to veterans of 1960s social movements who entered the withering vineyard of American labor back when cold warriors still held sway to build coalitions with non-labor groups that can "make union organizational rights as unassailable as basic civil rights." In so doing, Lichtenstein recommends finding a middle way between a renewed emphasis on class that downplays identity politics—"itself a pejorative term for rights consciousness"—and an exclusive emphasis on the latter that may indeed thwart efforts to unite workers around common concerns. In the past, Lichtenstein notes, "the labor movement has surged forward not when it denied its heterogeneity" but instead found ways to affirm it, using ethnic and racial pluralism within unions to build power in more diverse workplaces and communities.

Given the enormous external obstacles to union growth, the author's other proposals—summarized in a final chapter, "What Is to Be Done?"—seem a bit perfunctory. His "three strategic prescriptions for the labor movement" point in a better direction than where the AFL-CIO and some of its leading affiliates are currently headed. *State of the Union* calls for more worker militancy, greater internal democracy, and less dependence on the Democratic Party. These are all unassailable ideas, until one gets beyond the official lip service paid to them and down to the nitty-gritty of their implementation. Too often in labor today, particularly in several high-profile, "progressive" unions led by onetime student activists, participatory democracy is missing. Membership mobilization has a top-down, carefully orchestrated character that subverts real rank-and-file initiative, decision-making, and dynamism. The emerging culture of these organizations resembles the "guided democracies" of the Third World, in which party-appointed apparatchiks or technocrats provide surrogate leadership for the people who are actually supposed to be in charge. In politics, it's particularly disheartening to see that labor's "independence" is not being demonstrated through the creation of more union-based alternatives to business-oriented groups within the Democratic Party or by challenging corporate domination of the two-party system. Instead, we see SEIU and others making very traditional endorsement deals with Republicans like Governor George Pataki of New York.

This is not what Lichtenstein has in mind when he urges adoption of "a well-projected, clearly defined political posture in order to advance labor's legislative agenda and defend the very idea of workplace rights and collective action." His book applauds the authentic militants who battled contract concessions and the labor establishment prior to John Sweeney's 1995 election as AFL-CIO president. While the author backs "the new agenda of the Sweeneyite leadership," with its primary focus on the right to organize, he argues that the fight for union democracy is equally "vital to restoring the social mission of labor and returning unions to their social-movement heritage."

How labor is viewed, aided, undermined or ignored by men and women of ideas is, by itself, never going to determine its fate in any era. Workers themselves, acting through organizations they create or remake, are still the primary shapers of their own future, whether it's better or worse. Nevertheless, creative interaction between workers and intellectuals has helped spawn new forms of workplace and political organization in every nation—Poland, South Africa, Korea, and Brazil—where social movement unionism has been most visible in recent decades. In the United States, union activists and their new campus and community allies face the daunting task of developing ideas and strategies that will "again insert working America into the heart of our national consciousness." If they succeed, the labor movement may again have a broader impact on our society, and Lichtenstein's *State of the Union* will deserve credit for being a catalyst in that process.

IS THE STRIKE DEAD?

In the fall of 2002, the streets and office buildings in downtown Boston were the scene of inspiring immigrant worker activism during an unprecedented strike by local janitors. Their walkout was backed by other union members, community activists, students and professors, public officials, religious leaders, and even a few "socially minded" businessmen. The janitors had long been invisible, mistreated by management and, until recently, ignored by their own SEIU local union. Simply by making their strike such a popular social cause, they achieved what many regarded as a major victory. On the same day that the janitors' dispute was settled, a much larger strike—at Overnite Transportation—ended quite differently. Faced with mounting legal setbacks and dwindling picket-line support, the Teamsters were forced to call off their nationwide walkout against America's leading non-union trucker. The four thousand Overnite workers involved were not able to win a first contract. And, since their three-year strike was suspended, all have lost their bargaining rights in a series of "decertification" elections.

The intersecting trajectory of these two struggles—one hopeful and high-profile, the other tragic and now almost forgotten—raises important questions about the state of the strike and the future of labor in America. Maintaining "strike capacity" is no less important than shifting greater resources into organizing new members and just as essential to union revitalization and growth. Unfortunately, developing new ways to walk out and win has not been a big part of recent debates about "changing to win."

Labor's strike effectiveness and organizational strength have long been connected. Throughout history, work stoppages have been used for economic and political purposes, to alter the balance of power between labor and capital within single workplaces, entire industries, or nationwide. Strikes have won shorter hours and safer conditions, through legislation or contract negotiation. They've fostered new forms of worker organization, like industrial unions, that were badly needed because of corporate restructuring and the reorganization of production. Strikes have acted as incubators for class consciousness, rank-and-file leadership development, and political activism. In other countries, strikers have challenged and changed governments that were dictatorial and oppressive (plus union leadership no longer accountable to the membership).

In some nations—like Korea, South Africa, France, and Spain—where strike action helped democratize society, general strikes are still being used for mass mobilization and protest. In recent years, millions of Europeans have participated in nationwide work stoppages over public sector budget cuts, labor law revisions, or pension plan changes sought by conservative governments. In Brazil, voters have even chosen a one-time strike leader, Luis Inacio "Lula" da Silva, to serve as president of their country. In America, meanwhile, "major" work stoppages have become a statistical blip on the radar screen of industrial relations. As the recent experience of transit workers in New York City, graduate students at NYU, and mechanics at Northwest Airlines has shown, striking continues to be a high-stakes venture as well. It involves considerable legal and financial risks, particularly in the public sector, where walkouts are severely restricted and, as in New York, subject to draconian penalties. Since 1992, walkouts by 1,000 workers or more have averaged less than 40 annually. In 2003, there were only 14, with just 129,000 union members participating. In contrast, at the peak of labor's post-World War II strike wave in 1952, there were 470 major strikes, affecting nearly three million workers nationwide.

As strike activity continues to decline in the United States, the pool of union members and leaders with actual strike experience shrinks as well. That's why union activists need to analyze, collectively and individually, their strike victories and defeats—summing up and sharing the lessons of these battles so they can become the basis for future success, rather than a reoccurring pattern of failure. Attorney Bob Schwartz's new book, *Strikes, Picketing, and Inside Campaigns: A Legal Guide for Unions*, makes a valuable contribution to this educational process. It's the latest in a series of easy-to-read guides from Work Rights Press, which also publishes the author's best-seller, *The Legal Rights of Union Stewards*. As in his previous books, Schwartz provides useful sample letters, legal notices, and answers to commonly asked questions—in this case, about the many different types of union picketing and strike activity. There are also relevant case citations, tracking the development of labor law in this area over the past twenty-five years.[1]

Beginning with the PATCO disaster in 1981, when thousands of striking air traffic controllers were fired and replaced, the U.S. labor movement entered a dark decade of lost strikes and lockouts. Many anti-concession battles ended badly at Phelps-Dodge, Greyhound, Hormel, Eastern, Continental Airlines, International Paper, and other firms. Yet even during this difficult period for strikers, there were contract campaigns that bucked the tide of concession bargaining and Schwartz's book discusses some of the tactics and strategies they used. In 1989, for example, sixty thousand members of the Communications Workers of America and International Brotherhood of Electrical Workers waged an effective four-month strike in New York and New England over threatened medical benefit cuts at NYNEX. Telephone workers made extensive use of mobile picketing tactics, targeting top officials of the company and their allies in places where they least expected it.

At the same time, the United Mine Workers succeeded in making their twelve-month walkout against Pittston—conducted in geographically isolated Appalachian mountain communities—into a national labor cause. The union mobilized its members for sympathy strikes at other companies, linked arms with Jesse Jackson, used civil disobedience tactics, staged the first plant occupation since the 1930s, and created an encampment in southwest Virginia (Camp Solidarity) that hosted strike supporters from around the country. Even an avalanche of injunctions, fines, and damage suits did not deter the miners and their families.

West Virginia aluminum workers, locked out by Ravenswood, then applied many of the lessons of the Pittston strike in a wide-ranging corporate campaign orchestrated by the United Steel Workers of America. The USWA leveraged international union connections to put mounting pressure on key financial institutions and investors who were tied to the employer. (See Schwartz's chapter 5 on finding the pressure points of "integrated businesses," including their "foreign connections.") Despite massive hiring of replacement workers and other union-busting measures, Ravenswood was finally forced to end its lockout and settle with the USWA. Since that victory, the ILWU and UNITE-HERE Local 2 in San Francisco have both turned the table on offensive lockouts by employers responding to shop-floor action or a selective strike. (Boycott-related "consumer education"—of the sort conducted very effectively by the hotel workers—is discussed in several chapters, including one titled, "Buyer Beware.")

In 1997, the contract strike made its biggest comeback in recent years with the now-famous national walkout by 190,000 United Parcel Service workers. The backing of Teamster drivers has long been appreciated by other strikers. As Schwartz notes, IBT contract language has been "a boon to other unions who count on Teamster drivers to respect their picket lines." In 1997, it was time for the rest of labor to return the favor, which unions did in a tremendous outpouring of support for UPS drivers and package handlers.

How the Teamsters framed their dispute with UPS was a critical factor in gaining broader public sympathy. The main strike objective was creating more full-time job opportunities to thwart management's strategy of converting the UPS workforce into a largely part-time one. "Part-Time America Doesn't Work!" the Teamsters proclaimed, in a successful effort to invest their contract fight with larger social meaning. The UPS strike not only beat back the company's concession demands and made job security gains, it became a rallying point for everyone concerned about the societal impact of part-timing, with its accompanying erosion of job-based benefits.

Unions engaged in more recent struggles against health care cost-shifting have tried to borrow from the Teamsters' playbook at UPS by linking their strikes to the movement for health care reform. When 18,000 General Electric workers staged a two-day nationwide walkout in 2003, to protest medical plan changes, many locals organized around the slogan, "Health Care for All, Not Health Cuts at GE!" Strike-related rallies and publicity emphasized the common bond between union and non-union, insured and uninsured workers. (The UFCW's 2003–4 strike and lockout, involving thousands of grocery workers in Southern California, was far less successful in making the connection between management demands for benefit cuts and the need for universal medical coverage.)

As Schwartz notes, some unions are now striking with greater tactical flexibility than before, experimenting with limited-duration walkouts and inside campaigns to reduce the risk and cost of protracted shutdowns. HERE members at Yale University have repeatedly demonstrated creativity and unusual solidarity between separate white-collar and blue-collar units during their campus-based bargaining battles. In 2003, Yale workers skirmished effectively with the university for the ninth time in thirty-five years. Faced with aggressive picketing, mass rallies, and strike-related arrests, Yale sued for peace in the form of a long-term contract settlement.

In similar fashion, thousands of telephone workers in the Northeast entered regional bargaining with Verizon in 2003 with a record of five strikes in the previous two decades and a deeply ingrained "no contract, no work" tradition. Confronted with unprecedented strike contingency planning by management, members of CWA and IBEW shifted gears to throw their corporate adversary off balance. For more than a month, they worked without a contract (engaging in all the "job wobbling" activities described by Schwartz in chapter 2, "No Contract-No Peace"). Verizon incurred enormous strike-preparation costs, without ever getting the opportunity to replace its existing workforce with an army of scabs, as planned. The result was a new contract that preserved job security guarantees, plus fully-paid medical coverage for workers and retirees. (In 2004, a four-day national "warning strike" by 100,000 workers at SBC Communications—some of whom had not been on strike in twenty years—produced similar results, while avoiding the risk of an open-ended walkout.)

"Job wobbling"—in the form of work-to-rule and other "inside tactics"—has also figured prominently in recent rank-and-file discussions about how to respond to the deep wage and benefits cuts demanded by Delphi Corp., the nation's largest auto parts supplier. Both UAW leaders and some dissidents seem to have endorsed the work slow-down approach in a situation where walking out might actually facilitate the company's downsizing and plant shutdown plans.

Regardless of what form worker militancy takes, it helps to have adequate financial backing for strikes and contract campaigns. One bottom-line requirement is a big national strike fund, with the flexibility to pay out fixed weekly benefits (of at least $200 to $300 per week), either for strikers or for the disciplinary casualties of concerted in-plant activity. Some unions like CWA (which has a $400 million "Member Relief Fund") also maintain a separate source of contract campaign funding for use by workers who are prohibited by law from striking and for the payment of strikers' medical expenses and/or COBRA premiums. In a section titled "Benefit Daze," the author provides much valuable advice about COBRA coverage, unemployment claims, and other benefit eligibility that may aid strikers lacking a strong union safety net.

Creativity, careful planning, and membership involvement are essential to union success, whether workers choose to stop work or pursue a non-strike strategy. A big part of the internal planning process is sizing up the strengths and weaknesses of management's position and your own. Before (rather than after) walking out, union members need to line up labor and community support through solidarity coalitions like Jobs with Justice or local central labor councils. Otherwise, there is great danger that a small group of workers—and sometimes even a large one—will end up on picket lines isolated, frustrated, and impoverished.

Schwartz's book is a unique tool to use in membership education, leadership training, and union strategy discussions about what to do when a contract expires. In situations where striking is a necessary and viable worker response, he outlines what it takes to make a walkout effective, while helping unions anticipate likely employer countermeasures at the bargaining table, in court, and at the NLRB. The author has pulled together an enormous amount of material that has not been readily accessible to non-lawyers in the past—even to activists relying on the official strike manuals of the few unions that have them. Union members who fail to consult Schwartz's book while preparing for a contract fight will not be as ready as they could be to deal with the many legal and organizational problems that may arise. Any union bargaining team that doesn't have a copy of *Strikes, Picketing and Inside Campaigns* is missing out on information and advice that will make the hard job of winning good contracts just a little bit easier.

BACK TO THE FUTURE WITH EFCA?

In 1978, during President Jimmy Carter's first and only term, unions came closer to strengthening the Wagner Act than at any other time since Congress enacted labor's "Magna Carta" in 1935. They had the benefit of big Watergate-related congressional victories by the Democrats four years earlier and 61 Democrats in the Senate. Nevertheless, when a bill was introduced that would have speeded up National Labor Relations Board (NLRB) elections, helped fired organizers, and penalized union-busting employers, labor law reform got filibustered to death in the Senate, after tepid White House lobbying on its behalf. Three decades after that political setback—and partly because of it—American unions now represent only 12.4 percent of the total workforce. In the National Labor Relations Act-covered private sector, union density is down to 7.6 percent.

Thanks to the popular backlash against another discredited GOP administration in 2006 mid-term elections, Congress once again changed for the better, raising new hopes for labor law reform. In 2008, union members were urged to elect even bigger Democratic majorities in the House and Senate, plus a new president, so legislation called the Employee Free Choice Act (EFCA), described in more detail below, could be enacted in 2009. Since many in labor believe that amending the NLRA is more critical to union survival today than thirty years ago, it's worth examining labor's campaign for EFCA, whether or not it succeeds right now. Have the lessons of past political defeats been well applied in this latest bid for labor law reform, which may well require further efforts? Can the AFL-CIO and its Change to Win (CTW) rival really win on this issue when organized labor's size and political clout has been so much diminished since the late 1970s? Even if enacted, will EFCA enable unions to overcome widespread employer resistance to collective bargaining in the United States?

As a dress rehearsal for their push for EFCA in 2009, unions forced a House vote on EFCA in March 2007, even though their Democratic allies lacked a filibuster-proof "super-majority" in the Senate and then-President Bush would have vetoed the bill anyway. At hearings, rallies, and press conferences around the country, union officials and fired workers explained how EFCA would make a difference in union organizing and first-contract bargaining. Management would be compelled to recognize new bargaining units based on a showing that a majority of workers (in an appropriate unit) had signed union authorization cards. Employers would no longer be able to insist on NLRB elections, taking advantage of the accompanying delays and opportunities for legal (and illegal) anti-union campaigning. Workers fired for organizing would be eligible for "treble damages"—three times their lost pay—rather than just "back pay" minus "interim earnings." Other employer unfair labor practices—now "punished" with a mere notice posting—could result in a $20,000 fine (if found to be willful or repeated violations of the act). Finally, EFCA would create a Canadian-style process of first-contract mediation and arbitration. Unresolved first contract negotiations could, at union request, become the subject of binding arbitration leading to imposed contract terms. This would make it harder for employers to use bad-faith bargaining as their second line of defense against unionization, as many do now after losing a contested representation election.

EFCA opponents launched a well-coordinated drive against the bill in a dry run of the even bigger management counter-campaign anticipated in 2009. In op-eds, paid ads, anti-EFCA mailings, speeches, and websites, industry lobbyists defended the sanctity of secret-ballot NLRB representation votes, depicting labor's "card check" alternative as deeply flawed, undemocratic, and even "un-American." The result was a 241 to 185 House vote in favor. Three months later, 51 members of the Senate moved to bring it to a vote on the floor—far fewer than the 60 necessary to stop a Republican filibuster. Meanwhile, on the 2008 presidential campaign trail, every Democratic candidate endorsed the bill, although only John Edwards ever talked about EFCA much in front of non-labor audiences. When he was pursuing the "labor vote" in Ohio's Democratic primary, the eventual nominee, Barack Obama, told a blue-collar crowd in Lorain:

> If a majority of workers want a union, they should get a union. It's that simple. We need to stand up to the business lobby and pass the Employee Free Choice Act. That's why I've been fighting for it in the

Senate and that's why I'll make it the law of the land when I'm president
of the United States.[1]

Obama's primary rival, Hillary Clinton, also pledged her support for
EFCA, although in a private meeting with top AFL-CIO officials in early
2007, she suggested (somewhat gratuitously in light of her own "high
negatives") that labor's public image might be an impediment to its passage. As a candidate, Clinton carried the taint of her husband's dismal
record on labor law reform. During his first term, fourteen years after
Carter's attempted overhaul of the Wagner Act, Bill Clinton put labor's
top legislative priority on the back burner by creating a presidential
study commission. The "Commission on the Future of Worker-
Management Relations" spent 1993–94 collecting testimony and trying
to document links between "employee representation" and "economic
competitiveness." Unfortunately for labor, this two-year period was the
only time when the Democrats had a majority in both the House and
Senate and thus the ability to enact pro-worker legislation. Dunlop
Commission proposals—some of which were not even helpful to
unions—ended up being dead on arrival due to mid-term election victories in 1994 that gave Republicans control over Congress for the rest of
Clinton's presidency.

Having learned from that fiasco, labor law reformers hoped that their
preparatory activity in 2007 and continued agitation during the 2008 race
would result in a vote on EFCA early in any Obama administration. House
Speaker Nancy Pelosi and California Congressman George Miller promised to push the White House forward on the issue without any Clinton-
style commissions, delays, or political "triangulation." But not all of their
colleagues, old and new, were equally reliable. In a message to members of
the United Electrical Workers, the union's national political director Chris
Townsend warned "against political phonies who want us to think they are
in support of EFCA but who will get cold feet when big business lobbyists
(and campaign contributors) lean on them hard when the bill comes before
Congress again."[2] The 2007 House and Senate roll calls were an important
stepping-stone to labor law reform but, in terms of outcome, these were
votes that "didn't count." Everyone knew that EFCA wasn't about to
become law then, which made it possible for labor's more lukewarm
"friends" to take a "pro-union" stand of no actual consequence.

In addition to their campaigning for Obama, private sector unions
spent much of 2008 shoring up the shakier Senate Democrats and trying

to ensure that any Democratic candidates who joined them in January 2009 were already committed to EFCA. (In labor's best-case election scenario, Democrats would gain nine additional seats and, at long last, the ability to overcome a Republican filibuster.) Members of the Communications Workers of America (CWA) and other unions were deployed around the country to educate politicians about the experience of workers already covered by EFCA-type procedures for "card check" recognition. In Arkansas, for example, AT&T wireless customer service reps visited U.S. Senator Blanche Lincoln, a past EFCA fence-sitter, to recount how management had used threats, intimidation, and harassment to thwart previous union activity. When ownership of their call center in Little Rock changed, workers were able to unionize, without interference, under a negotiated agreement that obligated management to remain neutral and authorized the American Arbitration Association (AAA) to certify CWA based on its "card majority."

Among the 20,000 or more AT&T workers who have won bargaining rights in similar fashion since 2004 is a group of 600 located in Dover, New Hampshire. Their CWA organizing committee had a meeting with former N.H. governor Jean Shaheen, who pledged to become an EFCA sponsor during her 2008 race against a GOP incumbent, Senator John Sununu. The Dover workers explained to Shaheen how CWA Local 1298 became their bargaining representative after an AAA card count in October 2007. (This win was the biggest private sector organizing victory in the "Live Free or Die" state in three decades.) However, negotiations on a first contract with AT&T were delayed for several months due to the new notice posting and waiting period requirement imposed by the NLRB in its Dana/Metaldyne case decisions.[3] In those rulings, Bush appointees to the Board tried to undermine privately negotiated recognition agreements by giving anti-union workers 45 days, after certification via card check, to petition for a decertification vote. Thus if 30 percent of the workers in a new unit sign up, they can bring in the NLRB to hold an election even after a majority of the workforce has just authorized a union to represent them! At AT&T in Dover, an effective in-plant campaign thwarted any minority bid for a decertification vote; but nearly a year later, workers still had no first contract, illustrating the difficulty of getting one even at a "union-friendly" company (which, in this case, was not serving telecom customers but rather acting as a passport processing contractor for the U.S. State Department).

By placing a new obstacle in the path of card check recognition and, potentially, forcing more organizing back into the arena of NLRB elections, Dana gave unions most involved in "non-Board organizing" an additional incentive to win passage of EFCA. Even if NLRA reform failed under Obama, the Dana decision could be reversed eventually, without amending the law, through Democratic control of the White House. But any broader overturning of anti-worker rulings by the "Bush Board" requires the presidential appointment of more labor-friendly NLRB appointees and several years of case-by-case adjudication and/or agency rule making. As Max Fraser observed in *The Nation*, "Democratic labor board majorities have had little positive effect on organizing" in recent decades. "Private-sector union membership dropped steadily and by more than half between 1977 and 2000, while the two parties spent equal time in the White House. The Reagan years were particularly dismal, but labor didn't exactly thrive under the Carter and Clinton boards either."[4]

According to EFCA backers, unions won't be able to build on the success of card check and neutrality agreements (negotiated by SEIU, UNITE-HERE, CWA, IBT, UAW, UFCW, and others) without changing the NLRA itself. This confidence is not shared by all academic researchers. As Cornell University professor Richard Hurd noted in *New Labor Forum* in the spring of 2008, "Even a cursory review of the Canadian experience under provincial laws that parallel EFCA indicates that . . . expectations of union deliverance from organizing purgatory may prove to be overly optimistic."[5] Hurd cites the work of Canadian labor relations scholar Roy Adams, who points out that "union density and bargaining coverage are falling even in such provinces as Saskatchewan and Quebec that have card check and first-contract arbitration clauses." Adams predicts that U.S. management, like Canadian firms, will find new ways to resist unionization even if EFCA is enacted, and that its net impact will be minimal.[6]

Rutgers law professor James Pope is another EFCA skeptic and critic of overly narrow definitions of "labor law reform." Along with Peter Kellman, president of the Portland, Maine, AFL-CIO central labor council, and Ed Bruno, former organizing director for the National Nurses Organizing Committee (an affiliate of the California Nurses Association), Pope argues that "EFCA is merely the latest in a series of disconnected attempts to ram through the best bill that appears winnable at a particular moment in time." Earlier attempts they cite include the Carter-era Labor Law Reform bill that failed in 1978 and labor's unsuccessful

1992–94 push for passage of the Workplace Fairness Act. Never enacted, the latter measure was a union response to the widely publicized and usually quite devastating hiring of replacement workers during lost strikes in the 1980s. The Workplace Fairness Act would not even have prevented employers from hiring temporary labor during a walkout but it would have banned permanent striker replacements. To this day, in an economic strike without favorable return-to-work terms, employers still have no legal obligation to lay off "scabs" when a settlement is reached; strikers can return to their old jobs only as vacancies develop.

According to Pope, Kellman, and Bruno, EFCA's failure to close this loophole renders the "right to organize . . . of little use" because organizing and bargaining are so closely linked. The combination of card check and:

> compulsory arbitration to win first contracts . . . might make it easier for unions to sign up dues-paying members in the short run, but it will do little or nothing to strengthen the labor movement in the long run. When the first contract expires, the newly recruited members will discover that they have little or no bargaining power, that their "right to strike" consists of the right to be permanently replaced, and that stronger unions are banned from assisting them with sympathy strikes or secondary boycotts.[7]

Implicit in the critique above is the idea that labor law reform will always fall short if it doesn't overturn Taft-Hartley Act restrictions on real union solidarity *and* the Supreme Court's seventy-year-old sanctioning of the use of striker replacements. Unfortunately—except in the speeches of Ralph Nader—repeal of Taft-Hartley and a ban on permanent striker replacements is not a big part of political discourse today. The authors propose to change that by recasting labor's campaign as a fight for "the full acceptance of workers' rights as an essential component of American freedom." They reject "EFCA's slogan of 'free choice'" as "a short-term marketing sound bite" that "kowtows to our society's dominant ethos of individualism" and fails to "capture the labor movement's true objectives or its appeal to workers." In order to "win workers' rights, the labor movement needs to act like a genuine rights movement." Instead, they believe that EFCA inadvertently "plays into the hands of anti-union spin-masters, whose vision of the natural, union-free workplace is pervasive in the media, in academia, and in the public consciousness."

These EFCA critics call for a longer-term, more radical legal/political strategy, based on "the freedom of association model" and the early twen-

tieth-century labor idea that federal guarantees of the right to strike and
bargain collectively should be rooted in the Thirteenth Amendment's
protection against involuntary servitude—rather than the commerce
clause, which became the constitutional basis for the Wagner Act. Their
review of the history of labor law reform efforts based on "freedom of
association" highlights the Norris-LaGuardia Act instead. The authors
call it "the most effective pro-worker statute in U.S. history" because it
curbed "what were then perceived as the two greatest threats to 'full freedom of association,' namely federal court injunctions against peaceful
concerted activity and federal court enforcement of yellow-dog contracts"
(which prevented workers from joining unions not approved by their
employer).

Whatever one may think of the feasibility of their alternative strategy,
one point made by Pope, Kellman, and Bruno is indisputable and raises
yet another, more practical concern about EFCA—namely how does it get
passed without a lot of outside-the-Beltway agitation? As the authors note,
"a genuine rights movement relies primarily on the activity of its rank-and-
file members . . . and not on ordinary lobbying or staff-driven campaigns.
. . . [E]very major workers' rights statute has been preceded by widespread
collective action demanding and exercising workers' rights."

Key EFCA campaign strategists have not ignored this history.
Although "organizing unions" can't summon up a social movement out of
thin air, they can try to build on their collective experience of strikes, lockouts, and membership mobilization on behalf of organizing-related
demands. Some recent "bargain to organize" struggles have raised rank-
and-file consciousness about the importance of winning EFCA-type card
check language (plus employer neutrality) in new contracts.[8] Past labor
law reform efforts, such as the failed 1977–78 bid, had much less of a
grassroots orientation than the 2007–8 effort, relying instead on consult-
ant-driven Capitol Hill lobbying. The Carter administration backed
changes in the NLRA like it was just doing a favor for a nettlesome special
interest group. It provided a quid pro quo for past election support not
much different than congressional Democrats' repeated introduction,
years ago, of "common situs picketing" bills. This AFL-CIO-backed legislation was always viewed as a sop to the building trades and never garnered
enough support to loosen legal restrictions on worker solidarity in construction.

In key 2008 Senate races, business groups spent an estimated $50
million on ads depicting labor law reform as a dangerous "Big Labor"

power grab, financed by millions of dollars in union donations to the Democrats.[9] (No matter how much unions have shrunk, in the imagination of www.unionfacts.com and like-minded sources of disinformation, the bogeyman of "Big Labor" still stalks the land, just as it did in the late 1940s when Taft-Hartley was required to tame it!) In the January 2008 issue of *HR Magazine*, former management lawyer Rick Berman, now executive director of the Center for Union Facts in Washington, warned employers that if EFCA passes, "private sector union membership could double." In the same article, well-known union-busting consultant Stephen Cabot sounded the alarm about the proposed law's higher penalties for management misconduct. "Currently, many employers engage in initiatives to counter union campaigns they wouldn't dare do under EFCA," Cabot said. "With EFCA, it will be very costly." HR's conclusion: "If EFCA passes, it would be the most significant pro-labor legislation in more than two decades"—employers should rightly fear that it "will open the floodgates for organizing."[10]

To broaden support for EFCA, unions are depicting it, more accurately, as essential to their institutional survival. Friends of labor have been reminded that without NLRA reform unions will be further weakened as a defender of working-class living standards and an historic ally of progressive causes. For example, defending existing pension and medical benefits—not to mention protecting Social Security and replacing job-based health insurance with a Medicare-for-All system—will be increasingly difficult, if not impossible, without greater union density. The U.S. mortgage market meltdown and accompanying recession provides yet another compelling reason for congressional action on EFCA, since workers' rights could be a helpful part of any real "economic stimulus" package. As economist Dean Baker, from the Center for Economic and Policy Research, explained on the eve of Wall Street's collapse:

> While suppression of workers' right to organize may appear to have little direct relationship to the collapsing housing bubble that is the cause of this recession, on closer examination they are closely linked. . . . If workers are able to form unions and get their share of productivity growth, it can again put the country on the path of wage-driven consumption growth, instead of growth driven by unsustainable borrowing. . . . Restoring a wage-driven growth path will provide workers and businesses with much more stability than the current bubble economy.[11]

Yet policy arguments like Baker's—so redolent of the Depression-era rationale for passing the Wagner Act in the first place and so compelling again today—won't gain any traction in Washington without many more labor "boots on the ground" (and the accompanying sound of marching feet). At least that was the theory behind the AFL-CIO's "Million-Member Mobilization" for "bargaining rights worth working for and voting for" in 2008. Undertaken at the urging of CWA president Larry Cohen and others on the federation's executive council, the AFL-CIO resolved to get 10 percent of all union members signed up on pledge cards demanding that Congress and the White House take action on EFCA. To reach this proclaimed goal of one million petitioners, labor's campaign had both an internal and external component:

> Every national union, state federation, central labor council trade department, constituency group, local union and allied organization commits to massive membership mobilization about the assault on collective bargaining, the middle class, and our unions. . . . We must educate, mobilize, and enlist our members in the movement to pass the Employee Free Choice Act.
>
> Every segment of the labor movement also commits to engage and cultivate more allies, religious leaders, civil rights leaders, academics, think tanks, and other opinion leaders to speak out about the importance of restoring the freedom to form unions to build a just society.[12]

Organized labor is quite adept at "resolutionary activity," which papers over big gaps between rhetoric and reality. In the case of EFCA, one reality has been rather limited follow-up activity by several major unions that are predominantly public sector and won't benefit much, if at all, from private sector labor law changes. EFCA is also largely irrelevant to current strategies for regaining "union market share" in construction (although a few building trades unions have worked hard for it). Ditto for airline industry labor, which is covered by the Railway Labor Act rather than the NLRA. Among the industrial, (non-airline) transportation, service and retail unions with the biggest stake in EFCA, the follow-through on effective membership education and internal mobilization has varied widely. For some, having such an issue-oriented focus added a new wrinkle to political work during a presidential election year.

In March 2008, a core group of AFL-CIO unions stepped forward to provide initial leadership in the "Million Member" campaign. CWA, the United Auto Workers, the United Steelworkers, and the much smaller

International Federation of Professional and Technical Engineers (IFPTE) formed an alliance based on a professed shared commitment to "unprecedented workplace activity" on behalf of EFCA. All four, with a total membership of two million, had earlier balked at paying a $1 per member special assessment sought by the AFL-CIO to fund its more diffuse GOTV drive. The Alliance was critical of that plan because of its "deficient emphasis on laying the groundwork for enacting EFCA."[13] So, as part of labor's overall $300 million political effort, CWA, USWA, UAW, and IFPTE decided to pool resources to reach and engage 15 percent of their own members on the job, plus run a coordinated field campaign. Among the states targeted for worksite leafleting, door-to-door canvassing, and phone-banking by the Alliance were Virginia, Michigan, Pennsylvania, Kentucky, Louisiana, Minnesota, and Mississippi.

As Cohen of CWA argued: "Our own history, as well as that of other labor movements around the world, teaches us that we must act to create change—not sit back and hope for it, or hire others to make it happen for us."[14] Subsequently, Cohen became a bridge builder to Change to Win unions as well. He urged them to join Alliance union members in grassroots activity that would inject EFCA into 2008 races and build public support for its passage in 2009, by pushing candidates to talk about workers' rights in front of non-labor audiences. A group of seven unions, acting through American Rights at Work, raised $5 million for pro-EFCA ads on cable TV to help counter big business saturation of the airwaves with anti-EFCA propaganda. With a month to go before the November 4 election, CWA had signed up nearly 15 percent of its membership and had 97,842 pledge cards ready to be displayed in the U.S. Capitol in January, at the swearing-in of the new Congress. Around the country, some organizers tried to put a human face on the EFCA cards they gathered. They photographed rank-and-file endorsers of the bill so their pictures could be posted on campaign websites and sent to Washington too—demonstrating to legislators that EFCA is a real worker priority, not just a project of labor lobbyists.

In 2009 (and beyond), the Employee Free Choice Act faces plenty of competition for inside-the-Beltway attention, due to economic troubles that have now become scarily systemic. Even though union workers helped to put Obama in the White House, through their exertions in key "battleground states," the new president will not be spoiling for a knockdown, drag-out fight with corporate America over labor law reform, if recent history is any guide. Instead, he may be tempted to take a Jimmy

Carter-style dive or start bobbing and weaving like Bill Clinton. Only bottom-up pressure on the Democrats can ensure that this bout even occurs, not to mention ends favorably for labor during Obama's first year in office or any time thereafter.

PART FIVE

ORGANIZING IN THE GLOBAL VILLAGE

For much of the last century, American labor has had, at best, a mixed record of dealing with the successive waves of immigration that have transformed the nation's workforce. To make matters worse, as historian Paul Buhle and others have documented, the AFL-CIO was a longtime supporter of U.S. foreign and military policies that didn't benefit workers here or abroad. The articles in this section examine how union responses to immigration, foreign military intervention, trade deregulation, and corporate globalization have changed for the better in recent years, due to pressure from below and the need for real labor internationalism. Part 5 also illustrates the importance of alternative organizational models—whether in the form of the cross-border solidarity networks described by Kim Moody, David Bacon, and Robert Ross or the immigrant worker initiatives studied (and assisted) by Janice Fine, Jennifer Gordon, Manny Ness, and Biju Mathew.

TAKING CARE OF BUSINESS

The current more liberal tilt of AFL-CIO leaders and staff—as welcome as that may be—has tended to obscure organized labor's long history of conservatism on issues related to U.S. foreign and military policy. The

1995 election of John Sweeney's "New Voice" slate and its subsequent weeding out of Cold War apparatchiks at federation headquarters makes it appear that the slate has finally been wiped clean. As a result, a whole new generation of twenty-something union activists, many recruited directly from college campuses, has little historical memory of what the AFL-CIO was like B.S.—"Before Sweeney."

Two new books—one by a left-wing labor historian and the other by a mainstream biographer—provide a useful reminder of how bad it was in the bad old days not so long ago. Both are worth reading because organized labor still suffers from the debilitating, long-term legacy of the pre-1995 leadership. In the area of international affairs, the AFL-CIO's continuing dependence on government funding for its overseas programs remains controversial. Although heartened by Sweeney's "promise of a new, more inclusive and vigorous movement," Paul Buhle's *Taking Care of Business* cautions against putting too much faith in the new faces at the top of the federation. Their rise to power, Buhle believes, does not ensure fundamental institutional change, which can only be achieved by "ordinary working people acting as their own leaders."

A veteran researcher of union radicalism in the late nineteenth and early twentieth centuries, Buhle is a harsh critic of Sweeney's not-so-illustrious predecessors. (How many other labor historians have called for renaming the George Meany Center in Silver Spring, Maryland, after someone whose life in labor was more worthy of commemoration?) Buhle shows how the bumbling, business-oriented AFL-CIO bureaucracy run by Meany and Lane Kirkland developed over the twentieth century. What characterized AFL leaders, almost from the start, was not their aggressive defense of working-class interests, broadly defined. Rather, it was their common affinity for red-baiting, flag-waving, strike-breaking, and cozying up to whatever business and government leaders they thought might bestow favors on "the house of labor."

As Buhle observes, "From Gompers through the forgotten William Green to George Meany and the already obscure Lane Kirkland, they cast their fate with what they perceived to be society's winners," while turning their back on women, minorities, immigrants, and anyone else outside the craft union fold. Throughout the twentieth century, the labor establishment's search for partnerships with employers led inexorably to foreign and military entanglements that primarily served corporate interests. Yet, no matter how much wartime cooperation or U.S. foreign policy support organized labor managed to deliver, it was never enough—in either postwar period—to protect unions from a relentless business assault.

By no coincidence, the current era of union marginalization and decline began with the Cold War and labor's deepest entanglements with the State Department and Pentagon. Ted Morgan's *A Covert Life* tells the appalling story of Jay Lovestone, Meany's chief overseas operative for thirty years and the main architect of labor involvement with the Central Intelligence Agency (CIA). Morgan documents how CIA money flowed into a variety of projects designed to counter left-wing activism among workers in Europe and the Third World. These efforts often produced or exacerbated political splits that weakened foreign unions in the face of hostile employers or right-wing regimes. The resulting more favorable investment climate for U.S. firms facilitated the export of hundreds of thousands of U.S. jobs. The AFL-CIA alliance, which continued even after the AFL's 1955 merger with the more liberal Congress of Industrial Organizations (CIO), finally had its cover blown during the Vietnam War.

George Meany was a leading supporter of the war, throughout the Johnson and Nixon administrations. But, writes Morgan, as the antiwar movement eventually "caught fire in labor," he and Lovestone "found themselves unable to keep the rank and file in line." Their hawkish stance alienated many traditional union allies, divided labor as Vietnam had divided the nation, and ultimately led to Lovestone's downfall when his CIA ties and Meany's lies about them were publicly exposed. The top echelon of the AFL-CIO is now swarming with former anti-war protesters from the 1960s who later became labor activists and continued to challenge the AFL-CIO's kneejerk anti-communism in South Africa and Central America during Lane Kirkland's tenure. Meany's successor ended up devoting so much time to Cold War campaigning abroad—while American unions were under attack at home—that he eventually lost the support of key AFL-CIO affiliates.

Since their executive council rebellion in 1995 that forced Kirkland out—and overthrew his heir apparent, Tom Donahue—the federation's "free trade union institutes" have been overhauled. Former critics of their activities have been put in charge of labor's international work, more emphasis has been placed on building genuine solidarity, and the old ideological litmus tests have supposedly been scrapped. It would have been useful, however, if Buhle had concluded his book with a more detailed examination of the current funding, personnel, and goals of "New Voice" cross-border solidarity programs.

The AFL-CIO's glossy magazine, *America@Work*, provides glowing reports on every other Sweeney administration initiative, but discloses much less about any new directions in the field of international affairs. Without such information sharing—and the kind of critical scrutiny and debate encouraged by labor-based anti-intervention groups in the 1980s—there's no guarantee that the federation's overseas programs will, in fact, be run with greater independence from the U.S. government. To the dismay of some critics on the left, the latter continues to be the main financial backer of the AFL-CIO Solidarity Center via annual grants from the National Endowment for Democracy. Anyone at federation headquarters trying to move things in a better direction for workers overseas as well as at home, should welcome greater transparency, because, as Buhle and Morgan show, that's not how labor's foreign policy "business" has been handled in the past.

SLICING THE GLOBALONEY

Capital today is mobile and global, integrated, and powerful. Organized labor tends to be fragmented and much weaker than in the past. At a time when all workers need more than ever before to unite to defend their interests, most unions still operate within the framework of a single nation-state or, worse yet, one domestic industry, firm, or craft. Finding ways to overcome barriers created by organizational bureaucracy, geography, nationalism, or language is much harder for labor than management. Captains of industry can marshal and deploy their resources with far greater speed, discipline, and efficiency—operating now on a transnational basis as easily as they used to within most countries. Unions are quite parochial in comparison. The best are still groping for ways to move beyond traditional forms of labor internationalism, which include conference-going, speech-making, and resolution-passing by high-ranking officials in nice places like Montreal, London, or Geneva.

Workers in a Lean World is an ambitious attempt to analyze the fast-changing economic and political conditions facing labor on a global scale. Kim Moody has spent almost twenty years aiding rank-and-file networks in the United States as one of the founders of *Labor Notes,* a Detroit-based newsletter and labor education project. His previous book, *An Injury to All* (1988), chronicled the decline of American "business unionism" and predict-

ed that membership dissatisfaction with give-backs, lost strikes, and organizing defeats would lead to a leadership shake-up and revived militancy.

Now Moody is back with more bad and good news. Just when U.S.
unions seem to be getting their act together better on the domestic front,
the employers have raised the bar a lot higher. They've gone global on us,
creating "production chains" that span national boundaries. Everywhere,
they're shifting work from higher to lower-cost regions and using downsizing threats to extract new concessions from unions. In the workplace
itself, many long-standing labor achievements like full-time jobs, safety
rules, a reasonable work pace and limits on forced overtime are being sac-
rificed on the alter of "flexibility." Capital is meanwhile engaged in a
worldwide political offensive in favor of free trade, deregulation, privatization, and cuts in social spending, all of which undermine organized
labor and reduce workers' living standards. To make matters worse, many
traditional working-class parties—labor, social democratic, even
Communist—now embrace these "pro-market" policies. The so-called
alternatives to Thatcherism in Britain and Reaganism in the United States
offered by Tony Blair and Bill Clinton amount to little more than "neo-
liberalism with a heart," Moody contends. Their mantra about creating
"labor partnerships" with management to win what Blair calls "the crusade for competitiveness" just mimics the rhetoric of their predecessors
and echoes the demands of bosses everywhere.

The good news, according to Moody, is that many workers are reject-
ing their assigned role in this "dog-eat-dog world of lean and mean
transnational corporations and trimmed-down states." After all, why
should we act like a bunch of lab rats, running as fast as we can on tread-
mills in a race to the bottom against each other? From Mexico to the
former Eastern Bloc, neo-liberal reformers have promised prosperity but
so far have delivered only austerity, job insecurity, and greater unemployment. Moody provides a good overview of the mid-nineties strike wave,
which developed around the world in direct response to belt-tightening
demands on the job and in the community. He describes how the French
public workers' walkout in 1995, a series of one-day work stoppages and
anti-Tory demonstrations in Ontario in 1996–7, and nearly twenty other
"general" or "mass political" strikes on four continents have galvanized
popular opposition to governments of all stripes that are doing the bid-
ding of transnational corporations.

Few of these protests against the "austerity cops" were organized by
political parties, as they might once have been. Instead, because of the

"political vacuum created by the retreat of the old parties of the left, it was the working class itself, led or at least accompanied by its unions, that was taking on the right-wing/neo-liberal (conservative) agenda that had come to dominate the politics of most nations." While global economic change has pitted some groups of workers against one another, the trend toward internationalized production, regional integration, and free trade also produces far greater interdependence among labor organizations, particularly those dealing with common employers. The challenge facing labor is still enormous. How, for example, do workers go beyond strike resistance—as important as that is—to building unions that are more effective within each country and then linked together internationally? How can they move beyond defensive struggles to projecting labor-based alternatives to the "competitiveness agenda" of global capital? Based on extensive overseas travel, interviews, and hands-on solidarity work, Moody has some useful suggestions.

First, he believes North American and European activists should look to the newer, more vibrant labor movements of the Third World as "indispensable allies in the struggle with global capital" and as a source of inspiration and organizational models for "the social movement unionism" he favors. In South Africa, Brazil, South Korea, and Mexico, new formations have arisen since the late seventies as part of "the complex process of democratization that ended military or authoritarian rule" or undermined labor's traditional ties to a corporatist state. Their common feature is "a unionism that both organizes all who can be brought into unions and reaches beyond unions to the working class as a whole; a unionism that is prepared to take a class stand in the workplace, in the neighborhoods, and in political life, as well as reach across borders in all these efforts." (Among the North American unions whose activities Moody describes, only the breakaway Canadian section of the United Auto Workers seems to have approached, for a while, such a radical synthesis of labor and community activism.)

Second, *Workers in a Lean World* cautions would-be solidarity campaigners about relying too heavily on the alphabet soup groups—the I.C.F.T.U. (International Confederation of Free Trade Unions) and its fourteen ITSs (international trade secretariats)—that comprise the bureaucracy of international labor. (Says the author: "Linking together the walking wounded seldom wins a battle.") Even when doing good work, the industry-based trade secretariats cannot bypass their national affiliates and recruit union members directly for cross-border actions. So,

Moody argues, that leaves a key role to be played by unofficial groups like the Transnationals Information Exchange which facilitate worker-to-worker contacts and "sister local" relationships through low-budget, bottom-up strategy sessions, and the Internet. He describes, for example, how creative organizing by a rump group of locked-out Liverpool dockworkers in 1997 enlisted longshoremen around the world in what the *Journal of Commerce* proclaimed to be the "first coordinated global work stoppage."

Finally, and most important, Moody reminds us that solidarity begins at home. The most important thing that union members in advanced capitalist countries can do for embattled co-workers in other nations is stand up to their common employer over what are likely to be similar issues involving work reorganization, speed-up, scheduling, or "pay for performance." Any union, here or elsewhere, that has disarmed itself ideologically and organizationally by embracing labor-management cooperation schemes will offer much weaker resistance because its own members are divided, disoriented, and confused about who their real friends and enemies are.

While dispensing his valuable advice to labor, Moody cuts right through all the mass media "globaloney" about the inevitability of economic integration and restructuring on management's terms. He shows that workers can fight back and win, while creating new organizational forms better suited to the formidable tasks of the day. If Moody's manifesto, particularly the final chapter on redefining socialism, echoes one published 150 years ago, it's because united labor action today is both necessary and more technologically feasible than it was then—and the workers of the world once again have nothing to lose but their chains.

SLAVES TO FASHION

Samuel Gompers, the English immigrant cigar maker of Dutch-Jewish parentage, who helped found the American Federation of Labor in 1886 and led it for the next four decades, was no friend of immigrant workers. Having made it to these shores himself, Gompers was quite preoccupied with pulling up the gangplank behind him. How, he once asked, can we "prevent the Chinese, the Negritos, and the Malays from coming to our country? How can we prevent the Chinese coolies . . . from swarm[ing] into the United States and engulf[ing] our people and our civilization? . . . Can we hope to close the flood-gates of immigration from the hordes of semi-savage races?"

One hundred years and five labor federation presidents later, American unions have more enlightened views on immigration. As Robert Ross, from Clark University, and Immanuel Ness, from Brooklyn College, CUNY, both reveal in their respective books, a battered labor movement has been forced to join forces with immigrant workers and make their struggles for workplace justice a centerpiece of union revival efforts. In Ross's comprehensive survey of garment industry employment here and abroad, we see many encouraging signs that nativism—in official union circles—has been replaced by a nascent labor internationalism. Unable (like governments themselves) to impede the cross-border flow of cheap, unskilled labor, U.S. unions have finally embraced legalization of undocumented workers. They're also urging Congress to repeal penalties against firms which hire them. Once favored by the AFL-CIO, but rarely imposed, these "employer sanctions" now have the effect of depriving such workers of the legal standing necessary to fight dismissals for union activity.

Meanwhile, capitalism in the new millennium has linked the fate of factory workers from the global North and South (and within the latter) in such a way that effective campaigns against sweatshop conditions can't be restricted to any one nation. As Ross points out, not only does "competition among communities of workers in developing countries threaten to erode or hold back advancing labor standards and purchasing power," but the really ferocious competition in textile and apparel manufacturing will be among developing nations themselves. The "great sucking sound" of jobs leaving the country—so dreaded by foes of NAFTA—can now be heard in Mexico as well. Thanks to recent trade deals facilitating capital flight to China, runaway plants are on the run again to a land where labor costs are even lower than in the *maquiladora* zone. Better yet (from a management standpoint), privately owned Chinese factories are almost all union-free.

Back in the United States, as Ross notes, some still attribute the persistence of sweatshops to the growth of immigration itself. In the 1990s, 9.1 million new residents entered the country and headed for "the global cities of our new economy," Los Angeles, New York, Miami, and Dallas. *Slaves to Fashion* rebuts the notion that immigration restrictions are the policy solution. In apparel manufacturing, "the political and regulatory protections attained in the first half of the century" have been eroded, leaving a "large pool of disempowered workers with few legal rights" at the mercy of "unscrupulous and desperate entrepreneurs." According to Ross, "The pressures that generate low wages and substandard health and safety conditions are rooted in the neo-liberal trade regime and capital mobility of the current global capitalist era."

Immanuel Ness likewise challenges the view of labor economists like Vernon Briggs, who depict illegal immigrants as too passive and frightened to fight for workplace improvements. *Immigrants, Unions, and the U.S. Labor Market* suggests, to the contrary, that foreign-born workers are more apt to organize than the native-born. At least in New York City, the focus of Ness's study, the former have a "strategic advantage" because they typically work in labor markets shaped by employer and worker social networks. "Clustered together in the same labor niches and employment ghettos, with limited connections to mainstream U.S. society, immigrants can build camaraderie and class consciousness" that provides a basis for workplace solidarity and collective action. Low-wage workers born in the United States, meanwhile, are more apt to protest unfair treatment or bad conditions individually, by quitting and finding a new job—an option less available to many undocumented workers.

To support his thesis, Ness relies on fascinating and inspiring case studies of little-known labor activism by Mexicans, West Africans, and South Asians in Manhattan. The Big Apple has been the scene of recent organizing among its greengrocery employees, "black car" drivers, and supermarket baggers and deliverymen—all of whom formed their own groups and then got involved, for better of worse, with established unions. The cast of local union characters runs the gamut from extremely helpful organizers from the Union of Needletrades, Industrial and Textile Employees (UNITE) and Machinists to several disgraceful betrayers of immigrant workers, from the longshore and retail sectors of organized labor.

New York's 12,000 greengrocery clerks and deli workers come primarily from Mexico, but many are native Mayan speakers not fluent in Spanish. Their 1,000 or more store-owning bosses are immigrants too, usually Korean. Strikes, picketing, and boycotts organized by the Association Mexicano American de Trabajadores (AMAT) began targeting widespread minimum wage and overtime law violations in 2000. As a result, several hundred owners finally agreed to a code of better conduct and a monitoring scheme developed by the state attorney general.

At the same time, in larger food stores, French-speaking West Africans from Mali and Senegal were rebelling against their phony "independent contractor" status as baggers and deliverymen hired by middlemen instead of the retailer. They too staged work stoppages and made some gains in the form of belated and still inadequate representation by the Retail, Wholesale, and Department Store Union.

Manhattan's "black car" drivers provide the book's most impressive success story, since they formed their own 1,000-member "rank-and-file-led local" (affiliated with IAM District 15). Hailing from Pakistan, India, and Bangladesh, these owner-operators "worked long hours for many years to pay off their late model luxury car loans, send money back home, and survive in the city." Saddled with auto insurance and maintenance costs, most could never quite escape what the author describes as "virtual indentured servitude." Nevertheless, after winning union recognition at several limo services, they were able to negotiate contracts providing individual health coverage and other financial relief.

Whereas Ness emphasizes immigrant worker "self-organization" and on-the-job activity—often undertaken in the absence of reliable allies—Ross chronicles the growth of campus-based anti-sweatshop groups as a key union auxiliary in higher-profile, national campaigns. Formed in 1999, United Students Against Sweatshops (USAS) has used Sixties-style protests, including building occupations, to pressure colleges and universities into putting their logos on "sweat-free" caps and clothing. A founding member of Students for a Democratic Society (SDS), Ross applauds this contemporary activism and its more pragmatic goals but does identify one downside. Many USASers "emphasize the plight of sweatshop workers in other countries," not those in the United States, who number more than 250,000, earn about 55 percent of the average manufacturing wage, and are rarely visible in their campaigns. "It is," Ross explains, "more chic to advocate for people in the Third World" even though some of the most effective labor support work by students, at Harvard, Yale, Wesleyan, and elsewhere has involved campus workers, both immigrant and native-born.

Slaves to Fashion also faults USAS sponsor UNITE for its own seeming abandonment of "new organizing in clothing shops." Between 1998 and 2001, the union sunk to about 215,000 members, losing a quarter of its dues-payers. (Now, it has merged with the similarly sized Hotel and

Restaurant Employees.) Launched in 2002, UNITE's Global Justice for Garment Workers campaign tried to get more retailers to increase production in unionized U.S. shops. But, as Ross reports, "employment was still plummeting" in New York and UNITE "was frozen out of the clothing industry in L.A. So it decided to move on." Ness describes the union's new strategic focus and modus operandi as follows:

> Failing to organize garment workers, UNITE has redeployed its scarce resources into organizing industrial laundries and distribution centers bringing in some 40,000 new members who have proved pivotal to the union's survival. Under the leadership of Bruce Raynor, the national union has endeavored to control organizing at all levels of the union. Organizing drives carried out by independent local unions that did not fit the national's industry-based, top-down mission were vigorously discouraged, even though some locals had energetically engaged in dynamic campaigns.

Based on his research and personal experience in the greengrocers' campaign, the author of *Immigrants, Unions and the U.S. Labor Market* favors a more flexible, ecumenical, and worker-led approach to union-building, particularly in the "informal sector." Ness acknowledges the difficulty that unions face—amid all their other problems—marshalling the resources necessary "to organize workers employed in small businesses, which now employ two-thirds of the national labor force." Organizing shop by shop, in "appropriate units," as defined by the National Labor Relations Board, "is a monumentally difficult task." However, Ness makes a convincing case for a different kind of organizing, based on worker mobilization and direct action in the tradition of the Industrial Workers of the World (IWW). Such campaigns "may not start or end with a union contract" and shouldn't be "measured solely by membership gains or greater union density," he argues. If the only immediate result is the development of new workplace leaders, improvements in working conditions, and greater dignity and respect on the job, that constitutes "success" as well.

Both Ness's book and *Slaves to Fashion* are thus quite relevant to current debates about labor movement strategy and structure in the United States. They demonstrate the importance of academics being willing to address the shortcomings of trade union practice from a critical but sympathetic perspective—and one that defends the idea of unions as organizations run by and for workers themselves.

THE CHILDREN OF NAFTA

As American labor began gearing up for the 2004 presidential race, many activists joined high-profile protests against free trade, mistreatment of immigrants, and the erosion of union organizing rights. The Immigrant Workers Freedom Ride was the most widely publicized of these events, with stops throughout the country and a rally of 100,000 in New York City as its grand finale. Soon afterward, industrial union members marched in Miami, as part of heavily policed street demonstrations against the proposed Free Trade Area of the Americas (FTAA). And then, the AFL-CIO and Jobs with Justice held a nationwide day of action, with mass picketing and rallies in seventy cities, to promote "workers' rights as human rights" and labor law reform.

There are no better election-year guides to these interconnected issues—globalization, trade, immigration, and unionization—than David Bacon's *Children of NAFTA* and Leon Fink's *The Maya of Morganton*. Their work confirms what many John Kerry supporters in the ranks of labor already suspect. Even with a Democrat in the White House who has, on the campaign trail, professed belated concern about union-busting, outsourcing, and the adverse impact of free trade (which he helped to promote), unions—here and abroad—will still be in trouble. The climate for organizing, bargaining, and strike activity will remain unfavorable on both sides of the Rio Grande until there are major changes in labor law, trade policy, immigration rules, and our common political economy.

Bacon provides a sweeping, cross-border look at the deteriorating conditions of life and work in the decade since ratification of NAFTA—the North American Free Trade Agreement that FTAA would extend to all of South America. The author is a former United Farm Workers supporter and in-plant organizer for the United Electrical Workers (UE) in California. After retooling as a labor photojournalist, he devoted nearly a decade to interviewing and photographing Mexican workers in their homeland and in "El Norte." *Children of NAFTA* describes, in dismaying detail, how trade liberalization has intensified the exploitation of workers in the factories and fields of both countries.

Instead of raising living standards and promoting economic prosperity—as promised by boosters like Bill Clinton and John Kerry—NAFTA has spawned more child labor, horrendous health and safety conditions, downward pressure on wages and benefits, massive job loss, and increased management resistance to unionization. To add insult to injury, many employers in Mexico's *maquiladora* zone are now, on NAFTA's tenth birthday, picking up and leaving for places like China where labor is even cheaper.

Fink looks at a narrower but no less complex example of labor displacement and migration. His book traces the odyssey of peasant villagers who fled war-torn Guatemala in the 1980s to find work first as fruit pickers in Florida and later as chicken processors in western North Carolina. While teaching at the University of North Carolina, three hours away, Fink became a close observer of the Mayan community in rural Morganton that sustained a protracted organizing struggle at Case Farms, a 500-worker poultry plant.

Part of a larger Hispanic influx into the southern poultry industry, the Guatemalans hired by Case spoke four different indigenous languages (Q'anjob'al, Awakateko, Ki'ich'e, and Mam). Most had never worked in a factory before. Nevertheless, the Maya—mainly single men without families—were initially seen as a boon to productivity and much preferred to Mexicans (because of the latter's tendency to seek time off for holiday visits home). "Guatemalans can't go home," one Case Farms manager explained to Fink. "They're here as political refugees. If they go back home, they get shot."

For that portion of the Guatemalan civil war diaspora that landed in Morganton, sanctuary from right-wing death squads came at a price. Chicken-plucking is hard, dangerous, messy work, with high turnover and low pay. Not only were the new arrivals more willing to engage in this labor than local whites or African-Americans, they also proved far more resistant to factory discipline and management control. In September 1991, Case Farms made a sudden scheduling change that imposed speed-up and a pay cut on the night shift, triggering a walkout by twenty Guatemalans. This became the opening shot in an extraordinary shop-floor war—a kind of mini-J. P. Stevens saga, without the successful corporate campaign or happy ending. In addition to its insights into immigrant culture and community structure, *The Maya of Morganton* thus serves as a detailed case study in worker self-activity, organizing rights violations, and first-contract frustration.

As chronicled by Fink, labor-management skirmishing at Case Farms continued for ten years. Its highlights included another spontaneous in-plant work refusal in 1993, resulting in mass arrests; a four-day strike in 1995, which drew the Laborers Union into a winning NLRB election campaign; more protest walkouts in 1996, culminating in an eight-day strike over the company's legal foot-dragging and refusal to bargain; a Supreme Court decision compelling the start of negotiations in 1998; twelve months of fruitless talks, followed by further unfair labor practices that resulted in the company being cited for bad-faith bargaining again; and, finally, after another round of court-ordered negotiations in 2001, LIUNA's decision to abandon the costly campaign (in favor of a modest two-year commitment to fund a local "workers' center" to aid Case Farms workers).

Fink brings this heroic yet ultimately tragic story to life with vivid portraits of in-plant leaders, rank-and-file workers who waged (and sometimes gave up) the fight, their helpers in local churches and community groups, and various outside union organizers and lawyers, who joined the fray along the way. ("Prompted in part by publicity about the Case Farms conflict," the Clinton administration promised to intervene as well, with an investigation of "sweatshop conditions" in the poultry industry. Subsequent pressure from industry lobbyists, like Tyson Foods, caused Labor Secretary Alexis Herman to put the probe on hold instead.)

A similar cast of characters can be found in most chapters of *Children*. As Bacon reports, Case Farms-type situations arise routinely in Mexico in the context of bitterly contested independent union organizing drives. These are opposed by maquiladora managers, state and federal government officials, and the "charro" unions—corrupt labor organizations allied with the employers and the still-powerful Party of the Institutionalized Revolution (PRI). One-sided though it may be, the conflict between new and old political forces in Mexico has given rise to what one left-wing activist hopes will be:

> a new labor movement, more intelligent and more innovative. Already, people building independent organizations along the border are much better than the leadership of the old unions. They are more concerned about health, and the use of toxic substances in the work process. Their movement is very spontaneous and makes allies with neighborhood organizations, with farmers and with teachers, and with people from across the border.

Bacon's workplace tour includes a stop at Tijuana's Plasticos Bajacal. This plant relocated from the United States in response to a UFCW organizing drive and then, with its new, largely female workforce, became the scene of an early (but unsuccessful) workplace challenge to Mexican company unionism. The author devotes a key chapter to the better-known story of Han Young de Mexico, where a tangled union recognition fight became "the most important labor battle in Tijuana's history . . . whose repercussions were felt from the U.S. Congress to the Los Pinos residence of Mexico's president."

The Han Young workers were initially aided by Mexico's Frente Autentico de Trabajo (FAT), an anti-NAFTA dissident labor group with close ties to the UE. After the new union in the plant was denied government certification in 1997—despite winning a representation election—its U.S. allies attempted to utilize the NAFTA labor side agreement, which created a cross-border complaint process. Unfortunately, as twenty other complainants in similar cases also found,

> those side agreements, heralded as protection for labor and environmental rights . . . had already served their purpose long before. In 1993, their promise of protection provided political cover for liberal Democrats who wanted to vote with President Clinton, and thus produced the slim margin of Congressional votes needed to approve NAFTA.

The Han Young support campaign exposed this underside of NAFTA at a critical juncture, just as President Clinton was trying (in vain) to win "fast track" negotiating authority for future trade deals. At a hearing held in San Diego by the U.S. Department of Labor's National Administrative Office (NAO), Han Young workers testified about management's violations of both Mexican labor law and workplace safety rules. Neither had been enforced because that would be "contrary to the purpose for which NAFTA was negotiated in the first place—creating conditions favorable to investment."

Not surprisingly, given her Case Farms role, Alexis Herman arranged a toothless settlement of the Han Young case with her Mexican counterpart. It left workers still exposed to hazardous conditions, unfair dismissals, blacklisting, and strike-related violence by private thugs and police. Some were even roughed up when they attended a "Seminar on Union Freedom" organized by the Mexican labor ministry to explain the terms of the flawed NAO deal.

In Bacon's view, NAFTA has nevertheless been a useful, if painful, dope slap here—"stirring workers into a profound debate, surging up from the floors of union halls and workplaces, prodding them into an extensive reexamination of their relations with their Mexican counterparts." As a result, "the border isn't just a showcase for NAFTA's victims." It has become a laboratory for new forms of labor international-ism, as practiced by the various grassroots groups we meet in the book like the San Diego-based Support Committee for Maquiladora Workers, the Coalition for Justice in the Maquiladoras, the North American Worker to Worker Network, and others. According to the author:

> This cross-border solidarity movement not only provides material sup-port for embattled workers. As maquiladora-style production itself trans-forms the economies of developing countries like Mexico, this move-ment in response to it offers a proving ground for a new model of inter-national relationships between workers and unions.

Bacon's account of the tumultuous world of Mexican labor politics shows that cross-border cooperation is just one element of labor resist-ance to neo-liberalism. Another key ingredient is political independence. In Mexico, several important unions took a big step in this direction when, led by the telephone workers, they broke with the PRI-dominated Congreso de Trabajo (Labor Congress) and formed the rival National Union of Workers (UNT), which includes the FAT. As Bacon notes, the UNT has since led the fight for labor law reform in the Mexican Chamber of Deputies, relying on allies in the Party of Democratic Revolution (PRD), the left-leaning alternative to the PRI and President Vicente Fox's National Action Party (PAN). "We believe it's indispensable to democra-tize the world of work," says telephone union leader and UNT founder "Francisco Hernandez Juarez," because the workers have been kid-napped by their own unions."

In the United States—even in the AFL-CIO's progressive wing—there's far less consciousness of the need for a new unionism based on workplace militancy, internal democracy, and independent politics. If their campaigning for Kerry had succeeded in 2004, American unions would still have faced the harsh reality emphasized by Bacon: "Whether liberals or conservatives hold office, in Washington, Mexico City or Toronto, they're all committed to free trade." To challenge that bipartisan consensus—and the corporate domination it reflects—labor and the social movements must act together, more effectively, everywhere that workers are threatened "as the NAFTA model is extended southward."

CAN WORKER CENTERS FILL THE VOID?

If America had a union movement worth its salt, would there be any need for foundation-funded "worker centers"? Shouldn't unions themselves be places where workers go to get job-related legal advice, leadership training, and organizational backing for workplace campaigns? With a membership base of 16 million, collective bargaining rights, and thousands of full-time functionaries, doesn't organized labor have the capacity to wage "the fight for immigrant rights" so vividly described by Jennifer Gordon and Janice Fine in their new books on worker center activity?

The answers to these questions are, respectively, no, yes, and apparently not. As Gordon and Fine report, a network of more than 135 labor support groups has developed in the United States precisely because unions aren't meeting the needs of workers, largely foreign-born, who toil under terrible conditions in low-wage labor markets. *Suburban Sweatshops and Worker Centers: Organizing Communities at the Edge of the Dream* appears in the wake of a big win for the worker center movement against Taco Bell and the 2005 unraveling of the AFL-CIO, which made mainstream labor look even more disorganized than usual. The combination of these two developments has led some observers, like *Monthly Review* editor and author Michael Yates, to wonder whether "existing labor unions and leaders might not be the vehicle through which unions become relevant again. Maybe new organizations, outside traditional labor, will be necessary . . . [to] reinvent class struggle unionism."[1]

The Taco Bell fight involved a decade-long organizing campaign by the Coalition of Immokalee Workers (CIW). As Fine notes, the Coalition and its allies "succeeded at a boycott where so many others have failed in recent years," forcing Taco Bell's owner, Yum Brands, to take direct responsibility for the pay and conditions of the tomato pickers employed by its Florida subcontractors. The March 2004 settlement with the company has been hailed by United Farm Workers president Arturo Rodriguez as "the most significant victory" for agricultural laborers since the UFW's first California grape boycott in the 1960s. CIW volunteer Elly Leary, a retired UAW activist, contends that the Immokalee Workers and other "non-union working-class organizations" now play a key role in the labor movement because they can aid "poor, immigrant workers struggling for a just future" without the political baggage "associated with 'special interests' or 'big labor.'"[2]

Gordon and Fine would agree, although the authors' accounts of worker center funding and functioning reveal much about the limits and difficulties of this form of community-labor activism. In the long term, the only way to institutionalize and expand the worker protections that some centers have won is through stronger, more democratic unions, willing to embrace the creativity and dynamism of organizing currently being conducted outside the AFL-CIO and Change to Win (CTW). Now a law professor at Fordham University, Gordon founded and directed the Workplace Project on Long Island, a grassroots initiative that made her one of the few labor organizers ever to win a MacArthur Foundation "genius" grant. Her book is deeply rooted in the personal experience of aiding a largely Hispanic workforce of janitors, domestic workers, day laborers in landscaping and construction, low-wage factory hands, and fast-food restaurant help. These "suburban sweatshop" victims were drawn to her group because of its legal aid, popular education, collective action, and supportive community. While some staff focus on employment law violations, the Project does "intensive training" about labor history and immigration, organizing techniques, public speaking, and other skills necessary for members to play leadership roles in ongoing campaigns and the Project itself.

Gordon's book includes an interesting discussion of the relationship between "labor organizing and lawyering" and the use of "rights education" to promote engaged citizenship and rank-and-file participation. Invoking the tradition of left-wing lawyers like Lee Pressman and Maurice Sugar, who "used law to build collective power" during the early years of the Congress of Industrial Organizations (CIO), Gordon argues that "the standard labor lawyer" today has become a mere "technician . . . . pressing for the union's interests within the established rules of the game." In contrast, she writes:

> The Workplace Project's wealth of experience suggests several ways that law might support the organizing of the lowest-wage workers beyond the important straightforward approaches of litigating to enforce rights, lobbying to claim new ones, and defending organizing rights on the ground.

Janice Fine applies her experience as a labor, community, and political organizer (plus newly minted academic at Rutgers) to the task of surveying the larger network which includes the Workplace Project. Fine assesses the impact of dozens of groups engaged in service delivery, public advocacy, and workplace agitation. She also provides valuable historical context for the emergence of worker centers during a period of steady labor movement decline. That trend, plus related workforce changes, has stripped many industries of the "preexisting institutions" necessary "to integrate low-wage immigrants into American civil society and provide them with pathways to economic stability."

Nevertheless, worker centers—better than most unions—have been able to draw on the collective identity of workers who relate to one another more on the basis of ethnicity than on occupation or industry. Under such circumstances, Gordon argues, "a Latino organization," such as the Workplace Project, "united rather than divided the workforce" of "mobile and vulnerable" Long Island immigrants it was set up to serve. (Although, as Gordon admits, there can be a downside to operating within a single ethnic enclave: "most non-Latino immigrants, African-Americans, whites, and other people of color" could not easily join the Project, making it harder "to tackle the broader ways that employers used race to provoke job competition and stifle organizing.")

From Fine, we learn that some centers, like the New York Taxi Workers Alliance, have moved beyond their roots in "ethnically based organizations" and begun to function like unions themselves, winning wage increases through legislation, regulation, direct action, or informal bargaining. With 5,000 members (from South Asian, Middle Eastern, and Caribbean nations), the Alliance has developed both strike capacity and lobbying clout, despite the fact that many "lease drivers" are undocumented and all lack coverage under the National Labor Relations Act. In Los Angeles, the Korean Immigrant Workers Advocates (KIWA) has similarly pursued a "vision of building a community-based union" for ethnic grocery store clerks in Koreatown, despite a narrow NLRB-election defeat at immigrant-owned Assi Market.

Both Fine and Gordon examine relations between the centers and various national union affiliates. "From the outside," Gordon writes, "unions and worker centers seem like an ideal match, and yet their collaborations have been fraught with tension." Part of the tension derives from differing organizational priorities. In the Bay Area, for example, HERE Local 2 has made a strategic decision to focus its energies on the hotel industry, putting "any serious restaurant organizing" on the back burner for "at least three to five years," Fine reports. Nevertheless, Local 2 has found a way to work constructively with the Young Workers United (YWU), a "non-immigrant specific worker center" founded in 2002, which has jousted with the local restaurant industry over minimum wage levels and unpaid break time at non-union establishments like San Francisco's Cheesecake Factory.

Partnerships can be more problematic where there is worker disenchantment with what Fine calls "negligent unions." Gordon believes that worker centers should "help members who belong to a union address issues of non-representation." If such efforts are met with "hostility," a "more conflictive relationship may be appropriate." Unfortunately, the "resulting lack of trust" on the part of SEIU Local 32BJ in New York City has, according to Fine, led to its "total unwillingness" to work with the Workplace Project even though the latter "could have been a very valuable resource for the union's janitorial organizing drive on Long Island."

Elsewhere in the country, Fine finds additional evidence of union shortsightedness, as well as mutually beneficial labor support for some worker center campaigns. In response to the Korean grocery store organizing cited above, the United Food and Commercial Workers (UFCW) tried unsuccessfully to compete with the KIWA's Immigrant Workers Union (IWU) during its Assi Market card signing drive. Now, the IWU and UFCW are exploring "some form of joint affiliation." After a rocky start with a worker center in Maryland, the Laborers helped the National Day Laborer Organizing Network hold their first national conference, contributed $25,000 to the NDLON, and tried to turn the resulting "good feelings into joint organizing campaigns on the ground."

In Nebraska, Fine discovered that a collaborative meat-packing drive involving the UFCW and Omaha Together One Community (OTOC) "largely fell apart" after OTOC-developed in-plant leaders were "demobilized by the union once representation elections were won." OTOC had "helped build strong participation in the organizing drives." But then shop steward training and contract enforcement were subsequently neglected, leaving rank-and-file activists angry and frustrated. Fine concludes that the dispute is "quite typical" because:

> there is a dramatic culture clash between many unions and worker centers. Worker centers experience many local unions as top-down, undemocratic, and disconnected from the community; unions view many worker centers as undisciplined and unrealistic about what it takes to win.

In *Suburban Sweatshops,* Gordon touts the Workplace Project's own participatory culture and finds it relevant to recent union debates about the virtues of "democracy vs. density." While noting correctly that "the labor movement today faces challenges that bottom-up organizing alone cannot resolve," she argues that "the Project's experience lends support to the position that democracy can bolster organizing capacity." Even "the more activist unions" which "use innovative organizing tactics" remain "very top down in approach, equating organizing simply with mobilizing," Gordon contends:

> Members are not called on to understand or critique the context in which they work, to consider strategic options, or to make decisions about which course of action to pursue. The leadership of the union does all that. Once the decisions are made, union staff mobilize workers to carry them out. In this model, too, mobilizing is confined to critical moments.

Both authors admit there is a serious flaw in the "alternative model" of worker centers—namely, their lack of a self-sustaining, dues-paying membership base. As Fine notes, "Total numbers of workers directly participating are still modest," with most centers "reporting formal membership of one thousand or less." This leaves immigrant workers reliant on the kindness and political commitment of strangers. Notoriously fickle "social change" foundations (which have added worker centers to what Fine calls their "portfolio") provide 61 percent of their overall funding. Twenty-one percent comes from government sources, 16 percent from local fund-raising, and only 2 percent from membership dues. In the case of the Workplace Project, foundation money represents "upward of 80 percent of its small budget," according to Gordon.

In the United States, many workers have had trouble controlling institutions—namely, unions—which they fully fund themselves via dues payments. Can one safely assume that groups they pay little or nothing to join or which don't even have a formal membership structure are more likely to be "member-run," just because the staff people or donors involved are so democratic minded? I think that's assuming a lot. The apparent reluctance of many centers to reduce their dependence on philanthropy reflects a poor understanding of what actually gives workers "a sense of ownership over their organizations," as Fine puts it. When centers "begin with a model that is funded from outside sources, they are not forced to ask for significant commitments from members or to develop income generating strategies," she notes. Plus, grant-driven program development can lead to activity that doesn't even make grassroots sense but is undertaken anyway just because money is currently available for it.

Worker centers have also learned that striking the right balance between "organizing" and "servicing" is no easier for them than for the unions they often (and quite rightly) criticize. Although they don't have contract enforcement responsibilities, the successful centers clearly spend a lot of time on the legal case–handling equivalent of processing grievances. Job-related problems are, after all, what bring most workers to their door, not a natural predisposition toward building workplace or community organization. *Suburban Sweatshops* describes the elaborate methods it has developed to move workers "from a sense that the abuse they had suffered was an individual occurrence . . . to a broader under-standing of exploitation as a systemic problem that requires a collective solution."

Fine agrees that there is a "central tension in most centers" between "providing needed services" and mobilizing workers to have a broader impact. When a center is constantly pulled in the direction of "hot shops" by an endless stream of worker complaints, its "service provision—and even related organizing—can crowd out the time and resources needed for strategic campaigns."

Anyone interested in finding out more about the nexus between work-er center activity and efforts to revive the mainstream labor movement would be well advised to study both of these books. The authors have done an excellent job describing and analyzing the organizing experiments that may be moving, sooner or later, from the margins to the main-stream.

TEAMSTERS AND TAXI DRIVERS

In the late 1990s, it looked, for a while, like organized labor was making a comeback, particularly as a voice for contingent workers. As Deepa Kumar recounts in *Outside the Box*, 185,000 Teamsters went into battle against United Parcel Service (UPS) in 1997, under recently reelected reform leadership. The result was a successful ten-day strike that protest-ed mistreatment of part-timers not only at UPS but throughout the United States. Still basking in the glow of his own election two years before, AFL-CIO president John Sweeney applauded the walkout because it demonstrated the much broader appeal of unions when they defend the interests of all workers. As Sweeney noted, "You could make a million house calls, run a thousand television commercials, stage a hundred strawberry rallies [for the United Farm Workers], and still not come close to doing what the UPS strike did for organizing." In 1998, as Biju Mathew reminds us in *Taxi*, another group of drivers—24,000 cabbies—staged an equally inspiring work stoppage in New York City. Theirs lasted only a day but showed that a group of "independent contractors" known as the Taxi Workers Alliance could make gains through lobbying, publicity, and direct action even when deprived of formal collective bargaining rights.

Nearly a decade after the Alliance successfully challenged then-mayor Rudy Giuliani, TWA members again stopped work, producing what the *New York Times* called "frustrating waits on corners, long lines at airports, and angry exchanges" over whether cabs should have GPS devices and credit card machines. Drivers contended that the latter device would penalize them financially but were ultimately unable to block either form of "new technology." Other unions rallied behind the TWA, which has become the first "worker center" of its type to affiliate with a big city central labor council. In nearly twenty other cities, cabbies similarly lacking in coverage under the National Labor Relations Act have formed TWAs modeled on the New York one. Meanwhile, the much bigger and stronger Teamsters union, now under different leadership, celebrated the tenth anniversary of its UPS strike by bargaining away much of what it won on pensions and part-timing in 1997. The rank-and-file involvement, internal communication, and creative PR tactics described by Kumar were all jettisoned in favor of what Teamsters for a Democratic Union (TDU) calls "the most secretive negotiations in Teamster history."

Notwithstanding the different post-scripts to their books, Kumar and Mathew have both produced case studies of lasting value. The workers involved represent two ends of the spectrum of working-class life and organization in the United States. Unusual among worker centers, the Alliance has built a relatively stable dues-paying membership among South Asian, African, and West Indian immigrants struggling to earn $25,000 to $35,000 a year. Most NYC yellow cab drivers lease their vehicles for $130 a day and pay for gas themselves. They don't earn a dollar of their own until they've picked up enough passengers to recoup these fixed costs. They have no pensions or job-based health care coverage. Many operate outside the Social Security system and, according to

Mathew, "haven't seen a doctor in years, and if they have, it would be a different doctor in a different emergency room each time." TWA members are "predominantly dislocated males, unencumbered by the trappings of the full lives" (and sometimes professional jobs) they were forced to leave behind in the Third World. As Mathew movingly describes, the city's taxi-driving workforce—thanks to the forces of globalization—has been "structured almost permanently into a culture of masculine bachelorhood" due to the forced separation of so many drivers from wives and families in their country of origin.

In contrast, UPS Teamsters, both male and female, are employees of an $80 billion company, with America's largest private sector labor agreement. They work all around the country, with their ubiquitous brown trucks just as familiar in small towns as yellow cabs are in the teeming "global village" of New York City. Under their last contract, full-time UPS long-haul truckers and local delivery drivers earned $28 an hour, or about $75,000 a year with overtime, according to data provided by the International Brotherhood of Teamsters. IBT pension and welfare funds—still under siege—provide far better benefits than most Americans enjoy, including employer-paid health insurance for Teamster family members and retirees. That makes total compensation for full-timers more than $40 an hour (although, as noted above, contract concessions made in late 2007 will adversely affect part-time package sorters and leave many of them far behind in terms of starting pay and benefits). Seventy percent white and overwhelmingly native-born, Teamsters at UPS—if fully employed—could easily be mistaken for a "labor aristocracy" when compared to immigrant taxi drivers earning so much less.

The historical trajectory of upward and downward mobility among Teamsters and taxi drivers seems to intersect. New York cabbies were once "fleet drivers," direct employees of companies that owned city-awarded "medallions" permitting them to operate. In the 1960s and '70s, these outfits bargained with Local 3036, a union run by Central Labor Council President Harry Van Arsdale. Back then, cabbies had pensions and health benefits but started to lose them when the union agreed to internally divisive "differential commission rates." This two-tier pay structure weakened driver solidarity and helped pave the way for leasing in 1979. "Those left out in the cold—new occasional or part-time drivers badly served by the contract—felt no commitment to the union and had every reason to serve as a ready-made scab force," Mathew writes. To introduce leasing, a former cabbie explains, the industry "scare[d] one set of workers about losing their union benefits to create a system that robs every future worker of exactly the same."

In short order, the demographics of NYC cab driving changed dramatically and Local 3036 was out of business. "Prior to the advent of leasing, under the commission system, more than 50 percent of the drivers were European or African-American. Only a few were Third World immigrants.... By the late 1980s, you could hardly find a white driver." Today, owner-operators, the only true "independent contractors" in the industry, represent just 12 to 15 percent of the workforce. The remaining 22,000 or more active drivers "slave under the conditions of 'horse hiring'"—Mathew's term for the "primitive practice" of daily leasing. According to TWA director Bhairavi Desai, this makes taxi driving "one of the few professions in the world where not only are you not guaranteed an income, but you might end a long twelve-hour workday losing the money you started with."

As Kumar explains in *Outside the Box*, contingent labor at UPS has been used, just as in the taxi industry, to reduce labor costs, enhance management flexibility, divide the bargaining unit, and, whenever possible, weaken the union. Since part-time jobs were first implemented at UPS in 1962 in a deal negotiated by Jimmy Hoffa, the workforce has become 60 percent part-time. More than 80 percent of all new jobs created prior to the union's 1996–7 contract fight were part-time, with such slim opportunities for moving to full-time employment that turnover was huge and many new hires never even qualified for benefits. While analyzing how the media covered the 1997 walkout, *Outside the Box* reminds readers of what it took to reverse, at least temporarily within one company, the societal trend toward part-timing.

Unlike his benighted predecessors (or his not much better successor) then-Teamster president Ron Carey refused to treat the second-largest contract talks in the country—only GM bargaining was bigger at the time—like a special interest game, played out of sight from UPS members, their families, and the public. Carey's election in 1991 enabled the rank-and-file activity long promoted within UPS by TDU to become part of the union's official bargaining strategy. Scores of TDU members were finally able to mobilize their co-workers with national headquarters support, even if their own local union leaders remained in bed with the company. Many months of intensive education, discussion, and internal communication within the IBT's newly created "member-to-member networks" built a broad consensus about UPS bargaining goals and how best to articulate them.

The IBT's main goal was to convert more jobs from part-time to full-time, thus thwarting management's plan to further expand its part-time workforce. A second Teamster priority was keeping UPS as a lucrative participant in its multi-employer retirement funds at a time when management was already pushing the idea of coverage via a separate, less solidaristic company plan. As Kumar concludes, proper "framing" of the first issue proved to be a critical factor in generating unusual public sympathy for the strikers and an outpouring of picket-line support from other unions.

In all its innumerable pre-strike research reports, press releases, and Ron Carey interviews, the union insisted that "Part-Time America Won't Work!" The well-prepared Teamster rank and file was equally "on message." As Atlanta driver Randy Walls told Reuters on the first day of the walkout: "We're striking for every worker in America!" UPS is notorious for its authoritarian systems of workforce control, systematic internal propagandizing, and ever-vigilant supervisors. Nevertheless, management was caught off-guard by the unexpected unity between full- and part-time workers and the public pummeling incited by the union's high-profile contract campaign. "If I had known that it was going to go from negotiating for UPS to negotiating for part-time America, we would have approached it differently," company executive John Alden confessed in a *Business Week* postmortem.

Kumar is clearly a Carey fan, as evidenced by a rare interview with him appended to the book, which describes his personal jousting with the "Big Brown Machine" when he was a UPS worker himself. Like many others on the left, she laments Carey's post-strike ouster in a Teamster election fund-raising scandal that dealt a major blow to TDU. Yet, at one point, this Rutgers professor of Media Studies turns postmodern Marxist, faulting the now-retired "militant union leader" for his administration's use of a "nationalist narrative" in organizing the 1997 strike. She notes that strike publicity repeatedly invoked the "American dream" and denounced "big business for frustrating national aspirations for 'good, full-time jobs.'" According to Kumar, "Labor nationalism is based on a reformist ideology that claims that workers can fully realize their interests under capitalism or, more specifically, within a particular type of nation that ensures the fair treatment of its workers." In *Outside the Box,* a widely acclaimed and successful PR campaign—orchestrated by Matt Witt, Rand Wilson, Craig Merrilees, and others—is thus deemed insufficient because, among UPSers, "an international class-based identity was not counterposed to a national identity."

Kumar does not suggest alternative rhetorical devices that might have elevated the union's discourse to a more politically correct level. (Perhaps the slogan "A Part-Time World Won't Work?") And her book overlooks the fact that, under Carey, the IBT did try to build links with Western European UPS unions, some of which held coordinated workplace demonstrations of solidarity with Teamsters here in 1997.

Since Kumar's book was written, a more familiar obstacle to the forward march of labor at UPS has interjected itself—in the form of James Hoffa, son of the IBT negotiator who first opened the door for part-timing. Thanks to the current Hoffa administration, UPS management was indeed able to do things "differently" in the latest round of bargaining. During "early negotiations" in 2007 (on an agreement not scheduled to expire until a year later), the Teamsters dispensed with contract campaigning altogether, leaving future analysts like Kumar with much more to criticize than a flawed "narrative" about "nationalism." The IBT bargained away language, won ten years before, that turned 40,000 part-time jobs into 20,000 full-time ones. As *Labor Notes* reported, this deal will "end conversion of part-time into full-time jobs" and "widen the gap between full-time and part-time standards, freezing part-timers' starting pay [at $8.50 an hour for five years] and forcing new ones to work for a year before they are eligible for health coverage." In addition, the settlement moved "44,000 Teamsters out of the union's multi-employer Central States pension plan" and put them into a company plan with "benefits frozen at levels negotiated during the 1997 contract and accrual rates lower than those in other IBT funds."

Despite opposition in Carey's old home base in New York City (where rejection of the contract led to more favorable renegotiation of the Local 804 supplement to it), the results of the IBT's 2007 bargaining were generally accepted elsewhere out of a sense of fatalism and futility. (One selling point was a card check and neutrality agreement making it easier for the union to organize thousands of former Overnite workers now working for UPS Freight, a non-union subsidiary.) In 1997, as Kumar recounts, the full resources of the Teamsters were devoted to raising membership expectations and encouraging militancy, while elevating the consciousness of the general public as well. Ten years later, the propaganda machinery of the union was just put to work internally and only after a tentative agreement was reached. UPS workers who had heard little or nothing about bargaining for months were suddenly bombarded with PR mailings and robo calls to their homes urging them to "Vote Yes" in a fast-track ratification process.

With greater continuity in its core leadership and a more consistent rank-and-file approach, the TWA is, by necessity, still operating "outside the box." Mathew's book delves deeply into the daily lives, workplace and community relationships, and immigration-related legal problems of TWA activists. Their compelling individual stories are very well told and reflect the author's strong personal connection to New York cabbies, based on his ongoing TWA organizing committee role. Originally from India himself, Mathew is a professor of management at Rider University who personally bridges the gap between what he calls the "suburban immigrant middle-class" and TWA's far less assimilated or secure working-class members.

Taxi also lends itself more comfortably than Kumar's book to explorations of "international class-based identity" formation and related media coverage. In addition to his occasional invocations of Fanon, Foucault, and Robert Fitch, Mathew includes many telling anecdotes like the following:

> The atmosphere at strike headquarters [in 1998] was electric as the media tried to fathom how immigrants of so many different ethnicities had united in the action. Many reporters found it difficult to understand how, just one week after India's nuclear test, followed by Pakistan's ominous promise to respond in kind, Indian and Pakistani drivers could be brothers on the streets of New York. . . . "Listen, man," said Ilyas Khan, "when a New York cop stops me, he isn't asking if I am Indian or Pakistani. To him, we are all the same."

First published by New Press in 2005, it is hoped *Taxi* will now reach a wider audience via Cornell's paperback edition, which includes an updated introduction on recent TWA activities. My one disappointment with Mathew's book is the absence of a full-fledged portrait of Bhairavi Desai. As Mathew notes, she has "led the organization with rare vision and brilliance for all of its years of its existence." Perhaps out of modesty on her part and/or the author's deference to it, her role is downplayed in favor of a collective organizational portrait and personal details about rank-and-file members. Although this is a refreshing change from the usual tendency to focus on charismatic leaders, female organizers of

Desai's caliber get too little, rather than too much, attention and recognition. I'm sure other readers will be equally curious about how a young woman, with radical politics and a degree from Rutgers, became the key organizer of a large, diverse but almost entirely male immigrant workforce. Maybe we'll just have to wait until "Taxi-2," the sequel, appears to find out more about her.

PART SIX

CHANGING TO WIN?

Despite positive signs like the huge immigrant worker strikes and march-es in the spring of 2006, the new millennium has not been kind to American labor. With the exception of just two years so far (2007-08), union membership has continued to decline. In 2004–5, the challenges facing the AFL-CIO—which some critics defined bluntly as the need to "organize or die"—led to another round of public debate about whether the federation was moving fast enough to help its affiliates avoid further marginalization. Spearheading the campaign for change this time was a coalition of "dissidents" headed by Andy Stern, a former top assistant to John Sweeney (before the latter became head of the AFL-CIO) and Sweeney's successor as leader of Service Employees International Union (SEIU). Stern graduated from the University of Pennsylvania, where he was a student activist in the late 1960s. He began his union career as a Pennsylvania social worker in the early 1970s. He later moved to SEIU headquarters where he served as national organizing director before becoming president. As a member of the AFL-CIO executive board, Stern joined forces with hotel workers leader John Wilhelm and garment workers president Bruce Raynor (whose unions later merged to create UNITE-HERE). Together, their "New Unity Partnership" argued for additional union consolidation, expanded organizing, and a new political strategy focused on building "union market share" rather than pursuing broader social goals. Rather than force a debate on these issues at the 2005 AFL-CIO convention, SEIU, UNITE-HERE, and five other unions defected to form Change to Win (CTW). This new labor federation claimed one third of all AFL-CIO members. Some observers likened its emergence to the historic rift between craft and industrial unions that gave birth to the Congress of Industrial Organizations (CIO) seventy-four years ago.

This final section of the book surveys much of the recent literature on SEIU. It describes how America's second-largest union became its fastest-growing one under the leadership of Sweeney and Stern. "Reutherism Redux" doesn't stop there, however. It also takes a close look at the downside of SEIU's model for union restructuring and membership growth. Drawing on the work of multiple authors, this critique warns about the dangers of SEIU's top-down centralizing approach and some of the directions it was already taking prior to the AFL-CIO split. The same piece describes nascent membership resistance to Stern's policy of forced local union mergers and trusteeships, the imposition of non-member "leaders" in locals under trusteeship, and resulting diminution of worker control over contract bargaining. In 2006, Stern published a book that defends SEIU's organizational achievements, while providing insights into his own evolution and political thinking. The second article in this section compares Stern's "new agenda for labor" to *America Needs a Raise*, a volume published ten years earlier when John Sweeney's views were still being aggressively marketed by the AFL-CIO. The work of Ruth Milkman and Kim Moody also provides a useful vehicle for exploring different conceptions of "social justice" (or social movement) unionism and related debates about whether real change in labor comes from the top down, the bottom up, or some combination of both. Part 6 concludes by looking at their divergent assessments of the Sweeney era (not yet over) and the merits of Change to Win.

Throughout 2008, the *New York Times*, *Los Angeles Times*, *Wall Street Journal*, and other publications reported on the emergence of problems within SEIU, some of which were highlighted four years earlier in "Reutherism Redux." Recent developments include several embarrassing California corruption scandals, much wider public criticism of Stern, and a full-blown opposition movement. Led by United Healthcare Workers president Sal Rosselli, SEIU reformers tried to democratize their union, while Stern, in response to UHW dissent, threatened to dismantle Rosselli's local and/or put it under trusteeship. This controversial takeover of SEIU's third-largest affiliate was actively resisted by thousands of UHW members, for reasons described in the Epilogue following this section. In SEIU, as in many other unions, "La lucha continua." (The struggle continues.)

Reutherism Redux

> Don't they realize if they really push this organizing, the labor movement is going to wind up being a movement of strawberry pickers and chicken pluckers?
>
> —Anonymous delegate, 1997 AFL-CIO Convention, American Federation of Teachers (*New York Times*)

Despite stepped-up organizing among farmworkers and poultry processors, workers of this type have yet to take over the AFL-CIO. In fact, recruitment of "strawberry pickers and chicken pluckers" has generally flopped, thanks to employer resistance and the failure of labor law. Yet the influx of low-wage workers so much feared by this conservative member of the AFT has materialized at the base of the labor movement. Tens of thousands of janitors, nursing home workers, home health care aides, and hotel, laundry, and food service employees are now in the forefront of union struggles around the country. Under the post-1995 leadership of John Sweeney, the AFL-CIO has demanded a "living wage" for the millions of African-Americans, women, and recent immigrants who work in such jobs. Progressive allies of labor, including minority community activists, have widely applauded this new focus on the "most oppressed." Many believe it represents a renewed labor commitment to social justice, empowerment of the poor, and greater diversity.

Nevertheless, leading unions for the working poor—Service Employees International Union (SEIU) and the recently merged HERE and UNITE—remain frustrated with the overall pace of institutional change. Along with the Carpenters and Laborers, they've formed a New Unity Partnership (NUP) to promote their own ideas and strategies for membership recruitment and union restructuring. "As it is configured today the AFL-CIO has no hope of organizing the 90 percent of workers who are not in a union," SEIU president Andy Stern told HERE and

UNITE delegates at their merger convention in July 2004. "Sisters and brothers, it is time . . . we need to transform the AFL-CIO or build something new." Although they all helped elect a "New Voice" slate nine years ago so the federation could be transformed then, NUP members are now mulling a challenge to Sweeney's reelection next summer. If that fails (or doesn't extract sufficient organizational concessions), all or some NUPsters may leave the federation, as the Carpenters did three years ago, under the leadership of Doug McCarron.[1]

The key player in this constellation of "organizing unions" is Stern's SEIU, which is laying claim to a place in the liberal imagination once occupied by Walter Reuther's United Auto Workers. During the 1960s, the UAW was labor's leading voice for civil rights in the South, "Great Society" reform, and, belatedly, peace in Vietnam. Like Stern today, Reuther was a grand planner and big thinker. He wanted his union to be in the forefront of progressive activism (which in that day meant the Americans for Democratic Action instead of the Howard Dean campaign). Articulate, media-savvy, and self-promotional, the UAW founder financed student and community groups throughout the country to extend his influence. He also poured industrial union money into the efforts of others to organize public sector workers, like teachers. If the technology of his time had permitted, the voluble Reuther would certainly have had his own "virtual union"(like SEIU's PurpleOcean.org) and been a blogger as well (see www.fightforthefuture.org/blog). As announced in his recent blogging, Stern is now making a Reuther-style commitment of $1 million to fund "a network of workers and communities" to confront Wal-Mart, an organizing target not even within SEIU's current jurisdiction (unless, of course, it expands through merger with the UFCW).

NUP NOW, ALA THEN

Buoyed by the postwar economic boom, the Auto Workers reached its peak membership of 1.6 million under Reuther's energetic reign. (That's nearly the size of Stern's self-described "fighting Purple Army" today.) Back then, the UAW bureaucracy had similar esprit de corps, hegemonic ambition, and organizational discipline (although not the trademark purple T-shirts and jackets). Likewise, Solidarity House employed the best and brightest union technocrats. And it boasted its own army of field staff—including longtime leftists—who were loyal to the leader's vision and very adaptable, personally and politically, to the union's top-down culture. As defined by Reuther, American labor's crisis thirty-six years ago was the product of building trades backwardness, plus the AFL-CIO's own bureaucratic obstructionism and Cold War foreign policy meddling. The UAW founder was tired of playing second fiddle to George Meany, head of the federation since it was formed, in 1955, with UAW backing. According to Reuther, labor's failure to organize and grow, under the conservative Meany, could only be cured by the NUP of that era, a much-hyped, UAW-creation called the Alliance for Labor Action (ALA).

As Vanessa Tait recounts in *Poor Workers' Unions: Rebuilding Labor from Below:*

> In March 1968, Reuther challenged Meany to call a special AFL-CIO convention so the UAW could present its program for "revitalizing" the labor movement. When the AFL-CIO refused, the UAW withheld its per capita payments, then disaffiliated in July 1968. Just three weeks later, the UAW . . . announced the formation of the ALA, inviting other unions to join in organizing millions of unorganized workers and establishing community unions for the poor and unemployed.[2]

As an alternative pole of attraction for militant workers, the Alliance had several flaws (among them, the UAW's abhorrence of shop-floor militancy in its own ranks). The most glaring problem was Reuther's ALA partner—the racket-ridden Teamsters, who were already operating outside the AFL-CIO and (like McCarron's Carpenters today) playing footsie with White House Republicans. "These same Teamster 'allies' would shortly attack César Chávez's new United Farm Workers by signing sweetheart deals with California growers and would endorse Richard Nixon in the 1972 presidential election," Tait writes. "By mid-1972 . . . without a push to keep ALA alive from Reuther (who died in a 1970 plane crash), the UAW cut its per capita payments to the Alliance." Not long afterward, the ALA also expired.

Reutherism had its roots in the great radicalizing upsurge of the mid-1930s; three decades later, it was a far tamer and more confused political force (soon to be spent entirely, under subsequent UAW leaders who lacked Reuther's personal charisma or any pretense of fighting the boss). Similarly, many Service Employees officials have their own "movement history," linked, in this case, to the social and political upheavals of the 1960s, on campus and off. As Tait notes, some SEIUers even spent their younger days building independent unions as a grassroots alternative to the dysfunctional organizing methods and structures of the labor establishment in the 1970s and '80s. Today, they're part of that establishment in its Sweeney-era form, but still see themselves as promoting a brand of "social movement unionism" that's better and more successful than anyone else's. They tell other trade unionists and their own members that American labor faces a stark choice today: "Organize (our way)—or die."

THE SEIU MODEL

Since the mid-1990s, SEIU has doubled in size, through new organizing plus many mergers and affiliations with smaller unions. As one of its key strategists, Stephen Lerner, argues in "United We Win," an SEIU discussion paper, SEIU's increased "market share" has helped raise the living standards of many thousands of new members among the working poor.[3] For many activists and academics, this record of success ends any debate about the best way for other unions to grow. Some observers question whether the SEIU "organizing model" is easily transferable to other fields, however. They note that SEIU has, until now, had the singular advantage of operating mainly in the public sector, among smaller private firms, or within health care and home care entities that rely on public funding—a ready-made environment for union political leverage, lobbying and deal making. IBM, Toyota, Microsoft, Wal-Mart, Verizon Wireless, or even partially unionized GE operate in an entirely different league, as unions trying to organize them are reminded every day.

Against such adversaries, no amount of clever corporate campaigning, Justice for Janitors pageantry, or even craven political maneuvering—such as SEIU's embrace of industry-backed "tort reform" that would restrict lawsuits against elder abuse in California nursing homes—is likely to secure organizing rights or recognition anytime soon. In contrast, at the "for-profit" nursing homes that SEIU is now partnering with (to the dismay of California patient advocates) the union's new "alliance" with management may indeed boost its "market share."[4]

When workers win—by whatever method—a greater "voice at work," this doesn't guarantee that they'll have sufficient control over their union, its internal decision making or leadership. At the bargaining table in any industry, it's obviously better to have "union density" than not have it; but "density without democracy" is a deficiency that can, over time, seriously undermine union contract enforcement and rank-and-file militancy on the job. The lack of financial accountability and transparency, which goes hand-in-hand with undemocratic practices, leads to business unionism at its worst. Sooner or later, corruption scandals erupt, like the massive one that engulfed liberal, black-led AFSCME in its N.Y.C. District Council 37 under Stanley Hill in the late 1990s.

In *Poor Workers' Union,* Tait raises important questions about the empowerment of low-income members—or lack of it—within their own labor organizations, particularly those affiliated with SEIU. Read together, her study and the other books under review reveal much about the upside, downside, and development of the SEIU model, while also shedding light on NUP's "new labor metaphysic." That phrase is a favorite of Rick Fantasia and Kim Voss, two sociology professors clearly infatuated with SEIU's role in "remaking American labor." The authors of *Hard Work* view recent union developments through the narrow prism of academicians able to operate more freely within the AFL-CIO, thanks to their generational peers now holding key staff positions at the federation or SEIU, HERE, and UNITE. *Hard Work* argues that "new militants" from these unions have made a decisive break with the "relentlessly pragmatic business unionism" of America's past. They are now poised to take the "sea change at the AFL-CIO when John Sweeney was elected" to the next level of union transformation.

A "SACRED NARRATIVE"?

As suggested by such rhetoric, the authors tend to measure organizational change by how much strategically positioned NUPsters are "at ease with intellectuals and progressive activists, with whom they share both a measure of cultural capital and a set of experiences in social struggle that conjoin them as bearers of a sacred narrative." In Voss and Fantasia's six-point definition of "social movement unionism," union democracy or rank-and-file control are nowhere to be found as part of this "narrative."

Vanessa Tait also has a doctorate but a different kind of day job. She actually works for a local union, the CWA-affiliated University Professional and Technical Employees at the University of California. Perhaps that explains why her case studies are more rooted in reality and critical of union makeovers more rhetorical than real. In her view, "The new leadership of the AFL-CIO, along with many individual trade unions, has still not come to terms with a basic concept: trusting rank-and-file workers to organize and bargain for themselves." Whereas rank-and-file workers are "mobilized" in many SEIU campaigns, she notes, "they are not always the ones in control of the campaigns. SEIU, though politically progressive, is known throughout the labor movement as one of the most thickly staffed and highly centralized unions."

The perspective of Steven Henry Lopez, another young sociologist, is closer to Voss and Fantasia's than Tait's. He also has hands-on organizing experience, acquired while serving as an intern on several SEIU organizing and contract campaigns in western Pennsylvania during his research for *Reorganizing the Rust Belt*. Lopez's book is narrowly focused, very detailed, and with more academic trappings than Tait's—to the point where he tries to conceal the identity of most workers, employers, local unions, and officials profiled in his "inside study." In Lopez's view, SEIU's rejuvenation efforts in Pittsburgh did encounter some organizational speed bumps. Overall, however, he applauds its rebuilding of union membership among "post-industrial, low-wage workers" and its protracted unfair labor practice strike against "Megacorp Enterprises" (the Beverly nursing home chain).

Recruitment is not easy in a local service sector where the legacy of mill closings, plus the real or imagined past failings of manufacturing unions, weighs heavily on the minds of the unorganized. As Lopez observes, "Workers themselves often resist union efforts to organize or mobilize them." Social movement unionists must "overcome substantial working class anti-unionism to create new collective solidarities oriented toward collective action" and "directly confront the power of employers to intimidate, threaten, and punish their employees." Like Voss and Fantasia, Lopez views SEIU's "grassroots mobilization" and "strong social justice orientation" to be "an explicit rejection of traditional business unionism."

Last but not least is the more personal and confessional literature of the disaffected. *SEIU: Big Brother? Big Business? Big Rip-Off* is a self-published Internet book (available on Amazon.com) written by Harriet Jackson, an African-American building cleaner angry about SEIU members' loss of local control in Pittsburgh. Suzan Erem, the author of *Labor Pains*, is a white leftist and former SEIU staffer who found local union trusteeship work to be alternately frustrating, alienating, and exhilarating.

Erem's more polished Monthly Review Press memoir uses real names, just as Jackson does, and, in the latter's words, "feelings are not spared." In Erem's book, the main subject of embarrassing vignettes is her SEIU Local 73 boss, Tom Balanoff, scion of an Old Left family in Chicago long involved in local politics and the United Steelworkers.

Jackson's book draws on the author's twenty-four years as a rank-and-filer in SEIU Locals 29, 585, and 3 (one of which we meet, in *Reorganizing the Rust Belt*, as "Local A"). Jackson has had firsthand exposure to what Lopez calls "a new vision of participatory, powerful unionism" but she has not found it to be an improvement upon "the old-style business unionism of experience and cultural memory" in Pittsburgh. A former steward, local recording secretary, and bargaining committee member, Jackson describes workplace problems and contract violations that don't get addressed by her current union officials and their apparent coziness with management. According to Jackson, SEIU now "operates totally opposite from how it markets itself." Erem explores similar tensions and contradictions, from the standpoint of a harried, overworked servicing rep, who was hired from the outside, like so many other SEIUers around the country.

STAFFING UP FOR CHANGE

According to Voss and Fantasia, "staffing up" with non-members like Lopez, Balanoff, and Erem has been critical to the union's success. The process began under John Sweeney when he doubled SEIU dues "to support an increase in the staff of this traditionally decentralized union," which had "a strong tradition of local autonomy" and functioned "more as a loose configuration of urban fiefdoms than as a national union organization." Between 1984 and 1988 alone, national staffers increased from twenty to 200. (They now number about six hundred.) Many of those hired initially were veterans of the civil rights, welfare rights, antiwar, or women's movements. Some joined SEIU via affiliations involving workers in clerical, home care, food service, and other low-wage jobs. (Their prior work, building independent unions like the Rhode Island Workers Association and ACORN's United Labor Unions, is the subject of several interesting chapters in Tait's book.) As *Hard Work* describes it, this influx of "radical labor leaders and [their] innovative organizational experiments" brought "aggressive organizing techniques to SEIU":

Avoiding the core goods-producing, these activists focused their efforts
on rebuilding the labor movement in the service and public sectors,
which often entailed organizing immigrant, minority, and women workers—previously written off as unorganizable [in] the received wisdom of
business unionism.

There was, at the same time, another internal organizational trend
under way seemingly inconsistent with the grassroots spirit of SEIU's
newly affiliated "poor workers' unions." Having "staffed up," Sweeney
then "began to move toward centralizing the union, succeeding largely
because SEIU's expansion into the public sector gave it a growing treasury
and brought a more liberal membership into the union, both of which supported his efforts." (One of SEIU's first state government affiliates was the
Pennsylvania Social Service Union, home local of Andy Stern and Anna
Burger, who now serves as SEIU secretary-treasurer.) As *Hard Work*
notes, "Sweeney proved willing to use 'trusteeship'—the power to temporarily take over the affairs of locals—to advance a much more aggressive
organizing agenda." In fact, SEIU made "an institutional decision not to
tolerate local leaders who did not want to organize," according to building
service strategist Steve Lerner. Since 1996, when Stern replaced Sweeney,
40 SEIU locals—or 14 percent of its 275 affiliates—have been put under
trusteeship to implant new officers. Some of those ousted ran old-guard
fiefdoms and treated local union treasuries like their own personal piggy
banks. Others just balked at the industry-based local restructuring called
for in the union's "New Strength Unity" program.

Hard Work describes the coordinated Justice for Janitors campaign
that began in Denver, moved to Los Angeles in 1988, and then spread to
other cities, under Lerner's direction. Not surprisingly, the authors place
heavy emphasis on "the genius of J for J researchers," their "intensity and
commitment," the boldness of their union recognition strategy (which
bypassed the NLRB), and the creativity of SEIU's corporate campaign
tactics. Occasionally, they remember, that "to achieve success, the janitors
themselves had to be mobilized." But "here, too, research played a role,
for it showed workers how and why they could potentially win. Once the
janitors understood the big picture—and the J for J staff spent a lot of time
educating them—they too saw that pressuring the building owners and
big contractors was a key to victory."

AN AIR OF ARROGANCE

Voss and Fantasia admit that many SEIUers they admire "sometimes give off" an "air of arrogance and exclusivity"; their "attitudinal style would tend to make for a closer resemblance to Silicon Valley entrepreneurs than to veteran staffers of the trade union movement." (In the authors' view, this is quite excusable because, after all, the "political will for many of the dramatic changes that have occurred in the labor movement have come from the top, not the rank and file, who are usually believed to be the only source of democratic change.") Erem captures the "new militant" style nicely—in its trusteeship context—when she proudly describes her "privileged position as a senior staff member of a relatively wealthy union in the third largest city in the country." Only a few years out of college and already a Rainbow Coalition veteran, the author of *Labor Pains* was now an SEIU "communications specialist . . . part of a new breed of union staff."

> Tom [Balanoff] hired activists outside of the membership, people he'd identified as wanting to make change. . . . [We] were the new blood, instigators, agitators—people who wanted to shake up their work sites, their employers, the country. John Sweeney was leading SEIU and we would become his example of what new faces and ways could do to rebuild our movement. . . . We strutted around the office like nothing could get in our way.

By the late 1990s, when obstacles were getting in her way, Erem wonders whether she was "watching the slow motion death of a movement at its weakest moment or the labor pains of its dramatic rebirth." She also remembers lamenting that only the local's "staff and leadership had a vision but . . . the union members we served didn't want vision, they wanted a good contract and they wanted it now."

Labor Pains is very good at describing the day-to-day grind of full-time union work—the long hours, contract bargaining pressures, difficult-to-meet membership expectations, and constant need to resolve interpersonal tensions and conflicts that threaten workplace unity. Gradually, the stress of her job begins to wear the author down and she starts to have some very un-PC thoughts about the public service employees in Local 73. A onetime member of the Communist Party (which has a long history of promoting racial solidarity within the working class), Erem expresses particular disappointment with the local's African-American majority. Based on their reaction to the O.J. Simpson trial, she concludes that, for them, "the union was simply a vehicle for civil rights, not for black and white unity so we could all live better."

Other Erem frustrations include the "false starts" of 73's "member organizer" program, an effort to put SEIUers to work signing up new members or volunteering to help political candidates.

> A staffer named Cathy from the international union created [member organizing], though the best we could tell, "the program" entailed hitting up reps for their best stewards and asking them if they knew other members who might get involved. It faded away when the international assigned Cathy to another local. It came and went many times after that . . . the last time, years later, with me.

In *Labor Pains*, Erem finally admits that "for all our good intentions and forward vision, our dreams of expanding leadership and hopes of creating a new kind of union, we have made little more progress than the leaders before us."

"REFORM" VIA TRUSTEESHIP

Deputy trustee Balanoff remained very much focused on becoming Local 73's new leader, however. Other staffers might be "driving themselves to drink" because of their workloads, but "Tom's poison," Erem reports, "is not alcohol. It's power." According to the author, Tom's "desire for power, for responsibility and an ability to swing with the big boys, landed him where he is, and offered him opportunities beyond his wildest hopes." His biggest opportunity, which he doesn't fumble away, is to make the transition from appointed to elective office in the local.

> Chicago leftists were ecstatic when Tom was elected president of Local 73. Tom came from a famous progressive family, one which had reached positions of power. His extended family boasted a judge and a state representative. His mother was a professor and his father a legend in the Gary Steelworkers union.

As Erem observes sardonically, "There would be no class warfare, no overthrow of the state, and no socialism in Chicago" due to his election. In fact, "Tom had learned from those 'purists,' as he called them, in his own past. He considered himself a pragmatist and conducted his business that way." Before long, Balanoff is looking the part—"wearing a good suit and a new tie," smoking cigars, and lunching with lots of local big shots. Then he puts a "division director" system in place, "a new set of generals so he won't have to deal with each of his staff of twenty-five individually about the smallest issues at their work sites." This means there are now Local 73 "bosses and boss-ees" and an abundance of bad "attitude" at the union hall. But "Tom didn't notice. He was in his office, with the door closed, making the deals that would eventually make life better for our members . . . or so he thought."

In *Hard Work*, Voss and Fantasia offer a more sympathetic account of the SEIU trusteeship in Los Angeles that became a defining moment in the union's recent history of "advancing the difficult but crucial process of organizational change." This local takeover occurred after the 1990 Justice for Janitors' strike in L.A. spawned an internal struggle between fired-up members and the "old boy network" in Local 399. But it was the members, not just the "old boys," who were brushed aside. As Tait recounts:

> Latino, African-American, and white activists formed a coalition with health care workers called the Multiracial Alliance to run against existing officers in the first contested elections in 399's history. A 120-member mobilization committee spent months talking with voters about the need for democratic reforms and leadership diversity. . . . On June 8, 1995, Multicultural Alliance candidates won all 21 contested seats on the executive board in one of the largest turnouts in the local's history.
>
> A showdown shortly ensued with the local's president [who had been reelected] when the new officers wanted to fire some of the local's staff whom they accused of undermining democratic practices in the union. The president refused to fire the staff or allow the new officers to meet in any official capacity. In August 1995, Alliance members launched a hunger strike outside the union's headquarters in protest. For many rank-and-filers, this was about moving beyond the idea that members were just the front line troops at demonstrations, to building empowerment and democracy in their union. "We built this union," strike leader Cesar Oliva Sanchez told the *Los Angeles Times*. "We want to be able to make decisions."

According to Voss and Fantasia, however, the trusteeship imposed on 399 by John Sweeney—"in one of his last acts before leaving SEIU to become president of the AFL-CIO"—was a leadership decision made just in the nick of time. It "cleared the way for Los Angeles janitors to leave Local 399 and join other janitors in a statewide union local established just for janitors. Once this happened, the janitors were finally able to build a union that meaningfully involved workers in making decisions and running the union, revealing the extent to which the growth of social movement unions depends on *internal union reform.*"

MERGER MANIA

Tait correctly rejects this interpretation and, from her critical perspective, describes a more recent example of top-down "internal union reform" in northern California. When San Francisco janitors in 3,000-member Local 87 and its president Richard Leung balked at being merged into a larger SEIU entity in 2002, their local was put in trusteeship as well. As usual, this step was justified on the grounds that "master contracts," covering more members over a larger geographical area, were necessary to "build industry power" and that, somehow, negotiating such agreements is not possible if multiple locals are involved. According to Tait, however, the new regional local's first round of bargaining with janitorial companies resulted in significant health benefit concessions. "Instead of making the union more responsible to the rank and file, [SEIU] decided to take the corporate route through merger and acquisition to streamline their operation," Leung charges. "They're trying to mirror the corporations we bargain with, but we shouldn't be a mirror," says ex-Local 87 organizing director Olga Miranda. "We don't want to look like the corporations we're fighting against."

Forced mergers aren't just unpopular with ex-local officials, like Leung and Miranda, who get tossed out in disputes with the International. They're increasingly unpopular with working janitors as well. Here, for example, is how Harriet Jackson assesses the situation since her Local 29 was merged into a much larger health care local (585), parts of which are now being consolidated into a new tri-state building service entity, Local 3, representing over 10,000 workers in Pittsburgh, Toledo, Columbus, Cleveland, and Detroit:

The original structure of Local 29 was pretty unique. We were very much member-oriented. We had to inform the members about everything, and that is the way it is supposed to be. . . . When a president was not up to what the members thought in the way of honoring the contract, he was voted out. . . . Now, there is not much member input. It is basically the president who makes all the decisions, then says to the members what you are going to get. . . . We belong to an out-of-state local and we don't even know our officials. I do not even know the president's name. And most of the members don't. [But] SEIU tells us that these mergers are being done all across the country.

According to SEIU websites, the new president in question—or head of the "Local 3 Management Team"—is Peter Hanrahan, an appointee currently serving under a "provisional local charter." (Hailing from Chicago, Hanrahan is also still listed as vice president of 36,000-member janitors Local 1, covering Illinois and Wisconsin.) According to no less an authority than Andy Stern himself, Jackson's old janitor's Local 29 was an anachronism. On his blog, Stern argued recently that dividing workers into such "local unions" only "made sense years ago." Now, "in an era of corporate mergers," a "local union structure does more to handicap workers than it does to help." The real purpose of any "union structures is for workers to be able to unite, fight, and win together, not to make it easier or harder to elect or reelect leaders," he asserts. In Stern's opinion, only "intellectuals" interested in debating things "from an abstract point of view" care about democracy. And many of the unions that such "progressives" cite as "democratic models are losing members, losing strength, and are not the most effective." Says Stern:

Workers want their lives to be changed. They want strength and a voice, not some purist, intellectual, historical, mythical democracy. Workers can win when they are united, and leaders who stand in the way of change screaming "democracy" fail to understand how workers exercise the limited power they have in a country where only 8.2% of the private sector are in unions. They just don't get it!

As Stern's vision has been implemented, however, the key agents of change, engineers of "effectiveness," imposers of "unity," and would-be creators of "union power" are not rank-and-file members but full-time staffers instead. This has been true even when the "cleanup crews" dispatched from union headquarters had ready-made allies among rank-and-file opponents of old guard elements like the Bevona family in New York or the Sullivan clan in Boston Local 254. As New York *Daily News* columnist Juan Gonzalez reported in 2000, janitors who had courageously opposed John Sweeney's friend, Gus Bevona, the $400,000 a year president of Local 32B-J, were pushed aside by SEIU appointees during that local's trusteeship. The staffers anointed as the new leadership were so newly hired from outside that when they ran for local office they had to get an International union waiver of a 32B-J bylaw requiring candidates to be members in good standing for at least three years.

THE TAKEOVER CREW

Who are "these people" and where do they come from? (This question gets asked repeatedly in Harriet Jackson's book, as she expresses befuddlement about the revolving door, out-of-town staffing of her succession of locals.) As Gonzalez notes, many of SEIU's "well-educated organizers" are recruited "from universities and the community, as well as from other unions." They have, in common, "grand visions of a powerful new labor movement" but personally "may have suffered little in the trenches." According to Gonzalez:

> In their zeal, to build the new movement, they start to think that the workers under them are not as well educated or politically sharp as they are. Pretty soon, they want to run the unions with the members simply rubber-stamping their grand plans. Gradually, they begin to mistake the well-being of members for their own designs. Genuine democracy, which is not always efficient, gets sacrificed for paper democracy.[5]

Among SEIU's "best and brightest"—those who've made the union a career (as Suzan Erem did not)—there is another common denominator: most have never been a janitor, security guard, nursing home worker, home health care aide or public employee in their own local or anyone else's. According to 32B-J's website, Gus Bevona's successor as president, Mike Fishman, has been a "union leader for 25 years." Most of that time, however, Fishman worked for the Carpenters Union, then briefly with the

Teamsters, then at SEIU headquarters, and finally on the 32B-J trusteeship staff before securing the top job in a 70,000-member "local," which
now stretches from Trenton, NJ to Hartford, CT. (His executive vice
president, Kevin Doyle, likewise did his "janitoring" elsewhere, as director of SEIU/District 1199's New England Health and Pension Funds.)
Tom Balanoff, of *Labor Pains* fame, became a manager of Chicago locals
after previous stints at the Boilermakers Union and SEIU's Washington
research department. Since Erem's not-very-flattering portrait of Balanoff
was published, he has switched presidencies from Local 73 to 1, the latter being the Illinois-Wisconsin building service local whose VP is now
also "president" of all the unionized janitors in Michigan, Ohio, and western Pennsylvania.

Throughout the union, not having worked in an SEIU-represented
job is clearly no bar to upward mobility or lateral moves, either. When
SEIU executive vice president Tom Woodruff turned over the reins of
SEIU District 1199 (WV/KY/OH), it was not to any experienced member; his successor is a Cornell ILR school grad named Dave Regan, who
answered a "help wanted" ad in 1990, got hired as an organizer, and, six
years later, became president of a local now boasting 18,000 members!
In Massachusetts, meanwhile, two of SEIU's big public sector locals—
one just out of trusteeship and the other still in it—are headed by staffers
who weren't part of any state or local government units that their locals
represent. The state's new building service local officers have never been
unionized janitors there or anywhere else. In Oregon, a state worker
leader switched locals, via a trusteeship, to became SEIU's new Portland
janitors' president. In Seattle, the lead organizer in the union's southern
California home care worker drive, a former political operative, is now
president of Local 775, which represents 30,000 Washington State
home health care aides. Local 775's number-two slot is occupied by a
former SEIU staffer from Oregon (who's also never been a home care
worker).

Not all of those deployed as SEIU trustees are white or from college-
educated, middle- or upper-middle-class backgrounds. Sometimes they
match the demographics of their new assigned local more closely. But
their political mission remains the same—to build a base for themselves
and institutionalize international union control. They don't view their
local restructuring or trusteeship-related roles as an opportunity to develop the full leadership capacity of indigenous militants, who have, in some
cases, spent years struggling for change in a troubled local before the

International stepped in. Rather, these staffers operate with the clear understanding that they, not any longtime member, will become principal officers of the local—after running with all the advantages of "incumbency" in its first post-trusteeship election.

"What I'm looking at here, Sue, is my future," explained Balanoff, during Erem's interview for a job at Local 73, when he was still deputy trustee. "When this local comes out of trusteeship, I expect to be the president. Then I want to build real worker power in this city."

Organizer Eliseo Medina no doubt had similar plans in mind when he was hired away from the Communications Workers of America to take over a janitors' local in San Diego. Medina had been a Farm Workers activist and six-year CWA organizer in Texas but never an SEIU member; now he's one of the International's four executive vice presidents. To groom a new building service division chief for Boston janitors, SEIU parachuted in Mexican-born Rocio Saenz, a California Justice for Janitors staffer (with prior union experience at HERE and UNITE) who acted in Ken Loach's film, *Bread and Roses*. Saenz's second-in-command under the Local 254 trusteeship was Jill Hurst, an Anglo out-of-towner now serving as secretary-treasurer of the renumbered, re-organized, and heavily immigrant Local 615. When Hurst explained to the *Boston Globe* that "it's a real transition to have a leader who is part of that community," she meant, of course, immigrants generally, because Saenz has never been part of any 254 or 615 bargaining unit. In New York City, meanwhile, the post-Bevona administration of 32B-J includes another prominent Hispanic non-janitor, Hector Figueroa, who became, via the local's trusteeship, its secretary-treasurer after working as a researcher for SEIU and ACTWU (now UNITE).

A MEMBERSHIP BACKLASH?

Despite this well-established pattern around the country—and the degree to which new arrivals have entrenched themselves in multi-state mega locals—Voss and Fantasia still worry that SEIU's "new militants" may be "vulnerable to electoral defeat" because their focus on organizing has "forced them to devote fewer resources and less staff to servicing." Such fears would appear to be unfounded, in the short term. But an increasing number of SEIU members have begun to notice that in addition to being consolidated, many of their locals are being parceled out like McDonald's franchises to up-and-coming union "managers" who have influential patrons at corporate headquarters.

Jackson's book illustrates how this top-down leadership reshuffling looks from the bottom up. It often leads to membership resentment, alienation, and desperate casting about for (not always helpful) legal remedies. At various points in her narrative, we find Jackson reacting to her union experiences by disparaging a seminar on organizing (because she and her co-workers felt unrepresented themselves); criticizing union strike preparations to other members (because of SEIU misrepresentations about a strike settlement elsewhere); calling for "a serious overhaul of the National Labor Relations Board" (so it will better handle "duty of fair representation" cases); and proposing either an open shop ("People applying for jobs in the cleaning industry should have a choice whether to join SEIU or not") or, at the very least, new "laws that would allow members to withhold dues when the union doesn't uphold the contract."

More significantly, Jackson's *cri de coeur* contains distinct echoes of the angry complaints that militant black autoworkers once made about their union—its "social unionism" notwithstanding—in the late 1960s and early '70s. Says Jackson:

> Not only members from my building, but other buildings, too, are saying and asking, why are we in this union? SEIU is in with management. We may as well not file a grievance, nothing happens. The officials pick and choose who they are going to fight for and how hard. SEIU mocks the members, laughs in our face . . . and tells us that there is nothing we can do about it. They are taking our money and not fighting for us. The union is not about us, the members, anymore—it's about them, the union officials.

As Reuther biographer Nelson Lichtenstein recalls in *The Most Dangerous Man in Detroit,* UAW members were bearing "the brunt of a new speed-up" in the late 1960s and early '70s. This generated intense membership concern about shop-floor issues "that had animated UAW radicals from one generation to the next." But Reuther's generation of union officials had, by this time, become increasingly disinterested in fighting back via direct action on the job or even grievance-filing. Reuther himself was more often seen at someone else's protest than on a UAW picket line. Among black assembly-line workers, militancy thus mixed with bitter cynicism about the seeming hypocrisy of their union president's public identification with social causes like civil rights. "At the very moment Reuther sought to revitalize the labor movement and champion the insurgencies sweeping America, he faced the scorn of a newly politicized generation" within his own rank and file.[6]

Today's political context and SEIU's industrial setting are, of course, quite different. A few rumblings of membership discontent or an enterprising bit of Internet book publishing can hardly be described as the makings of a revolt on the scale of the black-led "revolutionary union movement" that unsettled Detroit auto plants thirty-five years ago. As Lichtenstein notes, that clash between radical black nationalists and social democratic union apparatchiks was also part of a far larger trend at the time, "a transatlantic surge that challenged workplace hierarchies in France, Italy, Great Britain, Quebec, and Poland."

STIRRINGS OF DISSENT

Nevertheless, even in a more quiescent era, mutinies and defections are spreading within the "Purple Army." A group of San Francisco janitors whose elected officers were removed, under circumstances described above, formed an independent union called the United Service Workers for Democracy (USWD) Local 87. In 2004, these former members of SEIU Local 87 challenged their new Local 1877 in a National Labor Relations Board election that resulted in a major defeat for SEIU in a unit of nearly 1,700 workers. By a margin of 947 to 573, USWD supporters working for the city's largest building service contractors voted to change unions, despite SEIU's flooding of San Francisco with out-of-town organizers, who tried unsuccessfully to stop the decert.

In Massachusetts, e-mail has become the whistle-blowing weapon of choice among other dissenters who, like Jackson, are still working within SEIU structures. In the wake of a controversial Boston janitors' strike settlement in late 2002, a young Harvard-educated staffer—who had just been profiled in the *Boston Globe* as the archetypal SEIU organizer—confided to strike supporters that he shared their concerns about the rift between disillusioned janitors and the union hierarchy. "My first concern with calling the strike a 'victory,'" said Aaron Bartley from Local 254 (now 615), "is that not a single worker I know believes it to be such."

Workers have two main responses upon seeing the settlement in written form. They either become deeply angry, call me or the union "vendidos" [sell-outs] and say they'll cease all union activity or, more commonly, they'll adopt a pose of resignation. . . . [The] workers have universally, almost obsessively, expressed that their overriding concern in this contract is with wages. . . . The settlement does not in fact change the wage scale much. I think many workers correctly sense that the International placed so much emphasis on winning something [on full-time jobs and health benefits for some part-timers] that they were willing to totally cave on wages.

The real disgrace and unvarnished loss is that the contract extends for five years. . . . Barring a reopener, workers are locked into shitty wages and the fact that the union can't mobilize in a powerful way for quite some time.

To Bartley, who worked for the 254 trusteeship, the main post-strike debate in Boston should be about the functioning of "the purple machine" itself— its problems with "hierarchical structure; member participation and power; leadership development; democracy, broader consciousness, etc." From his perspective as an organizer of immigrant workers, Bartley observed:

The fact that the International designed, implemented, and settled this strike without really giving a fuck about what workers, or [local] staff for that matter, had to say is bad enough. The fact that we have in our ranks 200 or so experienced union leaders and warriors from far more painful and powerful struggles in places around the world like El Salvador, Guatemala, Nicaragua, and the Dominican Republic makes some of what happened here a damn shame.[7]

More recently, another well-known labor activist in Massachusetts quit his field rep job to protest SEIU Local 888's belief "that members are incapable of intelligent decision-making and activity without almost total direction from staff." Local 888 is a recently restructured public sector entity and some of its 13,000 members have been under trusteeship for three and a half years. Their Washington-appointed leader has been in no hurry to hold elections or develop a new constitution and by-laws, preferring instead to cloak the latter process in secrecy and confusion. (At great expense, the local did pay for nearly forty hand-picked "observers" to attend SEIU's 2004 convention in San Francisco, twice the number of voting delegates a local its size would have been entitled to send if not in trusteeship.) That's why Ferd Wulkan, who helped organize 888's big unit at University of Massachusetts Amherst, resigned with this parting blast at "interim president" Susana Segat, a former SEIU political operative:

> The philosophy of the local's current leadership—especially regarding democracy and member empowerment—is so at odds with my own philosophy and long-standing practice that I believe a change in leadership is a prerequisite for the local's potential to be realized.

A newly formed 888 Members' Democracy Campaign (MDC) is now planning to run rank-and-file candidates who are committed to increasing "member involvement and control." MDC believes that union staff should "work for the members, not the other way around." It operates a website that posts warnings like the following:

> It appears that [Segat] is planning, as has happened in other SEIU locals, a hasty, superficial process to draw up a constitution that would include election guidelines. Then, a very quick election would follow—so quick as to insure no viable opposition to her election as president.[8]

Philadelphia janitors were faced with a similar situation in late 2003. Fortunately, their opposition proved viable enough to unseat a $100,000-a-year trustee, a young African-American who had been special assistant to SEIU secretary-treasurer Anna Burger in Washington. To secure his election as president of Local 36 in its first post-trusteeship vote, Wyatt Closs teamed up with members of the "old guard" in the local who had been accused of past collusion with management. Denys Everingham and Wayne MacManniman, two former stewards-turned-staffers under the trusteeship, broke ranks with Closs. They formed a broad-based, multicultural "Philly Home Team" slate, which won 60 percent of the vote in the largest turnout in the local's history. Among the issues in the election was the trustee's handling of contract negotiations and a ratification vote so poorly publicized that less than 150 of 2,200 eligible members ended up participating. Says Elba Mercado, a janitor who took time off from his job to campaign for the "Home Team":

Contracts that are bad for the members and good for management win five stars from the International and get signed. When we fight for changes in our union, we get harassed, transferred, called names, race-baited, and pushed aside like we have rabies. People who do janitorial work and clean toilets often get laughed at, discriminated against, sexually harassed, and treated like an outcast at work. We don't need to pay forty dollars a month to people in our union with $200 suits on their backs so they can treat us in the same manner.[9]

Of course, the irony of alliances between angry workers like Mercado and dissident staffers like Everingham or Wulkan is that SEIU local politics is so staff-dominated that, often, only a split among payrollers themselves makes it possible for members to mount a successful challenge to International appointees running, in effect, as incumbents.

UNION DEMOCRACY OR CARTEL UNIONISM?

From the standpoint of creating real rank-and-file power, SEIU's top-down, technocratic, transformation-by-trusteeship strategy is deeply flawed. Voss and Fantasia try to contrast SEIU's modus operandi with the practices of those post-World War II "business unionists" who weren't shaped by "the class war of the 1930s." Their legacy was a "system of labor relations increasingly governed bureaucratically," through institutions dependent on "deal making" and "organized in various subdivisions that relied on many layers of specialized staff." Unfortunately, that's a very accurate description of what former Sixties activists and their newer campus recruits have wrought in much of SEIU. And in other NUP unions like the Carpenters, Andy Stern's "vision of a highly centralized labor movement which restrains membership initiative in an authoritarian straitjacket" is, as Herman Benson points out, "already in operation." In the name of "changing to organize,"

Carpenter locals have been reduced into impotent units. Merged into sprawling regional councils, locals . . . have lost all control over collective bargaining. No member can hold any paid staff position in the council or any local without the permission of an all-powerful executive secretary treasurer. Local delegates, who elect the EST, cannot hold a paid union job without his or her endorsement.[10]

The danger inherent in the SEIU/NUP strategy is clear. If successful, it may foster a smaller-scale, U.S. version of the "cartel unionism" that has trapped so many Mexican workers in deeply compromised collective-bargaining relationships, as part of their country's corporatist labor-management system. In Mexico, decades of political wheeling-and-dealing by "charro" union officials—increasingly unaccountable to those they represent—has resulted in tremendous union "density" on paper but very little positive union presence on the shop floor or in workers' lives. The lesson of that experience is quite relevant to current debates about the organizational restructuring promoted by NUP unions, under the leadership and inspiration of SEIU. Put simply, the lesson is that you can't "remake," "rebuild," or "reorganize" unions in any society without workers and what goes on in their workplaces being central to the project—unless you're no longer interested in having the union function as a genuine workers' organization.

SEIU deserves credit for "pushing organizing" harder and further than most AFL-CIO affiliates. But, reassuringly enough for that AFT delegate to the AFL-CIO convention in 1997, this new member recruitment hasn't led to any takeover of the labor movement or even SEIU itself by low-income dues-payers. For that to happen, "poor workers," as Tait calls them, must first stage two, three, many rank-and-file "takeovers" of their own local unions, and then build from there. As Tait writes in her concluding chapter, "Imagining a New Movement":

> The idea of union democracy must be developed further than its current state of "democracy by consent," where members have a formal vote but no real control at all levels. Union strength and internal democracy are linked, as is clear from study after study that shows rank-and-file organizers build stronger unions.
>
> Top-down, staff driven unions offer little to the masses of non-unionized workers who want a voice in their workplaces and communities. Union members need to be more than "mobilized" for a street demonstration; they need to be activists integral to the movement in all its aspects. They need ownership of their movement.

Challenging staff domination and top-down control within SEIU will require additional "hard work" by a great many working-class "leaders and warriors," of the sort described above by Aaron Bartley in Boston. Their current and future efforts deserve strong support from other trade unionists and friends of labor, at least those able to distinguish, like Tait and Jackson, between SEIU's brand of "progressive" managerialism and organizational transformation that puts members in charge of their own unions.

FROM MONSIGNOR SWEENEY
TO REVEREND ANDY

As politicians pursued voters and media coverage around the country in the fall of 2006, labor's most voluble and highly visible national spokesperson was out on the hustings as well. A non-candidate himself, at least for now, SEIU president Andy Stern had a new book to promote. It is packaged very much like the "campaign bios" manufactured every four years to burnish the image of Democrats and Republicans seeking the presidential nomination of their respective parties. Stern's *A Country that Works* also reminds one of John Sweeney's 1996 manifesto *America Needs a Raise*, which landed in bookstores during the AFL-CIO president's own brief ascendancy as a widely acclaimed "new voice" for labor.

To find out how the political thinking (and book marketing) of American labor leadership has evolved, for better or worse, during the intervening decade, it's worth examining these two slim volumes. Laid side by side, they shed considerable light on the overlapping SEIU careers of the authors and the dramatic developments, within the AFL-CIO, that gave birth to their respective ghost-assisted literary efforts. (The title page of *America Needs a Raise* credits former White House speechwriter David Kusnet as Sweeney's main wordsmith; meanwhile, *A Country that Works* buries its "special acknowledgment" of Jody Franklin's "excellent writing and editing skills" on page 201.)

Each book appeared in the wake of a high-profile AFL-CIO shake-up. Sweeney's collage of childhood memories from the Bronx, SEIU war stories, public policy prescriptions, and a modest account of his 1995 bid for the federation presidency was published when he was still basking in the glow of that election victory—the first by a non-incumbent in one hundred years. Aided by a chorus of outside academic boosters (in Scholars, Artists, and Writers for Social Justice), Sweeney's PR handlers were trying to position him as the main spokesperson for "social movement unionism" in America. He was a labor leader who would not shun

"appearances on national television" like his pallid, conservative predecessor Lane Kirkland often did, leaving labor without "a strong voice and
a visible presence in the debates of the 1990s."

Instead, as the head of a new, media-savvy AFL-CIO, Sweeney
received rave reviews from leading figures in politics, feminism, the civil
rights movement, and academia. The author of *America Needs a Raise*
was hailed as a "visionary leader" (Cornell West) who, "with the audaci-
ty and diligence of FDR during the Hundred Days, has transformed
American labor" (Daniel Patrick Moynihan). After Sweeney's election,
progressives looked to "a newly militant labor movement for a larger
vision of American business than the next quarter's stock market index"
(Betty Friedan) and "a compelling strategy for how working Americans
can restore not only their living standards, but also the traditional
American values of work, family, and community" (Marian Wright
Edelman). Said Julian Bond: "Anyone concerned with economic democracy and social justice must read *America Needs a Raise*."

Reading Sweeney's book-jacket copy ten years later, it's hard to recognize, in such descriptions, the low-key septuagenarian still hanging on
to the federation presidency long past his promised retirement age.
Nearly seventy-three and quite passé, Sweeney looks more like an old
Irish-Catholic priest than a "labor militant" or "visionary leader." He is,
in fact, presiding—with extremely low visibility (but still very high pay)—
over a greatly diminished flock. Five million of his former parishioners
belong to another congregation.

The media spotlight has shifted accordingly to the flashy "mega-
church" minister down the block who spirited them away and replaced
Monsignor Sweeney on the public stage as America's most-quoted labor
leader. A number of former SAWSJ members have left Sweeney's parish as
well, moving to new pews specially reserved for the amen chorus of Change
to Win (CTW). According to one of them, best-selling author Barbara
Ehrenreich, "the future of the American dream" is now "in the hands of
Andy Stern," who has a "vital agenda for change" and "a bold vision for
reform" (as opposed to Sweeney's dusty old sermons from a decade ago).

Stern first seized the microphone (not to mention the blogosphere)
from his onetime mentor during the 2003–4 media campaign that accompanied his creation of a "New Unity Partnership" with Bruce Raynor and
John Wilhelm, leaders of the yet-to-be-married UNITE and HERE.
Round Two of Stern's PR blitz unfolded in 2005, when NUP morphed
into CTW, its affiliated unions stopped paying dues to the AFL-CIO, and

then boycotted the federation's national convention. Stern's resulting "fifteen minutes" of personal fame and media acclaim—in outlets ranging from *Business Week* and *Fortune* to *60 Minutes* and *The New York Times Magazine*—has been very long indeed. It was recently extended further via the fall 2006 nationwide book tour that followed publication of his new book.

Stern's superior preaching style notwithstanding, his emergence as labor's premier pitchman in the marketplace of ideas leaves us with a "messaging" problem. The SEIU president may be a much better "talking head" than Sweeney on TV, radio, in print, or in person. But his recent statements, on a number of political and economic issues, have aroused growing concern among progressive trade unionists, including members of his own union. His conservative pronouncements—usually made in front of business audiences and dressed up as creative new thinking—don't improve with repetition or further elaboration between hardcovers. In Stern's book, the Change to Win demand—"Make Work Pay"—comes across as a cosmetic reworking of Sweeney's mantra, "America Needs a Raise." Furthermore, Stern's "bold unassailable plan" to "get America back on track" actually falls short of Sweeney's 1996 proposals on similar topics such as workers' rights, retirement, health care, education, energy, and taxation. And definitely missing from Stern's laundry list of "vital reforms" is the warm and fuzzy feel of Sweeney's valiant defense of the postwar "social compact" and the good old days of the Great Society and New Deal.

According to Stern, "anyone who might long wistfully for a return to the New Deal policies of 1935 should consider that America today is as far from the time of FDR as the New Deal was from Abe Lincoln and the Civil War." Instead of such liberal nostalgia or the politics of Democratic Socialists of America (a group that still counts Sweeney as a member), Stern serves up a brand of futurism that's just plain fuzzy. Inspired by the likes of Alvin and Heidi Toffler, *A Country that Works* is a breathless celebration of "change processes" in politics, government, the economy, and unions that fails to assess the actual positive or negative impact of particular changes on workers or society. (The word *change* is used 50 times in just 212 pages; in the mind of the author, it always denotes something good coming down the pike, regardless of content or circumstances.) In fact, in the church of Reverend Andy, Americans are urged to: "[p]ause and take the time to appreciate the glory and grandness of our future. Humanity faces a quantum leap forward, and we are engaged in building a remarkable new civilization from the ground up. No single generation has ever been offered such possibilities; we should seize them with passion and zest."

Not surprisingly in light of florid passages like the one above, Stern has started communing with a fellow "change agent" named Newt Gingrich. The author and Change to Win chairperson Anna Burger were "pleasantly surprised" by the former House Speaker's "thoughtfulness and candor," plus his "smart, contemplative demeanor," when they all met at a Republican Main Street Partnership meeting in Chicago (where the speakers included Burger). Reports Stern:

> As only a history scholar can, Gingrich talked in broad historical terms of the change-making process, the challenges facing our country, and America's need to confront its future. . . . He argued [that] labor would have to continually rethink its role in the changing economy—specifically, how it could deliver increased productivity and better services to its members and employers. *Gingrich's thinking reinforced much of my own.* [emphasis added]

As a personal memento of their conversations, Gingrich presented Stern with "a set of diagrams he called 'Designing Transformational Change' that communicate twelve steps to promote organizational transformation." Newt embellished this "parting gift" with "his handwritten comments" on the diagrams and "followed up" by later sending his new friend Andy "a personally annotated edition of the Tofflers' *Creating a New Civilization.*"

The U.S. Army is among those civilizing institutions that Gingrich, joined by Stern, applaud for "consciously and continuously conforming itself to changing times." In their talks, "Gingrich cited his respect" for "the army's management" because the military "accepts change as a fact of life and has worked for decades to reshape itself to meet changing security needs. It actually integrates change into its planning process." Stern notes that some Americans are still wondering, nevertheless, whether the army is to blame for the quagmire in Iraq. Drawing on the insights of Gingrich, Stern believes instead "that our political leaders rushed to war in Iraq without a plan and enough troops to secure peace—over the objections of many in the military, as some former generals have revealed." He concludes reassuringly, "If the Iraq fiasco was the outcome of ineffective planning, then my guess is the army will evaluate their planning process and make any necessary"—yes, you guessed it—"changes."

This example of what Stern's book-jacket copy calls his "eye-opening analysis" would be fairly eye-opening even if the paragraph above wasn't the only reference to "Iraq" cited in the book's index. One would think that a $2 billion a week war, not to mention America's costly post-9/11 military buildup, might warrant a little more discussion in a book that, on its cover, claims to be a dissection of what's "Wrong with a Country that Helps the Rich Get Richer while Most Americans Get the Squeeze."

To be fair, Sweeney's book, *America Needs a Raise*, was similarly silent on the price that workers pay for the ruinous foreign and military policies of their own government. (Yet the AFL-CIO president wasn't writing in 1995 as the head of a union like Stern's that had just adopted an antiwar resolution at its national convention and then allied itself, through many of its local affiliates, with U.S. Labor Against the War.) Like Stern, Sweeney indicts "mean- spirited business leaders"—not capitalism or the military-industrial complex—for making life worse for millions of Americans. Both denounce corporate downsizing, the erosion of job-based benefits and employment security, and the resulting wage stagnation, income inequality, and longer working hours that take a terrible toll on family life and opportunities for civic engagement among working people.

The root cause of such problems, as Sweeney defines it, is "corporate America doing business the wrong way." Too many shortsighted employers are meeting "the challenge of global competition" by taking the "low-wage path" of "driving down wages and living standards." Instead of "cooperating with workers and improving the quality of goods and services," they've "decided to break the postwar social contract" and utilize anti-union decisions by the National Labor Relations Board to undermine labor and destroy the Wagner Act's Depression-era "promise of industrial democracy."

Enter Andy Stern, after a decade of failed efforts by Sweeney to "save our bosses from themselves." In *A Country that Works*, Stern uses management consultant jargon to offer up a series of "twenty-first century policies to ensure America's continued economic leadership" based on "a bold future-oriented vision . . . new ideas and a thoughtful, collaborative, nonpartisan approach." Stern wants to entice management into the same "value-added" partnerships proposed more sparingly by Sweeney but apparently spurned by employers after they perused *America Needs a Raise*. So the SEIU president distances himself from the "class-struggle mentality" that he implies is still widespread in labor today. According to

Stern, union reluctance to embrace labor-management cooperation is an unfortunate and counterproductive "vestige of an earlier, rough era of industrial unions."

Stern believes that organized labor should, like SEIU, better "appreciate employers' competitive reality and attempt to create or add value to their business models" as "a basic operating principle." In the apt description of political consultant Donna Brazile, Stern favors a "strategy of adaptive cooperation." In essence, if you can't beat them, join them. In his book, he cites "alliances with hospitals and nursing home owners" on both coasts, lauding Kaiser Permanente in California and the health care industry in New York. To achieve the Kaiser partnership, angry union members had to shed their attachment to "their own ineffective strikes and concession bargaining." In New York, SEIU's "partnership approach challenged many leaders' traditional 'class struggle' attitudes about employers," a hang-up they've apparently overcome while lobbying together for legislative funding (and, more recently, a plan to close hospitals around the state).

To build "new relationships with public employers in the South and Southwest," SEIU introduces what Stern calls "the 'IQ' program—innovation and quality," while "eschewing traditional collective-bargaining issues and focusing on improving public services." However, in states like North Carolina, Mississippi, or Texas, it's not hard to eschew "traditional collective bargaining" because it doesn't exist in the public sector. One would think that the real challenge there (which has been taken up by other unions) is to build membership organizations that can fight for and eventually win collective bargaining rights for government employees. Although it's always a good idea to link demands for better pay and benefits to public service improvements funded through progressive taxation, Stern's focus, as usual, is on forging SEIU's own institutional "relationships with employers." Worker activity, community engagement, and political action that might actually change the balance of power between labor and management all get short shrift—unless "the power of persuasion" fails, and the union must then resort to the "persuasion of power."

As Stern admits, most employers are not being persuaded, either way, that they need a union "partner" (proving that Jesse Jackson–style alliterative rhetoric only gets you so far, even if you're Jesse). As part of his peripatetic speech-making to human resources managers and open letter writing to Fortune 500 CEOs, Stern has been promoting the idea that "responsible unions" should embrace outsourcing. At the PC Forum, a national meeting of high-tech entrepreneurs, he "shared a variation on the outsourcing concept," providing "a straightforward intellectual argument that made solid business sense—but there were no takers." Much to Stern's dismay, "Changing nonunion employers' attitudes . . . remains a monumental challenge. They often don't believe that partnerships with unions are possible, nor are they able to overcome their prejudices against unions in order to establish a different kind of relationship that could add value to their bottom line."

A Country that Works contains no thoughtful discussion about the pros and cons of the labor movement "moderniz[ing] its strategic approaches to employers in order to take into account their competitive business needs." The California Nurses Association has compiled an impressive record of organizing, bargaining, and legislative success, while remaining a leading foe of "jointness" in health care. Yet its ideological and organizational dissent merits only a two-sentence dismissal from Stern. "Not every union agrees with our approach," he writes. "To this day, the CNA still criticizes SEIU's arrangement with Kaiser and has chosen not to join us in the process." Readers of the book are left to find out on their own what the downside of health care partnerships might be for the quality of patient care. (Among other things, CNA has objected to SEIU's joint lobbying with Kaiser to limit the right of patients to sue their HMO.)

On the subject of legislative and political action, Sweeney and Stern agree that Democrats are often a disappointment waiting to happen, particularly in the area of worker rights and job-killing free-trade deals. Sweeney recalls that labor was extremely unhappy with the results of Democratic control of both houses of Congress and the White House during President Clinton's first term. "After two years in which working people had relatively little to show from their friends, it is not surprising that, with their abstentions and even their votes, they helped elect their enemies [in 1994]."

Sweeney urges unions to move beyond "politics as usual"—i.e. just making COPE endorsements and donations to candidates—to greater membership involvement in grassroots political initiatives, whether issue-oriented campaigns or election fights. He has few good things to say about Republicans. Stern, meanwhile, says that "hitching our fate to . . . Democratic politicians [has] proved to be a losing strategy for American workers." Unfortunately, his "alternative" is more deal making and check writing involving the GOP. In this bipartisan vein, *A Country that Works* praises Republican officeholders like George Pataki, John McCain, and

Mitt Romney, all for their dubious contributions to workers' rights, immigration reform, or universal health care. We learn also that, after his election as SEIU president in 1996, Stern

> reached out to the Republican Party chair, Jim Nicholson, and SEIU became an "Eagle"—a $10,000 donor to the Republican National Committee. "It was an expression of my interest in engaging Republicans on issues of concern to America's workers, and I was promised a conversation."

Stern remained undeterred when "the Committee accepted SEIU's contribution" but never got around to having "the conversation." Ever the optimist, he reports:

> SEIU continues to keep an open mind and open door: At the Republican Convention in 2000, we honored several Republican legislators. We also employ Republican advisors. In 2004, SEIU was actually the largest contributor to both the Democratic and Republican Governors' Associations, a fact that confused both party establishments.

Nevertheless, Stern admits, "the Republican Party's agenda on issues of work" is still "often not in our members' best interests," particularly in states like Indiana and Missouri where SEIU dollars helped elect GOP governors who proceeded to roll back already limited bargaining rights for state workers (an outcome Stern neglects to mention). During the same round of elections, SEIU also aided a Republican gubernatorial candidate in North Carolina who was running against a Democrat backed by the rest of the local labor movement.

Although his book touts this "independent, non-partisan approach," Stern's true political identity appears to be deeply Clintonite. As *Atlantic Monthly* editor Joshua Green recently observed, "Veterans of Bill Clinton's White House often speak of themselves as having been a 'modernizing force' in the Democratic Party. . . . Their guiding idea was that a more pragmatic, results-oriented approach held greater promise for achieving traditional liberal goals." Stern, who positions himself as labor's leading "modernizer," couldn't agree more, in terms of both medium and message. "If the Democratic Party wants to win elections," he argues, "it needs a permanent infrastructure, not controlled by the party's elected officials," that "employs and integrates the modern techniques of data management, marketing, mobilizing and new communications technologies."

Bill Clinton's two [presidential] victories were not due to a Democratic Party infrastructure but were the result of his self-assembled, highly talented campaign staff and consultants, his finely honed, disciplined message that directly addressed issues of concern to voters, and his extraordinary charisma and leadership.

The tragedy of Stern is the tragedy of Clinton, a fellow-product of Sixties liberal idealism whose similar ambition, media savvy, organizational drive, and personal charisma could have helped advance a real progressive agenda. Instead, Clinton's formidable political skills have always been deployed on behalf of a cramped, technocratic, and triangulated politics, which has achieved very few "traditional liberal goals." Like Clinton, Stern is part of that generational cohort shaped by Vietnam-era campus activism and the liberal antiwar politics of the McCarthy, Kennedy, and McGovern presidential campaigns of 1968 and 1972. In Clinton's career, youthful idealism quickly gave way to a pragmatic centrism and the search for business-friendly policy prescriptions that broke with the Democrats' traditional New Deal nostrums, like reliance on "big government." Since Stern became a social worker union activist in the early 1970s, his ascendancy in labor has followed a similar political trajectory. Like the former president, he sees himself as courageously challenging official orthodoxy on behalf of "new ideas." In the media and before business audiences, he counterposes his persona—as a smooth, sophisticated, globally minded "change agent"—to that of blue-collar troglodytes in the rest of labor who "just don't get it," don't want to "change to win," and, instead, remain sadly wedded to "class-struggle unionism."

In their respective arenas, Stern and Clinton both command continuing attention because they represent "success." In the case of the former president, his is based on being the only Democrat in four decades to serve more than one term in the White House; in Stern's case, proof of success comes from being, as his book jacket proclaims, "the newsmaking president of the fastest-growing, most dynamic union in America" who has "led the charge for modernizing the 'house of labor,' taking unions out of the past and into the twenty-first century." Within labor, Stern's message boils down to this: he and his union are "winners," most of the others are "losers," so, if any of them really want to be winners too, they'd better get with the SEIU/Change to Win program. His message for America is that we need *A Country that Works* and that "government, business, and labor must work together as a team in order for America to prosper in the new global economy." In Sweeney's concluding chapter—entitled "Changing Lives, Changing America"—there's at least a little hint that the motor force needed for major change might be mobilization of the rank and file. "For all our problems," he observes hopefully, "the labor movement can still draw on the energy, experience, intelligence, and resources of more than thirteen million members"—if working people can better "organize themselves to transform the economy."

In Stern's closing argument for "commonsense ideas" that would "get America back on track," there's barely a nod to "the power of protest" or the role that various social movements played during the 1960s, "when the winds of change were gusting." The author's list of "course-correction reforms" in the area of taxation, education, health care, and retirement policy are said to be "so compelling, simple, and achievable that readers will find themselves enraged that they haven't yet been enacted." Yet it's more likely that readers will end up wondering how any future Democratic administration or Congress might be pressured to adopt such an agenda, without some real big gusts of wind.

A Country that Works is thus far less convincing and coherent as a brief for reform than *America Needs a Raise* because it deals so little with the dynamics of successful, grassroots movement building. (Even the immigrant worker upsurge around the country in the spring of 2006 rates a mere two sentences in Stern's book.) We're left with the impression that what really brings about "change" is not mass mobilization, but rather some well-oiled union organizational equivalent of the Clintons' political machine. In Stern's union, not surprisingly, one finds the same kind of finely honed message discipline, "highly talented staffers and consultants," nonstop fund-raising (i.e., "doubled dues" because "you can't have a champagne union with beer money"), and last but not least, a maximum leader (or two) long on personal charisma, political opportunism, and relentless self-promotion.

REFORM FROM ABOVE
OR RENEWAL FROM BELOW?

The veterans of Sixties radicalism who became union activists in the 1970s belonged to a variety of left-wing groups. Regardless of other political differences, most of them shared one common belief—namely, that union transformation and working-class radicalization was a bottom-up process. As Stanley Aronowitz observed in *Socialist Review* (nee *Socialist Revolution*) when *L.A. Story* author Ruth Milkman belonged to its Bay Area Collective in 1979, young radicals usually became "organizers of rank-and-file movements" and builders of opposition caucuses. They immersed themselves in "day-to-day union struggles on the shop floor" and the politics of local unions, often displaying in the latter arena "almost total antipathy toward the union officialdom." Because "union revitalization" also required organizing the unorganized, rather than just proselytizing among existing union members, Aronowitz approved, "under some circumstances," leftists becoming "professional paid organizers." But he encouraged those who took this path to "see their task as building the *active* rank and file, even where not connected to caucus movements."[1]

Three decades later, the shrinkage of organized labor and the Left within it has produced more than a few deviations from the shining path of "revival from below." Kim Moody, author of *U.S. Labor in Trouble and Transition*, remains a true believer in the transformative potential of rank-and-file movements. A founder of *Labor Notes* and author of several previous books on contemporary trade unionism, Moody was a leading theoretician of the International Socialists when it sent college-educated cadres into the auto, steel, telecom, and trucking industries during the 1970s. What Moody and his comrades contributed to the workplace-organizing debates of that era (and more recent decades as well) is "the rank-and-file strategy"—the idea, simply put, that radicals should orient themselves toward the strata of worker activists, at the base of unions, who are most engaged in shop-floor militancy and resistance to management, rather than "attempt to gain influence by sidling up to the incumbent bureaucracy or its alleged progressive wing." Moody's newest volume is a wide-ranging account of the economic forces, domestic and international, that have eroded American unions, since their last, turbulent period of grassroots insurgency from 1966 to 1978. As in the past, he argues that "rank-and-file rebellion"—despite its many setbacks and defeats in recent years—is the only proven method of projecting a genuine "alternative view of unionism, to force changes on reluctant labor leaders, and challenge the top-down culture of business unionism . . . [which] provides little or no education and leadership training for rank-and-file workers."

Both Moody and Milkman, in *L.A. Story,* see great potential in the immigrant worker organizing and strike activity of the last several years. Based on her case studies of Latinos in construction, building services, garment manufacturing, and port trucking, Milkman believes that these newcomers can "take the lead in rebuilding the nation's labor movement." Moody even discerns "the beginnings of an upsurge in direct action in workplaces and communities by a variety of groups," both unions and allied "workers' centers," that could lay "the basis for a new class politics" in America. Unlike Moody, however, the author of *L.A. Story* downplays rank-and-file initiatives as a catalyst for institutional change.

Now a professor of sociology at UCLA and director of its Institute of Industrial Relations, Milkman has watched how the Service Employees International Union (SEIU), United Brotherhood of Carpenters (UBC), and Hotel and Restaurant Employees (HERE) have revitalized themselves and/or the L.A. County Labor Federation. In her view, looking to union members to rebel against corrupt, ineffective, or undemocratic unions and refashion them into something better is an exercise in wishful thinking and existential frustration—*Waiting for Lefty* reborn as *Waiting for Godot.* According to Milkman, proponents of the rank and file approach long championed by Moody naively assume that "if only the legions of top union brass would step aside and allow the rank-and-file's natural leaders to take command, labor would no longer be so impotent." In reality, she writes, "this approach glosses over the complex and multi-layered character of union leadership and various political configurations that are possible across those layers."

Milkman believes that, "when International leadership is progressive, it can be a powerful force for promoting innovation at the local union level" and rooting out "business unionism:"

> As is now well documented, many of the most successful initiatives of the SEIU [and other Change to Win affiliates] have actually been "top-down" efforts, engineered not by the rank and file but by paid staff in the upper reaches of the union bureaucracy. . . . The recent ascension of leaders with both extensive formal education and activist experience in other movements to high-level positions in key unions has injected dynamism into the labor movement. . . . The most vibrant and innovative unions are those that combine social movement-style mobilization, with carefully calibrated strategies that leverage the expertise of creative, professional leaders.

Moody is far less impressed by what Milkman characterizes as the "daring, intrepid character" of Change to Win. Nor is he similarly inclined to drape the new labor federation with the mantle of "social movement unionism." Moody makes a more nuanced three-way distinction between "business unionism," which everyone on the left agrees is bad; "democratic social movement unionism," born of real "struggle with the employers" here and abroad; and what he calls "the new corporate unionism." He argues that the ongoing internal reorganization of SEIU and the Carpenters into "huge administrative units" represents "a step beyond business unionism in its centralization and shift of power upward in their structure away from the members, locals, and workplace." Providing a detailed analysis and critique of the undemocratic "corporate side of SEIU's culture," Moody concludes that the union's much-envied gains in "market share" are too often the product of "shallow power" or partnership deals. According to Moody, SEIU has achieved "a density suspended from above by a layer of 'talent' recruited mainly from outside the union rather than upheld from below by deep roots in the workplace and local unions."

In contrast, Milkman regards SEIU's Justice for Janitors (JfJ) campaigns to be an unqualified success and model for union builders everywhere. "Justice for Janitors originated as part of a strategic union rebuilding effort. It was conceived by SEIU's national leadership and relied heavily on research and other staff-intensive means of exerting pressure on employers." To their credit, JfJ organizers helped pioneer comprehensive, community-based campaigns that bypassed the NLRB to win union recognition via card check and neutrality by targeting building owners who were the real power behind cleaning service contractors. SEIU employed direct action tactics, including civil disobedience, built strong ties with immigrant communities, and presented the workers' cause in a way that elicited sympathy and support from that part of the broader public concerned about social justice and better treatment of oppressed minorities.

According to Milkman, in the original JfJ struggle in Los Angeles in 1988-9 and similar efforts elsewhere, "rank-and-file mobilization played a critical role in its success." Nevertheless, as Moody notes, this "mobilization" has rarely translated into a leading role for immigrant workers in managing the affairs of their own SEIU locals. By the mid-1990s, JfJ activists in Los Angeles were complaining about Local 399's out-of-touch leadership, its neglect of day-to-day workplace issues, and the lack of rank-and-file participation in union decision making. Many janitors supported a successful electoral insurgency, led by the "Multiracial Alliance Slate." But, in 1995, the SEIU national leadership quickly nullified the Alliance's election victory by throwing the local into trusteeship and later moving L.A. janitors into a much larger, regional local. In *L.A. Story*, Milkman barely acknowledges that there was "widespread criticism" of SEIU over this pivotal development. She dismisses "Multiracial Alliance" organizing activity as an unfortunate "outbreak of factionalism" that, only "on the surface, appeared to involve rank-and-file rebellion against the local SEIU officialdom."

Moody, on the other hand, takes the 399 matter very seriously. He believes the trusteeship and transfer of L.A. janitors into a "mega-local" beyond their effective control had a negative impact on subsequent collective bargaining, which produced wage gains of 12.3 percent between 1990 and 1995 and only another 6 percent between 1995 and 2000 for downtown L.A. janitors. Thus, in the decade after their 1990 victory:

> L.A. janitors with the best conditions saw their real wages fall 10%. In this same period, 1990 through 2000, average real hourly wages in the U.S. *rose* by 4.8%. It is just possible that had the L.A. janitors been in their own local instead of statewide Local 1877, with its low wages, minimal benefits, and long contracts, they could have pressured the industry for more and set a better pattern for others.

Where Moody sees troubling continuity with conservative union practices of the past, Milkman waxes enthusiastic about "AFL organizational legacies" that she finds uniquely empowering. A major thesis of her book is that Change to Win unions have paradoxically proven more "adept at crafting new survival strategies for labor in the post-industrial economy" because of their past experience of taking "wages out of competition in unregulated, highly competitive labor markets" and winning union recognition in pre–New Deal fashion, without utilizing the National Labor Relations Board. In *L.A. Story*, the allegedly superior "strategic and tactical repertoire" of CTW affiliates—and resulting "organizing successes"—are attributed to their roots as "old AFL craft and occupational unions." According to Milkman:

> As the L.A. janitors' campaign and other recent organizing successes illustrate, this repertoire is highly adaptable to contemporary economic

conditions, which in many ways resemble those of the pre–New Deal era. By contrast, many of the CIO's strategies and tactics were tailored to the historical conditions of the 1930s and 1940s—conditions that have been largely swept aside over the past three decades by deindustrialization, deregulation, and deunionization. . . . That unions—once seen as bastions of conservatism and corruption—have emerged in the vanguard of current labor revitalization efforts is a powerful testimony to the renewed relevance of the AFL's historical legacy.

Unfortunately for the credibility of her book, there is little evidence to support Milkman's sweeping claim that CTW unions, with the exception of SEIU and perhaps HERE, have responded more effectively to damaging "political and economic transformations" than any other battered labor survivors of the last thirty years. As Moody shows, in the five-year period prior to the AFL-CIO'S 2005 split, the International Brotherhood of Teamsters (IBT), United Food and Commercial Workers (UFCW), and Laborers International Union (LIUNA) all lost members (whereas the Carpenters registered only 1.4 percent growth)—a record inferior to that of CWA, AFSCME, AFT, and the independent NEA. Only SEIU registered membership gains of 20 percent or more but, percentage-wise, the AFT's growth during the same period was nearly as great. The smallest of CTW's seven affiliates—the still struggling United Farm Workers—remains only a fraction of its peak size twenty-five years ago.

Far from just decimating former CIO unions, deindustrialization has also been a major cause of membership shrinkage within Change to Win (particularly in affiliates with a mixed craft and industrial union heritage). The three unions—Textile Workers, Amalgamated Clothing Workers, and Ladies' Garment Workers, which merged over time to form UNITE—lost hundreds of thousands of dues payers in plant shutdowns prior to UNITE's 2004 marriage with HERE. These factory job losses were so devastating that, even today, the combined membership of UNITE and HERE—a claimed 450,000—is less than ACTWU's alone in 1976.

The notion that the Teamsters somehow dodged the bullet of deregulation is even more far-fetched. The IBT today is one-third smaller than it was before the Carter administration introduced trucking deregulation in the late 1970s. As Moody notes, "By 1985, the number of workers covered by the Teamsters' National Master Freight Agreement had dropped from over 300,000 in 1970 to as low as 160,000" and it's half that number today. Non-union competition, including the growth of a huge owner-operator sector, undermined national bargaining and led to what Moody calls "a long string of concessionary contracts."

Likewise, CTW's third-largest affiliate, the United Food and Commercial Workers, has hardly been in "the vanguard" of thwarting deunionization. Although its systematic campaign for organizing rights at Smithfield Foods in North Carolina is well deserving of praise, UFCW's record generally in meatpacking is one of failing to maintain wage standards and unionization levels. Meanwhile, non-union "big box" chains like Wal-Mart have grabbed a huge share of total retail sales in recent decades; their much lower labor costs have led to similar management pressure for union give-backs in the shrinking organized sector of the industry. The UFCW's disastrous 2003 walkout by 60,000 Southern California grocery workers was a case study in *un*-successful resistance to this trend. As Moody observes, "The UFCW's record of lost strikes and failed organizing drives is too consistent and too visible to make this union the likely David to Wal-Mart's Goliath."

Finally, "conservatism and corruption" also remain very much a part of the negative "AFL organizational legacies" that Milkman glosses over or ignores entirely when assessing Change to Win. For example, the IBT and UFCW are both guilty of wasting membership dues money in a manner quite inconsistent with being a "mean, lean organizing machine" or part of a "new union reform movement." Thanks to Teamster president James Hoffa's undoing of real reforms dating from the Ron Carey era, the IBT now squanders more than $8.5 million a year on extra paychecks for 175 of the Teamster officials throughout the country who get multiple salaries. As the *Detroit News* reported last August (2007), UFCW local officials "are among the highest paid in the United States with 33 making more than $200,000 in base salary in 2006 and many earning thousands more by drawing additional paychecks from the union's international headquarters. Meanwhile, the average UFCW member earns between $25,000 and $30,000 a year, with many at Michigan grocery stores earning less." In a not atypical profile of an individual UFCW regional leader—Local 588 president Jack Loveall—the *Sacramento* (California) *Bee* reported that Loveall's total compensation for 2003 was more than $565,000 (in a 23,000-member local that has two of his sons on the payroll, plus a twin-engine jet for the officers' use).

Nevertheless, when the AFL-CIO split was still brewing in 2005, Milkman insisted that the IBT, UFCW et al. had embraced the "reform agenda" of SEIU president Andy Stern, including the latter's call "for a one-union-per-industry model" that would curb inter-union competition for unorganized workers. Meanwhile, Hoffa declared that his multi-jurisdictional amalgamated union had no intention, then or now, of concentrating only on certain "core industries" and ceding workers in any other field to labor organizations, CTW or AFL-CIO, with more relevant experience! In *L.A. Story*, Milkman likewise depicts CTW unions as advocates of "extensive structural changes in the labor movement," including "a strengthened central body that would have the power to enforce its policies with the affiliates." The new mini-federation's actual practice, in the two years since its founding, has been quite different, of course.

Even with only seven affiliates (as opposed to fifty-plus in the AFL-CIO), CTW has found policy unanimity to be elusive and certainly hasn't developed any "strengthened central body" with the power to impose it. As promised, CTW has launched some laudable joint organizing projects. Yet CTW unions have been unable to agree on the war in Iraq, trade or immigration issues, which Democratic primary candidate to endorse for president (even SEIU was split internally on that one), or the appropriateness of working with Wal-Mart for "health care reform." A disagreement between Stern and UFCW president Joe Hansen over this last issue led to a public spat in 2007, followed by UFCW picketing of a joint appearance by Stern and Wal-Mart CEO Lee Scott. In another display of disunity, Doug McCarron's Carpenters Union didn't even bother to show up for the CTW's second anniversary convention in 2007. As was the case before the UBC's defection from the AFL-CIO, the Carpenters have apparently stopped paying dues to CTW; according to *In These Times*, "rumors persist that the union will soon leave the new group."

None of this messy organizational reality, most of it well known or very predictable before publication of *L.A. Story*, ever intrudes on Milkman's upbeat narrative. On some subjects covered in the book—for example, SEIU's doubling of its membership to 1.8 million in the last ten years—the author's boosterism is certainly more warranted. But, unlike Moody, she never addresses the serious concern, now being raised by union insiders, that SEIU growth in some sectors has been achieved at the expense of contract standards, community allies, workers' rights, membership participation, and leadership accountability. Milkman's infatuation with the vanguard role of the union's "innovators"—college-educated organizers, researchers, strategic campaign coordinators, local officers and trustees—also leaves little room for examining more incisively how SEIU operatives actually interact with the working members who nominally employ (and, more rarely, elect) them.

To Moody falls the task of imagining how the rank and file can rise again, in SEIU or any other union in need of a different, more democratic form of organizational "dynamism." This challenge is particularly daunting in light of developments like home-based workers being the largest single source of new union growth. Brokering deals with labor-friendly state officials around the country, SEIU (and now other unions as well) have created collective bargaining units composed of 500,000 or more home-based workers previously regarded as "independent contractors." When SEIU was certified as the representative of one such unit—74,000 home health aides in Southern California—it described this 1999 victory as the biggest for labor since the Flint sit-down strike. In reality, many home-based workers are imprisoned in the post-Clinton system of "workfare" that replaced welfare. Largely female, non-white, and/or foreign-born, this workforce cares for the young, old, and disabled while struggling to survive on poverty-level incomes, even when union-represented. One of the usual quid pro quos for union recognition is continued exclusion of these workers from standard public employee health care or retirement coverage.

Unlike the Teamsters, Transit Workers, or other more traditional union members (whose past assertions of rank-and-file power are lionized by Moody), these workers have atomized, high-turnover, part-time jobs in settings quite unlike the large industrial workplaces of the past. The fact that their "non-traditional workplace" is their own or someone else's home increases the likelihood that unions won't help them build real organizations or a functioning steward system. Already, many such workers remain "agency fee payers" or members with little consciousness of or connection to their union. Their experience of collective action, if any, comes from initial community-based mobilizations for bargaining rights and better pay. The poor and/or immigrant neighborhood, not the shop floor, is the only possible nexus for solidarity among co-workers.

If one of the continuing shortcomings of organized labor today, as noted by both Moody and Milkman, is that it's still too pale, male, and stale, what better way to achieve greater diversity than by developing the leadership potential of this vast "new rank and file"? Can such workers or the immigrant janitors and hotel workers in other Change to Win recruitment drives ever succeed in becoming leading actors in their own organizations, rather than bit-players in union-orchestrated street pageantry or political campaigns? It won't be easy in a staff-run "mega-local" like SEIU's 190,000-member United Long Term Care Workers Union in California for all the reasons identified by Moody.[2] But, as he concludes hopefully, the initiatives of rank-and-file-oriented radicals and reformers "can help lay the basis for better things to come, just as inaction, timidity, bureaucracy, or 'more of the same' can stifle them."

A PURPLE UPRISING IN OAKLAND

As an infrequent visitor to the West Coast, I've never experienced the earthquake tremors that are so familiar to millions of Californians. But in a union hall in downtown Oakland, one didn't have to be a seismologist to see and feel the fault lines shifting in America's second-largest union on a late March day in 2008. Several hundred members and staffers of United Healthcare Workers (UHW) were jammed into their local headquarters for a raucous press conference and pep rally. Arriving by bus, BART, on foot and by car, the crowd was chanting, clapping, whistling, and making an enormous racket with union-issued yellow plastic clackers. Almost everyone wore the signature purple T-shirts and jackets of their parent organization, the Service Employees International Union (SEIU).

The event could have easily been mistaken for an SEIU strike vote, a contract ratification meeting, or an organizing rally involving some portion of the UHW's statewide membership of 150,000. Since a few workers even wheeled in the disabled people they care for in neighboring homes, it also looked like a union protest against state budget cuts in Sacramento.

The gathering of African-American, Asian, and Latino home care workers, nursing home aides, and hospital employees was convened for another purpose, however. Their call-and-response chants were not directed at any recalcitrant employer or tightwad Republican governor.

Instead, UHW members were venting against top officials of their own union.

"What do we want?" Someone with a bullhorn shouted. "Democracy!" the crowd responded. "When do we want it?" The answer, delivered by all present, was a thunderous "Now!" And that was before they broke into another spirited chant, reminiscent of Bay Area protests past: "Hey, hey, ho, ho—Andy Stern has got to go!"

Andy Stern is, of course, the powerful, high-profile and increasingly heavy-handed president of SEIU. Much to the chagrin of many of his members, he and union democracy are like oil and water. On March 27, the day before their Oakland rally, UHW rank-and-filers awoke to a headline in the *San Francisco Chronicle* that read: "SEIU Leader Moves to Oust West Coast Dissident."

The article reported that Stern was preparing to put UHW under "trusteeship," a form of martial law in which local elected leaders are replaced by International union appointees from Washington. Since Stern became SEIU president, in the mid-1990s, he has named trustees to run the affairs of nearly 80 locals. Originally, his professed goal was to root out corruption and promote organizing. But more recently scores of SEIU affiliates have been merged, restructured, and saddled with unelected leaders so Stern can exercise greater personal control over their dealings with politicians and employers. (For SEIU's public sector members, these are often one and the same.)

In UHW, there are no crooks in need of ousting and the local's membership recruitment record has been exemplary. Between 2001 and 2006, UHW added nearly 65,000 new members, more than any other SEIU local in the country. Nevertheless, in a March 24 letter that was clearly designed to lay the legal groundwork for a takeover, Stern accused UHW of violating the national union constitution by "developing a secret plan to destabilize and decertify bargaining units." As part of this conspiracy to "sabotage" SEIU, UHW members would become part of a breakaway "independent union" formed in alliance with the AFL-CIO and the California Nurses Association. (CNA is a longtime rival of SEIU, now affiliated with the AFL; SEIU left the AFL in 2005 and formed Change to Win, a rival federation.)

The main target of any trusteeship, based on such false charges, is UHW president Sal Rosselli. He is a well-known Bay Area labor activist and past supporter of myriad progressive causes, including gay rights. Since resigning from SEIU's national executive committee so he could speak more freely—as he is entitled to do under the Landrum-Griffin Act— Rosselli has turned his local into a hotbed of dissent. He has criticized Stern's leadership in *Labor Notes*, on *Democracy Now*, and in major newspapers like the *Wall Street Journal*, *Chicago Tribune*, and *New York Times*. Meanwhile, UHW has launched a lively website (www.seiuvoice. org) to stimulate internal debate about the need for "real member participation" in SEIU and a more democratic, bottom-up approach to building the union.

As the *Chronicle* noted on March 27, Rosselli is trying to generate grassroots support for reform proposals at SEIU's 2008 convention in Puerto Rico. There, Stern's critics say they will push for a Teamster-style direct election of top union officers, so all 1.8 million SEIU members can vote on the leadership, instead of just a few thousand convention delegates every four years. UHW also wants to give local unions more protection against forced mergers which dilute membership control. Critical of recent deal making by Stern and his associates, SEIU dissidents want to ensure that workers have a stronger voice on the bargaining committees and "unity councils" that deal with large, multi-state employers.

According to Rosselli, Stern's threatened trusteeship over UHW is simply "retaliatory because we are speaking out against his ideology, his direction. The simplest way I can say it is, it's top down versus bottom up, corporate unionism versus social unionism." Based on its size, UHW is entitled to have one of the largest delegations at the SEIU convention. But, if Stern puts UHW in trusteeship, none of its 146 elected representatives will be able to attend or lobby other delegates about democratizing the union's structure and functioning. Fellow SEIU dissidents, now organizing nationally in a group called SEIU Member Activists for Reform Today (SMART), would then have a much harder time getting other union officers and stewards to engage in reform activity. That's why Rosselli accuses Stern of using the UHW trusteeship threat "to eliminate his political opposition."

In a March 27 statement, Rosselli disclaimed any intention of encouraging membership decertification from SEIU. UHW reasserted its public position that, "despite profound disagreements" with Stern's leadership, "leaving is not an option. SEIU is OUR union, that's why we're fighting to change it." At the anti-trusteeship rally in Oakland, Rosselli proudly introduced an organizing committee member from St. Francis Medical Center in Lynwood, California, where 600 service and maintenance workers had just voted to join the union. Due to its membership growth around the state, UHW is negotiating new contracts for 75,000 hospital and nursing home workers in 2008 alone.

Given such a heavy bargaining calender and the challenges UHW faces from various employers, its elected rank-and-file board members are very concerned about the chaos, division, and disruption that will ensue if SEIU tries to oust them and Rosselli—plus purge their local's most experienced staff reps and organizers.

Their concerns are clearly shared by others in California labor who've worked with Rosselli for years—even union officials who disagree with him and leftists who doubt his sincerity as a union reformer. For example, Mike Casey, a prominent Bay Area trade unionist who heads Local 2 of the Hotel Employees, has ignored the usual protocol that "members or leaders of other unions should not interfere in the internal disputes of another union" and issued an open letter about the UHW-SEIU rift. In his March 28 missive, Casey addresses, among others, his own UNITE-HERE national officers, Bruce Raynor and John Wilhelm. They both joined Stern in launching Change to Win in 2005, after subjecting AFL-CIO president John Sweeney to withering public criticism of the sort Stern now doesn't like when directed at him from within SEIU.

"I believe that there must always be room within organized labor for legitimate and principled dissent, if our movement is to survive and ultimately grow," Casey says.

"The questions and issues raised by Sal meet the threshold of such dissent. . . . [These] are matters that must be addressed by any union looking to organize on a large scale. The public discourse initiated by UHW and Sal may well be kicking up a lot of dust, but it has also provoked a closer examination of the direction of our movement."

To date, Casey notes, SEIU spokespeople have responded to Rosselli largely with personal attacks and claims that "his behavior is 'shameful,' 'unprincipled,' and 'dishonest.'" Says the HERE leader: "The Sal Rosselli I know is anything but shameful, unprincipled, and dishonest." And he goes on to heap praise on Rosselli and UHW for their concrete expressions of solidarity and support when Local 2 members faced a "two-year war," the strike and lockout that roiled San Francisco's hotel industry in 2004–6. "Such a union and leader has more than earned the right to air objections to union practices without being vilified or demonized."

Nevertheless, in some daily press coverage and the spin of SEIU media handlers, the UHW affair is still depicted as a narrow turf battle between Stern and Rosselli, both veterans of Sixties student activism, now unfortunately feuding, in late middle age, over the perks of institutional power. Conversations with UHW rank-and-filers suggest that they see it differently—as a much broader fight that they didn't start, but have a huge stake in. "We're on a mission to hold Andy Stern accountable," says UHW board member Eloise Reese-Burns, one of the thousands of nursing home workers that Stern wants to transfer against their wishes to a local in Los Angeles. "We believe that the rank and file should be involved in making contract demands and helping to raise our contract standards. Andy's just a bully—but he's going to find out that it's not a good idea to piss off the union people who pay your salary."

Ella Raiford, another African-American leader in UHW who belongs to SEIU's national black caucus (AFRAM), is equally vehement. Speaking at a meeting in Berkeley attended by sixty-five SEIU dissidents from locals around California, Raiford noted that there were many in the room "who've worked long and hard over the years to have a democratic union." Now, "Andy Stern is telling us where we have to go and what we have to do—and we don't have any say in the matter. It's time for us to stand up and say, 'No!'"

Applauding the formation of SMART and UHW's own alternative vision for the union, Raiford called on her fellow reformers "to make a real 'change to win'" for our members, so they have a voice in the union." "We're going to find," she predicted, "that a lot of people in SEIU want to be part of *that* 'change to win.'"*

*Note: Despite the opposition of thousands of members like Raiford, SEIU placed UHW under trusteeship ten months later, on January 27, 2009. Most Elected leaders of the UHW, including its deposed president Sal Rosselli, resigned from SEIU in protest and began building a new organization, the National Union of Healthcare Workers (NUHW). In its first month, NUHW filed petitions with the NLRB seeking elections that would enable 90,000 UHW members to switch unions. For more information on this development, see http://nuhw.org/

READING, WRITING, AND UNION BUILDING

"It's a well-established fact," reports the *New York Times Book Review*, "that Americans are reading fewer books than they used to."[1] According to the National Endowment for the Arts, more than 50 percent of those surveyed haven't cracked a book in the previous year. In labor circles, the percentage of recent readers may be even smaller. Eric Lee, the UK-based founder of Labour Start, recalls an encounter he had a few years ago at a union conference in Chicago. There, a "labor intellectual" was "bemoaning the fact that even the most intelligent and best-informed union leaders he knew simply did not read the books that they should be reading, if they read any books at all."

"Even though there are millions of union members," Lee notes, "the books aimed at unionists are never listed" on best-seller lists. "If you're a gardener or a cook or a moviegoer, the books targeted at you may sell in the tens of thousands. History books are sometimes big best-sellers—but not books about labor history."

Lee's own online promotion of labor books notwithstanding (see www.labourstart.org/books.shtml), he now offers the following advice to authors seeking large audiences:

> Don't write books about and for trade unionists. Our movement does many things well, but one thing we do not do well is buy and read books that are written for us.[2]

As evidenced by the contents of this collection, I've opted for "optimism of the will," rather than "pessimism of the intellect," on the subject of reading, writing, and union building. Yet, as a key labor education project, helping to link labor writers to readers is a challenging task. Unless they are national union presidents—with the ability to use dues money to promote their book or purchase it in bulk for internal distribution—labor-oriented authors must work very hard to reach a working-class audience.[3] Few writers on the subject of work have the creativity, journalistic ability, and mainstream media cachet of Barbara Ehrenreich. Her 2001 work, *Nickel and Dimed*, represents the gold standard of commercial publishing success involving a labor-related book. Only Tom Geoghegan's *Which Side Are You On?* comes anywhere close to Ehrenreich's best-seller in terms of crossover appeal. And, as some reviewers (including this one) have noted, Geoghegan's 1991 account of his career as a Chicago labor lawyer was not really intended for the rank and file, which he sometimes reduces to humorous stereotypes. Rather, it was aimed at an audience of yuppies—liberal-minded, upper-middle-class readers (including friends and classmates of the author long puzzled by his post-Harvard affinity for blue-collar causes and clients).

The first constraint faced by many labor writers is publishing with a university press, rather than a "trade" bookseller like Henry Holt or Farrar, Straus and Giroux, the publishers of Ehrenreich and Geoghegan respectively.[4] Academic publishers are quite proficient at turning doctoral theses into books that can help junior faculty members get tenure (no matter how small their press run or sales figures). But university press marketing departments are not well equipped to attract the attention of working-class readers or the general public. The United States boasts more than one hundred campus-based publishing houses but altogether they account for only 1 percent of all books produced.[5] The number of university presses that specialize in labor history, culture, politics, industrial relations, and/or contemporary union issues can be counted on one hand. Within that small group, even a very committed backer of labor books like the Cornell ILR Press finds it a challenge to reach a large audience. According to longtime editor Fran Benson, the average ILR Press book sells about 2,000 to 2,500 copies (in hard and soft cover). Thus, as *Labor Studies Journal* editor Bruce Nissen observes, "Any labor book selling over 5,000 copies is a 'best-seller.'"

The relative "success" or "failure" of such books depends on several factors. One is their accessibility and appeal to non-academic readers.

Benson reports that books in her labor series often do better than Cornell titles generally because labor activists, not just fellow academics, buy them if the material is topical and well-written. Among these non-academic book buyers are the large number of college-educated young people who have gravitated toward the labor movement after being involved with campus workers, anti-sweatshop campaigns, or graduate student unionization.

Some of Benson's "best-sellers" have gotten a boost from the bulk order patronage of unions whose organizing, bargaining, or strike activity has been chronicled by Cornell authors. For example, then-USWA president George Becker was sufficiently pleased with the favorable portrait of himself—and his union's campaign on behalf of locked out West Virginia aluminum workers—that he ordered 5,000 copies of *Ravenswood: The Steelworkers' Victory and the Revival of American Labor* by Kate Bronfenbrenner and Tom Juravich. To demonstrate SEIU's interest in nursing issues and provide RNs with free books, Andy Stern bought 5,000 copies of Suzanne Gordon's *Nursing Against the Odds*, published by Cornell in 2004. (As noted above, Stern's bulk buy of his own book was presumably much larger, since *A Country that Works* was promoted everywhere in SEIU, not just in health care locals.) A popular speaker at nursing conferences and training sessions, Gordon has tried to maintain friendly ties with many different RN organizations, not all of which are on speaking terms. Her most recent book, *Safety in Numbers,* highlights the successful campaign for state-mandated RN-patient staffing ratios waged by the California Nurses Association (CNA), a bitter rival of SEIU. Yet some CNAers were displeased that the book was, in their view, insufficiently critical of SEIU's stance on ratios. Though Gordon's latest work was reviewed in *Registered Nurse,* CNA's national magazine, the union has, according to the author, otherwise distanced itself from a book that actually burnishes its own reputation.[6]

Intra-union politics can limit book publicity even more than inter-union rivalries, as Texas law professor Julius Getman has discovered. When Cornell published his valuable account of a pivotal strike at International Paper in the late 1980s, the response of the United Paperworkers International Union (UPIU) was chilly indeed. Getman's title alone—*The Betrayal of Local 14: Paperworkers, Politics, and Permanent Replacements*—created marketing problems within the UPIU, since no union likes to be criticized for failing to support a militant local during a difficult contract struggle. Now part of the Steel Workers, UPIU officials detested Getman's book and completely ignored it in their national union newspaper. As a result, *The Betrayal of Local 14* received far less notice than it deserved in the labor press, except in those unofficial publications, like *Labor Notes*, which had previously covered the IP strike in Jay, Maine, and other mills.

Assuming their material is not as controversial as Getman's, authors who maintain a well-designed website and line up book-related speaking engagements can boost their sales via online marketing and personal networking. Adjunct professor Joe Berry collaborated with the North American Alliance for Fair Employment to create an excellent site (www.reclaimingtheivorytower.org) publicizing Berry's 2005 Monthly Review Press book aimed at non-tenure-track teachers in higher education. The site highlights upcoming appearances by the author, relevant biographical information, recent reviews of *Reclaiming the Ivory Tower*, and news about adjunct faculty organizing around the country. (According to Berry, NAAFE also partnered with Monthly Review Press to co-publish the book, "kicking in enough dollars to assure MRP that they would not take a bath on the title.")[7] Jack Metzger, a fellow labor educator in Chicago, was similarly able to utilize personal and professional contacts, developed over many years, to promote *Striking Steel*. The son of a steelworker, Metzger grew up in a Pennsylvania mill town and later became the co-founder and editor of *Labor Research Review*. His book was praised in the pages of *Steel Labor,* the USWA's national magazine, by former USWA president Lynn Williams; the author also made a special effort to reach union retirees (whose work lives in the 1950s and 1960s are movingly described in the book). Nevertheless, according to Metzger, "even getting a book in the hands of people you know takes a long time and a lot of work."

With this challenge in mind, some labor-oriented writers have taken matters into their own hands and turned to self-publishing to expedite the process of book production and marketing, from start to finish.[8] More than twenty years ago, Boston labor lawyer Bob Schwartz approached the Bureau of National Affairs (BNA), a leading publisher of legal newsletters and case reports, with a proposal for a steward's guide to labor law. BNA wasn't interested. So Schwartz started Work Rights Press, now based in Somerville, Massachusetts, to distribute his *Legal Rights of Union Stewards* and other books for union activists (all priced between $13 and $24). Since the late 1980s, Schwartz's stewards' handbook has sold 600,000 copies (and continues to sell, in both Spanish and English editions, at the rate of about 25,000 per year). His next best-seller is a guide to the Family and Medical Leave Act; since publication of its first edition a decade ago, that book has sold 100,000 copies. An explanation of "workers' comp" in Massachusetts, which Schwartz has repeatedly updated over the years, has 50,000 to 60,000 copies in circulation, and a broader guide to state employment law has sold 25,000 copies in multiple editions. Only Schwartz's most recent work, on *Strikes, Picketing, and Inside Campaigns,* has yet to sell out its original press run of 5,000, notwithstanding a glowing review of it by this author (based on the book's introduction). Lagging sales are no doubt related to the abandonment of the strike weapon by too many unions.

What's the key to Schwartz's overall success? Well, unlike other authors of heavily footnoted volumes, his discussion of legal decisions, legislative history, and the workings of labor-related administrative agencies is highly accessible. Schwartz writes short, punchy, understandable sentences and paragraphs, uses sidebar boxes, and Q&A sections at the end of each chapter. He also employs an excellent cartoonist to illustrate his work in humorous fashion. His Work Rights Press series draws on the broader publishing tradition of "do-it-yourself" and "self-help" books, a genre that's far more familiar to union activists than dense volumes of labor history or industrial sociology. Local union work, when combined with family life, community activities, and the demands of bargaining unit employment, doesn't leave much time for educational reading on the side. The only book that many stewards have time to bury their nose in is the contract itself. Nevertheless, both full-time union officials and what the British call "lay representatives"—working members who represent their co-workers on the job—are expected to be familiar with a large body of additional information related to job rights and benefits, collective bargaining procedures, and, in some cases, union administration and financial record keeping.

So when Schwartz's Work Rights Press or the Detroit-based Labor Education and Research Project (LERP) produce easy-to-read guides for being a good steward, running a better local union, or conducting effective contract campaigns, there is a ready-made market for them. LERP has sold over 32,000 copies of its *Troublemaker's Handbook,* volumes I and II, edited by Dan LaBotz and Jane Slaughter. The Project's 1999 book, *Democracy Is Power* by Mike Parker and Martha Gruelle, attracted 5,000 readers and every issue of *Labor Notes,* the monthly newsletter LERP has published for nearly thirty years, promotes other books by authors like

Kim Moody, Sheila Cohen, Dan Clawson, and Vanessa Tait. To sustain its labor education and publishing, *Labor Notes* relies on an international network of trade union militants, sympathetic local unions, and local or national union reform caucuses. This far-flung community of supporters comes together every other year—most recently in April 2008—at a conference in Michigan attended by a thousand activists (plus a few authors and publishers) who share *Labor Notes*' goal of putting "the movement back in the labor movement."

On their own (or in connection with similar book promotion ventures), several other worker education projects have encouraged reading as well. The American Labor Education Center—run by Matt Witt, a former communications director for the Mine Workers, Teamsters, and Service Employees—publicizes "out of the mainstream" books (and films),which is to say those dealing with labor. Witt's online reviews appear eight times a year at www.TheWorkSite.org and are also published in *New Labor Forum*. In addition to producing a newsletter for stewards and a labor news and graphics service for union editors, David Prosten's Union Communication Services (UCS) publishes a labor book catalogue once a year. Distributed to 70,000 potential readers, this 60-page brochure features volumes on labor history, economics, and bargaining, plus union-oriented books for children and young adults. Prosten's catalogue (which can be found at www.unionist.com) includes both practical "tools for union leaders and activists" of the sort published by WRP and LERP and popular biographies of Mother Jones, Eugene Debs, A. Philip Randolph, and César Chávez. Prosten's own nuts-and-bolts handbook, *The Union Steward's Complete Guide*, has sold more than 50,000 copies, thanks to UCS marketing efforts like its annual catalogue.

On Labour Start, Eric Lee's cross-border labor campaign site (see link above), book reviews are regularly posted to generate orders from both Prosten's catalogue and Powell's, the unionized bookseller in Portland, Oregon. (Labour Start now lists almost 300 recommended titles in its online bookstore and, at www.powellsunion.com one can find books favored by the ILWU Local 5 members who work at Powell's.) Even the AFL-CIO has made book buying easier via its own online retail store for labor activists. The federation's Union Shop has a much smaller selection of books competing for "shelf space" with union posters, sweatshirts, golf balls, mugs, movies, games, and other merchandise. For reasons noted above, none of the fifteen books on labor history or contemporary union affairs that it features are likely to ruffle any feathers among AFL affiliates.[9]

The website of the independent United Electrical Workers markets two classic labor books—*Them and Us: The Struggles of a Rank-and-File Union* by journalist James Higgins and the UE's first organizing director, James Matles, and *Labor's Untold Story* by Richard Boyer and Herbert Morais. (Originally published commercially in 1974, *Them and Us* was updated and reissued by the UE in 1995; first published half a century ago, the Boyer-Morais account of U.S. labor history is now in its third edition and 26th printing, thanks to the UE's commitment to keeping it available for labor educator use, inside and outside the union.) Meanwhile, on the West Coast, every issue of *Dispatcher*, a publication of the International Longshore and Warehouse Union, carries a plug for ILWU-approved labor history books and videos, including several bios of union founder Harry Bridges, accounts of the 1934 San Francisco general strike, and David Wellman's 1995 Cambridge University Press study, *The Union Makes Us Strong: Radical Unionism on the San Francisco Waterfront*.[10]

Unfortunately, other national union sites offer little in the way of good reading. As Lee reports, "The Teamsters sell a whole range of products including watches, clocks, jewelry, clothing, leather goods, glassware and hats—but not a single book." (In the July/August 2008 issue of *The Teamster* magazine, the IBT did find space for an author interview with *St. Louis Post-Dispatch* reporter Philip Dine, who wrote *State of the Unions*.) Meanwhile, the American Federation of Teachers' website provides a Powells.com link so members can order the latest Harry Potter from a union shop; yet, according to Lee, the AFT "doesn't recommend any book that teachers might find useful and interesting as trade unionists." (In 2008, the union proved Eric wrong by finally touting one book on its site—a flattering biography of late AFT chieftain Albert Shanker, written by Richard Kahlenberg and entitled, *Tough Liberal*.)

Such an underplaying of books seems particularly inexcusable in a white-collar union whose members have acquired four-year (and advanced) degrees to teach reading and writing, among other subjects. As longtime AFT member Joe Berry explains: "Teachers themselves don't necessarily read much more than an average reader—which is to say, not as much as you might hope or wish." In his own role as a recruiter of students for labor education programs run by the University of Illinois, Berry visits labor councils and attends local union membership meetings around the state. There, he keeps alive the old labor education tradition of a "bookstore in a box" by setting up a literature table at every stop. (His car is, in fact, a rolling bookstore, full of such boxes!) In addition to displaying his own recent book (mentioned above), Berry offers titles ranging from Howard Zinn's *People's History of the United States* to the Lenny Moss mystery series authored by Tim Sheard (in which a hospital union steward in Philadelphia moonlights as a detective). Months after setting up his book display at a labor event—and, often, making many sales—Berry sometimes receives emails from satisfied customers, telling him how much they enjoyed a non-fiction book or novel he sold them.

In my own experience, doing labor education work within the Communications Workers of America (CWA), book promotion efforts were always well received by the rank and file. For many years, Cornell's Lee Adler and I jointly organized a week-long leadership school for CWA activists in the Northeast. Since this program was held every year in Ithaca, home of the ILR Press, and at the Industrial and Labor Relations School conference center, I began organizing a Cornell "book-and-author" event for the CWA students involved. The authors were usually recruited locally—among them, ILR School faculty members like Lance Compa, Jeff Cowie, Kate Bronfenbrenner, and Bill Sonnenstuhl. Their topics included workers' rights as human rights, runaway shops in manufacturing, successful organizing tactics, and local union involvement in Employee Assistance Programs.

Either at breakfast or during a lunch break, speakers would talk to our CWA group about a recent book they had written, take questions about it, and sign copies for any buyers. CWAers were encouraged to make purchases from the large selection of other books laid out on a table manned by ILR Press staffers so they could start building a library for themselves or their local union back home. For most of the hundred CWAers participating, this was the first book signing they had ever attended. Some responded so enthusiastically that they returned to their locals with stacks of ILR Press titles, catalogues, and order forms. To underline the importance of reading as part of what would hopefully be a career-long quest for personal self-improvement, I told the first-year students at one such CWA school that buying, reading, and writing a review of an ILR Press book was a requirement for returning to Cornell the next year. (This "homework" assignment was later waived, but the point was made.) When I asked ILR extension program staffers and the ILR Press whether any other labor organization using Cornell's conference center had ever sponsored any similar book-and-author events, they confirmed that none ever had.

If more unions took similar initiatives, there could be far greater book-selling synergy with university presses (or any cooperating labor book publisher) whenever union members are being trained at university facilities like Cornell's or union-operated education centers, like the George Meany Center or the Maritime Institute in Maryland. In an earlier era, some unions like the UAW even operated book clubs for their members. Les Leopold's *The Man Who Hated Work* recalls how OCAW leader Tony Mazzocchi, a ninth-grade dropout, launched a book discussion group among local union activists on Long Island in the mid-1950s.

> Tony's group saw itself as part of a working-class culture that encouraged self-education. Soon there were more than twenty people enrolled in the University of Mazzocchi. The introductory curriculum packed a political wallop. It started with Howard Fast . . . books such as *Freedom Road*, *Spartacus* and *Citizen Tom Paine*. Then the group turned to the history of American class struggle through such works as *Labor's Untold Story* and *The History of the Fur and Leather Workers*. For some, the reading group opened the door to more traditional literature as well. [One member] recalled how they passed around the *Iliad* and the *Odyssey*.[11]

In the larger left-liberal community today, the idea of a liberal—if not left-wing—book club is making a comeback. In June 2008, a group of politically active journalists, novelists, and non-fiction writers launched a new venture that "combines the offerings of a traditional book club with the interactive features of an online social network and the ideals of a grass-roots political party."[12] The Progressive Book Club (PBC) is backed by magazines and/or Internet blogs like *The Nation, Mother Jones, The Huffington Post, Daily Kos, Salon*, and others. It hopes to attract a membership of several hundred thousand in the next few years, with the participation of major publishers and smaller houses like Chelsea Green Publishing and Soft Skull Press. (Founded more than forty years ago, the PBC's well-established counterpart on the right, the Conservative Book Club, boasts more than 80,000 members today.)

Among the PBC's two hundred initial offerings, there are fewer than ten labor-related titles. One of them is PBC editorial board member Andy Stern's own book, *A Country that Works*. (To its credit, SEIU is also an organizational sponsor of the club and the only union involved so far.) Stern's fellow board member, Katrina vanden Heuvel, editor and publisher of *The Nation*, cites the conservative movement's success in spreading its ideas, via books, as one reason why more of the liberal left, including labor, should get on board. Says vanden Heuvel: "It seems like a good time to rededicate ourselves to the notion that ideas have power and consequence, and that the grassroots can use those ideas to create change."

> The Progressive Book Club was established to help restore balance to American discourse by bringing progressive voices and issues to the forefront. It offers a strong social networking platform—members can learn, debate, interact, and exchange ideas through PBC's vibrant online community. Offline there will be opportunities to interact with authors, progressive opinion leaders, and fellow members at local events, readings, and book discussions.[13]

Preoccupied as they may be with their own survival struggles, more unions would be well advised to join SEIU in promoting the PBC or, better yet, starting their own smaller-scale version of it. This could be done in conjunction with the handful of labor-oriented journals that regularly review or run excerpts from labor-related books, or by a group of cooperating labor studies centers. Either way, it's long past time for progressives in labor to find new methods of encouraging rank-and-file reading or to revive some of the old-fashioned ones.

Notes

INTRODUCTION

1. Eric Lee, "Educate, Agitate, Organize: Selling Labor Books On-Line," *The Industrial Worker*, May 2005, 4; available at www.labourstart.org/books. shtml.

2. The collected works of Farrell Dobbs—*Teamster Rebellion, Teamster Power, Teamster Politics*, and *Teamster Bureaucracy*—are still worth reading. They are available from the Socialist Workers Party's Pathfinder Press. See www.path finderpress.com.

3. George Orwell, "Confessions of a Book Reviewer," in *The Collected Essays, Journalism and Letters of George Orwell*, ed. Sonia Orwell and Ian Angus, 4 vols. (New York: Harcourt Brace Jovanovich, 1968). Quoted in Gail Pool's *Faint Praise: The Plight of Book Reviewing in America* (Columbia: University of Missouri Press, 2007), a wonderful exploration of the past, present, and future of book reviewing.

4. For more on the lessons of union reform struggles three decades ago, see Steve Early, "The Enduring Legacy and Contemporary Relevance of Labor Insurgency in the 1970s," and other contributors to *Rebel Rank and File: Labor Militancy and Revolt from Below*, ed. Aaron Brenner, Robert Brenner, and Cal Winslow (New York: Verso, 2009).

5. For more on internal criticism of Stern, see Kris Maher, "Union Hears Rumbling in Its Ranks," *Wall Street Journal*, Feb. 29, 2008, A10; Steven Greenhouse, "A Leader at the Point of Union Growth and Criticism," *New York Times*, Feb. 29, 2008, A17; and Mark Brenner, "California SEIU Leader Mounts Battle for Local Control, Union Democracy: An Interview with Sal Rosselli," *Labor Notes*, March 2008.

PART ONE: LABOR AND THE LEFT, OLD AND NEW
FROM REBEL PENS TO REBEL HANDS

First published in *Against the Current*, July/August 2003, as "From Rebel Pens to 'Pencil Hands': The Rise and Fall of Labor Journalism." Books under review included *Writing the Wrongs: Eva Valesh and the Rise of Labor Journalism*, by Elizabeth Faue (Cornell University Press, 2002); *Rebel Pen: The Writings of Mary Heaton Vorse*, edited by Dee Garrison (Monthly Review Press, 1985); *Mary Heaton Vorse: The Life of an American Insurgent*, by Dee Garrison (Temple University Press, 1989); and *Strike!* by Mary Heaton (University of Illinois Press, 1991, reprint).

1.   See Frank Swoboda, "The Decline of the Labor Beat," *The Guild Reporter*, October 22, 1999, 6–7, an article based on the 19th A. J. Liebling Memorial Lecture, delivered by Swoboda at the 1999 convention of International Labor Communications Association (ILCA).

2.   See unpublished paper by Zipser, "Some Thoughts on Labor Journalism and ILCA's Role in Preserving—or Challenging—the Status Quo," distributed at ILCA meeting in Washington, D.C., November 17, 2000. Available from the author at azipser@cwa-union.org.

FROM CRIMSON TO COAL SEAM

First published as "From Crimson to Coal Seam," a review of *From Harvard to the Ranks of Labor: Powers Hapgood and the American Working Class*, by Robert Bussel (Penn State Press, 1999), in *The Nation*, March 20, 2000.

RADICAL UNIONISM

First published as "The Rise and Fall of a Radical Union," a review of *Radical Unionism in the Midwest, 1900–1950*, by Rosemary Feurer (University of Illinois Press, 2006), in *Socialism and Democracy*, March 2008.

ON CULTURING A UNION

First published as "On Culturing a Union," a review of *Not For Bread Alone: A Memoir*, by Moe Foner (Cornell ILR Press, 2002), in *The Nation*, September 30, 2002.

1.   See *New Labor Forum* 9 (Fall/Winter 2001), for more on Esther Cohen's account of the Bread and Roses Project, NLF editorial on the state of relations between labor and the arts generally, and Freeman's view of the need for rejuvenation of left/labor culture.

REVOLUTION IN THE AIR

First published as "Revolution in the Air," a review of *Revolution in the Air: Sixties Radicals Turn to Lenin, Mao, and Che*, by Max Elbaum (Verso, 2002), in *New Politics*, Winter 2003.

1.   See Christopher Phelps, "Mao and Then," *Left History* 9/1 (Fall/Winter

2003); http://www.yorku.ca/lefthist/.

2.   See David Garrow, "Mao Mix," *The Village Voice*, July 3–9, 2002; http://www.villagevoice.com/2002-07-02/books/mao-mix/1.

LABOR'S WORST NIGHTMARE
First published as "With Friends Like These," a review of *An Unlikely Conservative: The Transformation of An Ex-Liberal (or How I Became the Most Hated Hispanic in America)*, by Linda Chavez (Basic Books, 2004); and *Betrayal: How Union Bosses Shake Down Their Members and Corrupt American Politics*, by Linda Chavez and Daniel Gray (Crown, 2004), in *The Nation*, November 22, 2004.

WORKING-CLASS INTELLECTUALS
First published as "Rediscovering the Legacy of Two Labor Intellectuals," a review of *Singlejack Solidarity* by Stan Weir, edited by George Lipsitz (University of Minnesota Press, 2004); and *Punching Out & Other Writings*, by Martin Glaberman, edited by Staughton Lynd (Charles H. Kerr, 2002), in *WorkingUSA: The Journal of Labor and Society* 8 (December 2004).

THE MAN WHO HATED WORK
First published as "He Conjured Up a Labor Movement," a review of *The Man Who Hated Work and Loved Labor: The Life and Times of Tony Mazzocchi*, by Les Leopold (Chelsea Green Press, 2007), in *The Progressive*, January 2008.

PART TWO: RACE, CLASS, AND GENDER
First published as "A Long Tradition of Bias," a review of *American Work: Four Centuries of Black and White Labor*, by Jacqueline Jones (W. W. Norton, 1998), in the *Philadelphia Inquirer*, April 5, 1998.

THE MOST DANGEROUS WOMAN IN AMERICA
First published as "Most Dangerous Woman in America," a review of *Mother Jones: The Most Dangerous Woman in America*, by Elliot Gorn (Hill and Wang, 2001); and *Race, Class, and Power in the Alabama Coalfields, 1908–21*, by Brian Kelly (University of Illinois, 2001), in *Socialism and Democracy*.

LEFT OUT: BLACK FREEDOM FIGHTERS IN STEEL
First published as "Race, Radicalism, and Industrial Union Democracy," a review of *Black Freedom Fighters in Steel: The Struggle For Democratic Unionism*, by Ruth Needleman (Cornell University Press, 2003); and *Left Out: Reds and America's Industrial Unions*, by Judith Stepan-Norris and Maurice Zeitlin (Cambridge University Press, 2003), in *WorkingUSA*, Winter 2004.

FIGHT IN THE FIELDS—AND BEYOND

First published, in different form, as "A Timely Story of César Chávez and the Farmworkers Movement," a review of *The Fight in the Fields*, by Susan Ferriss and Ricardo Sandoval (Harcourt Brace, 1997), in the *Philadelphia Inquirer*, April 27, 1997; and as "From David to Goliath?" a review of *Beyond the Fields*, by Randy Shaw (University of California Press, 2008), in *Z Magazine*, December 2008.

AMERICA'S BEST-KEPT SECRET

First published as "Labor Thinking Needs a Touch of Class," a review of *The Working-Class Majority: America's Best-Kept Secret*, by Michael Zweig (Cornell University Press, 2000); and *Striking Steel: Solidarity Remembered*, by Jack Metzger (Temple University Press, 2000), in *The Guild Reporter*, July 21, 2000.

PROLE LIKE ME

First published as "Prole Like Me," a review of *Nickel and Dimed: On (Not) Getting By in America*, by Barbara Ehrenreich (Metropolitan Books, 2001), in *The Nation*, June 11, 2001.

ON THE WATERFRONT

First published as "On the Global Waterfront," a review of *On the Global Waterfront: The Fight to Free the Charleston 5*, by Suzan Erem and Paul Durrenberger (Monthly Review Press, 2007), in *Z Magazine*, January 2008.

PART THREE: VOICES OF DISSENT AND REFORM

NOT YOUR FATHER'S UNION MOVEMENT

First published as "Checking the Union Labels," a review of *Not Your Father's Union Movement: Inside the AFL-CIO*, by Jo-Ann Mort (Verso, 1998); and *The Transformation of U.S. Unions: Voices, Visions, and Strategies from the Grassroots*, edited by Ray M. Tillman and Michael S. Cummings (Lynne Rienner Publishers, 1999), in *The Nation*, February 8, 1999.

FROM THE ASHES OF THE OLD

First published as "From the Ashes of the Old," a review of *From the Ashes of the Old: American Labor and America's Future*, by Stanley Aronowitz (Houghton Mifflin, 1998), in *Dollars & Sense*, Fall 1998.

THE NEW RANK AND FILE

First published as "The New Rank-and-File," a review of *The New Rank and File*, by Staughton and Alice Lynd (Cornell University Press, 2000), in *WorkingUSA*, Spring 2001.

LABOR'S HEARTLAND LOSSES

First published as "Six Strikes," a review of *Three Strikes: Labor's Heartland Losses and What They Mean for Working Americans,* by Stephen Franklin (Guilford Press, 2001); and *Three Strikes: Miners, Musicians, Salesgirls, and the Fighting Spirit of Labor's Last Century,* by Howard Zinn, Dana Frank, and Robin D. G. Kelley (Beacon Press, 2001), in *WorkingUSA,* Spring 2002.

SOLIDARITY SOMETIMES

First published as "Solidarity Sometimes," a review of *Coalitions across the Class Divide: Lessons from the Labor, Peace, and Environmental Movements,* by Fred Rose (Cornell University Press, 1999), and *Taking History to Heart: The Power of the Past in Building Social Movements,* by James Green (University of Massachusetts, 2000), in *The American Prospect,* September 11, 2000.

1.   For more on the cast of characters involved in "'Teamster Donorgate," and how that scandal came about, see the series of articles written under my pen name at the time, Jim Larkin: "What Went Wrong: The Campaign Money Scandal of Ron Carey," *In These Times,* December 14, 1997, 18–21 ; "Teamster Tragedy," *The Progressive,* January 1998, 20–22; and "Teamsters: The Next Chapter," *The Nation,* January 4, 1999, 17–20.

THE NEXT UPSURGE

First published as "Is Labor's 'Next Upsurge' Just Around the Corner?" a review of *The Next Upsurge: Labor and the New Social Movements,* by Dan Clawson (Cornell University Press, 2003), *New Labor Forum,* Spring 2004.

AFTERTHOUGHTS ON SWEENEY

First published as "The Crisis in Organized Labor," a review of Bill Fletcher and Fernando Gapasin, *Solidarity Divided: The Crisis in Organized Labor and a New Path toward Social Justice,* by Bill Fletcher and Fernando Gapasin (University of California Press, 2008), in *New Politics,* Summer 2008.

1.   See Bacon interview with Fletcher, *The Progressive,* March 2000, 31–35.
2.   See "The Future of the Labor Left," *Monthly Review,* July/August 2000, 60–83.

PART FOUR: WORKERS' RIGHTS AND WRONGS
WHICH SIDE ARE YOU ON?

First published as "A Persuasive Defense of Organized Labor," a review of *Which Side Are You On?: Trying to Be for Labor When It's Flat on Its Back,* by Thomas Geoghegan (Farrar, Straus & Giroux, 1991), in the *Boston Globe,* and as "Quirky Account of Labor's Woes," in *USA Today,* both of which appeared on August 12, 1991.

WITH FRIENDS LIKE THESE
First published as "Workers' Rights: Looking for the Union Label," a commentary on the preliminary report of the *Presidential Commission on the Future of Worker-Management Relations*, in the *Boston Globe*, June 5, 1994.

UNFAIR ADVANTAGE
First published as "How Stands the Union?," a review of *Unfair Advantage: Workers' Freedom of Association in the United States under International Human Rights Standards*, by Lance Compa (Human Rights Watch, 2000), and *Labored Relations: Law, Politics, and the NLRB—A Memoir*, by William Gould (MIT Press, 2000), in *The Nation*, January 22, 2001.

OUR COLLECTIVE BARGAIN
First published as "Our Collective Bargain," a review of *State of the Union: A Century of American Labor*, by Nelson Lichtenstein (Princeton University Press, 2002), in *The Nation*, February 25, 2002.

IS THE STRIKE DEAD?
First published as "Is the Strike Dead?," a review of *Strikes, Picketing, and Inside Campaigns: A Legal Guide for Unions*, by Robert Schwartz (Work Rights Press, 2004), in *MRzine*, January 1, 2005.

1. For a longer account of strike activity during this same period, see Steve Early, "Strike Lessons from the Last Twenty-Five Years: What It Takes to Walk Out and Win," and other contributors to *The Encyclopedia of Strikes in American History*, ed. Aaron Brenner, Benjamin Day, and Immanuel Ness (Armonk, N.Y.: M. E. Sharpe, 2009).

BACK TO THE FUTURE WITH EFCA?
First published as "Labor Law Reform Thirty Years Later: Back to the Future with EFCA," in *Labor: Studies in Working-Class History of the Americas* 5/4 (November 2008), a commentary on union efforts to amend the Wagner Act, now and in the past.

1. Brian DeBose, "Obama Banks on Union's Support," *Washington Times*, March 3, 2008, 14.
2. Chris Townsend, "The Deck's Stacked against Labor," *The UE News*, February, 2008, 15.
3. Kim Moody, "Card Check Takes a Hit," *Labor Notes*, December 2007, 4–5.
4. Max Fraser, "Beyond the Labor Board," *The Nation*, January 21, 2008, 6–8. For a critique of the performance of the NLRB during the Clinton years, see Steve Early, "How Stands the Union?" *The Nation*, January 22, 2001, 25–27.
5. Richard Hurd, "Neutrality Agreements: Innovative, Controversial, and Labor's

Hope for the Future," *New Labor Forum* (Spring 2008): 35–44.

6.   See Roy Adams, "The Employee Free Choice Act: A Reality Check," Proceedings of the 58th Annual Meeting of Labor and Employment Relations Association, 2006.

7.   See James Pope, Peter Kellman, and Ed Bruno, "The Employee Free Choice Act and a Long-Term Strategy for Winning Workers' Rights," *WorkingUSA: The Journal of Labor and Society* 11 (March 2008), 125–44.

8.   See, for example, the 2005-6 "Hotel Workers Rising" campaign that, according to UNITE-HERE president Bruce Raynor, produced neutrality agreements that have added 6,000 new members to the union. Cited in Hurd, n. 5 above. For an account of the strike by 75,000 CWA and IBEW members against Verizon in 2000 that occurred, in part, due to a long-running (and still unresolved) union fight over organizing rights at Verizon Wireless, see Steve Early, "Verizon Strike Highlights New Union Role," *Boston Globe*, September 3, 2000.

9.   Kris Maher, "Labor Dispute Takes to Airways," *Wall Street Journal*, July 16, 2008.

10. Robert J. Grossman, "Reorganized Labor," *HR Magazine*, January 2008.

11. See Dean Baker, "The Recession and the Freedom to Organize," posted February 6, 2008, by AFL-CIO at http://www.aflcio.org/mediacenter/speak-out/dean_baker.cfm.

12. For full text of AFL-CIO Executive Council's March 10, 2008, statement, see http://www.aflcio.org/aboutus/thisistheaflcio/ecouncil/ec030420081.cfm.

13. See Harold Meyerson, "A Fractured Labor Movement Is Throwing Everything into Its Campaign for Obama," *The American Prospect*, August 28, 2008 (Web edition only: http://www.prospect.org/cs/articles). Meyerson doesn't approve of the Alliance. He finds the formation of this "political action sub-group" to be a further disappointing "splintering of a movement whose watchword, supposedly, is solidarity."

14. See "Working Together," Larry Cohen's column in *The CWA News*, April–May 2008, 2.

PART FIVE: ORGANIZING IN THE GLOBAL VILLAGE

TAKING CARE OF BUSINESS

First published as "Tale of the AFL-CIO's Sorry Record Overseas," a review of *Taking Care of Business: Samuel Gompers, George Meany, Lane Kirkland, and the Tragedy of American Labor,* by Paul Buhle (Monthly Review Press, 1999), and *A Covert Life, Jay Lovestone: Communist, Anti-Communist, and Spymaster,* by Ted Morgan (Random House, 1999), in *Labor Notes*, September 1999.

SLICING THE GLOBALONEY

First published as "Slicing the Globaloney," a review of *Workers in a Lean World: Unions in the International Economy* (Verso, 1997), by Kim Moody, in *The Nation*, February 16, 1998.

SLAVES TO FASHION

First published as "Labor, Immigration, and Globalization," a review of *Slaves to Fashion: Poverty and Abuse in the New Sweatshops,* by Robert J. S. Ross (University of Michigan Press, 2004), and *Immigrants, Unions, and the U.S. Labor Market,* by Immanuel Ness (Temple University Press, 2005), in *Socialism and Democracy* 19/2 (July 2005).

THE CHILDREN OF NAFTA

First published as "Union Building in the Global Village," a review of *The Children of NAFTA: Labor Wars on the U.S./Mexican Border,* by David Bacon (University of California Press, 2004), and *The Maya of Morganton: Work and Community in the New South,* by Leon Fink (University of North Carolina Press, 2003), in *New Labor Forum,* Fall 2004.

CAN WORKER CENTERS FILL THE VOID?

First published as "Can Worker Centers Fill the Void?," a review of *Suburban Sweatshops: The Fight for Immigrant Rights,* by Jennifer Gordon (Belknap Press of Harvard University Press, 2005), and *Worker Centers: Organizing Communities at the Edge of the Dream,* by Janice Fine (Cornell University Press, 2006), in *New Labor Forum,* Summer 2006.

1. Michael Yates, "Do Unions Still Matter?," available at http://mrzine.month-lyreview.org/yates041105.html.

2. See Elly Leary, "Immokalee Workers Take Down Taco Bell," *Monthly Review* 57/5 (October 2005).

TEAMSTERS AND TAXI DRIVERS

First published as "Leave the Driving to Us," a review of *Taxi! Cabs and Capitalism in New York City,* by Biju Mathew (Cornell University Press, 2008), and *Outside the Box: Corporate Media, Globalization, and the UPS Strike,* by Deepa Kumar (University of Illinois Press, 2007), in *New Labor Forum,* Summer 2008.

PART SIX: CHANGE TO WIN
REUTHERISM REDUX

First published as "Reutherism Redux: What Happens When Poor Workers' Unions Wear the Color Purple," in *Against the Current,* September/October 2004. Books under review included *Poor Workers' Unions: Rebuilding Labor from Below,* by Vanessa Tait (South End Press, 2005); *Hard Work: Remaking the American Labor Movement,* by Rick Fantasia and Kim Voss (University of California Press, 2004); *Reorganizing the Rust Belt: An Inside Study of the American Labor Movement,* by Steven Henry Lopez (University of California Press, 2004); *Labor Pains: Inside America's New Union Movement,* by Suzan Erem (Monthly Review Press, 2001); *S.E.I.U.: Big Brother? Big Business? Big*

Rip Off? by Harriet Jackson (AuthorHouse Books, 2004).

1. Aaron Bernstein, "Can This Man Save Labor?" *Business Week* cover story, September 13, 2004. For earlier coverage and commentary on the emergence of NUP, see Bernstein, "Breaking Ranks with the AFL-CIO," *Business Week*, September 5, 2003, 64–67; and "Pooling Our Resources for Growth," *Business Week Online*, September 5, 2003; Harold Meyerson, "Organize or Die," *American Prospect*, September 2003, 39–42; JoAnn Wypijewski, "The New Unity Partnership—A Manifest Destiny for Labor," *CounterPunch*, October 6, 2003; William Johnson and Chris Kutalik, "New Unity Partnership: Five Guys in a Room Plan the Future of U.S. Labor Movement," *Labor Notes*, October 2003, available at http://labornotes.org/archives/2003/10; and   Johnson's "The New Unity Partnership," *Z Magazine*, March 2004, 15–17.

2. One significant difference between the ALA's reform program and NUP's is that Reuther, before leaving, challenged the AFL-CIO to create a joint defense fund for strikers. While shifting tens of millions of dollars into organizing and politics every year, SEIU has made no effort to build a national strike fund— even for its own members—that would guarantee fixed weekly benefits of any amount—much less the $200 to $300 a week that UAW or CWA strikers receive. How NUPsters plan to rebuild union power without strengthening workers' strike capacity has yet to be explained.

3. See "United We Win: A Discussion of the Crisis Facing Workers and the Labor Movement," an unpublished document circulated by SEIU, dated 1/8/03. For a different presentation of the same argument, see Stephen Lerner, "An Immodest Proposal: A New Architecture for the House of Labor," *New Labor, Forum*12/2 (Summer 2003): 9–30.

4. See Matt Smith, "Partners in Slime," *San Francisco Weekly*, June 30, 2004. Also William Johnson, "Some Unions Join Employers Seeking to Limit Lawsuits," *Labor Notes*, September 2004, 3–4. For more on union recognition deal making by NUP unions, see Steve Early (and others), "Will Endorsing Republicans Teach Turncoat Dems the Right Lesson?," *Labor Notes* June 2002: 7–11.

5. See Juan Gonzalez, "Bevona Battler vs. National's Cleanup Crew," New York *Daily News*, June 20, 2000. For more on NUP union recruitment of former students as organizers and future labor leaders, see Steve Early, "Thoughts on the 'Worker-Student Alliance'—Then and Now," *Labor History* 44 (2003): 5–13; and a follow-up exchange with Lance Compa on this subject in *Labor: Studies in Working-Class History of the Americas* 1/2 (Summer 2004): 23–26.

6. See Nelson Lichtenstein, *The Most Dangerous Man in Detroit: Walter Reuther and the Fate of American Labor* (New York: Basic Books, 1995), 434–35.

7. For more on the 2002 strike by building cleaners in Local 615 (then 254) of SEIU, see Amy Offner, "Boston Janitors Say Strike Settlement Is No Victory," *Labor Notes* 285 (December 2003): 1, 11.

8. For more information on the Members' Democracy Campaign, see http://www.888democracy.org/home.html. The activities of Local 888 "interim president" Segat were the subject of Steve Bailey's column in the *Boston*

Globe, "Union's Tactics Are a Bust," February 27, 2004.

9.   For more details on the "Philly Home Team" campaign, see William Johnson, "Philadelphia Service Employees' Local Election Becomes Battleground for Union Democracy," *Labor Notes* 299 (February 2004): 5.

10.   See Herman Benson, "Sweeney Critics Would Bureaucratize to Organize," *Union Democracy Review* 149 (December 2003–January 2004): 1–3.

FROM MONSIGNOR SWEENEY TO REVEREND ANDY
First published as "From Monsignor Sweeney to Reverend Andy," a review of *America Needs a Raise: Fighting for Economic Security and Social Justice,* by John Sweeney (Houghton Mifflin, 1996), and *A Country that Works: Getting America Back on Track,* by Andy Stern (Simon & Schuster, 2006), in *WorkingUSA,* January 2007.

REFORM FROM ABOVE OR RENEWAL FROM BELOW?
First published as "Remaking Labor—From the Top-Down? Bottom-Up? or Both?" a review of *L.A. Story: Immigrant Workers and the Future of the U.S. Labor Movement,* by Ruth Milkman (Russell Sage, 2006), and *U.S. Labor in Trouble and Transition: The Failure of Reform from Above and the Promise of Revival from Below,* by Kim Moody (Verso, 2007), in *Working USA,* March 2008.

1.   Stanley Aronowitz, "The Labor Movement and the Left in the United States," *Socialist Review* 9/2 (March–April 1979): 42–43.

2.   In August 2008, Tyrone Freeman, the Andy Stern–appointed president of SEIU's United Long Term Care Workers Local 6434, was removed from office after it was reported in the *Los Angeles Times* and other publications that nearly $1 million in dues money had been misappropriated. For more details on the challenges facing union reformers in that local, see Steve Early, "Tyronegate and Trusteeship," *CounterPunch,* September 3, 2008.

EPILOGUE: A PURPLE UPRISING IN OAKLAND
First published as "A Purple Uprising in Oakland," in *CounterPunch,* April 1, 2008.

AFTERWORD: READING, WRITING, AND UNION BUILDING
1.   Rachel Donadio, "You're an Author? Me Too!" *New York Times Book Review,* April 27, 2008, 27.

2.   Eric Lee, "Educate, Agitate, Organize: Selling Labor Books On-Line," *The Industrial Worker,* May 2005, 4. Available at   http://www.labourstart.org/books.shtml.

3.   Stern's 2006 book is not the first to benefit from a "captive market" of union members. See, for example, *From Telegraph to the Internet,* another ghost-assisted volume, published in 1998 by then-Communications Workers of

America president Morty Bahr. With a foreword by his good friend Senator Edward Kennedy, a longtime recipient of CWA political contributions, Bahr's book was "marketed" within the union much like Stern's has been inside and outside SEIU—as "part autobiography, part labor history, and part vision of how unions can proceed into the next century."

4. Since *Which Side Are You On?* and *Nickel and Dimed* appeared, two of the few remaining daily newspaper reporters assigned to the labor beat have turned their reportage into widely publicized trade press books on the state of working life and/or organized labor in America. In 2007, *St. Louis Post Dispatch* reporter Phil Dine published *State of the Unions* (McGraw-Hill), followed by *New York Times* staffer Steve Greenhouse's book, *The Big Squeeze: Tough Times for the American Worker* (Borzoi Books, 2008).

5. André Shiffrin, "How to Pay for a Free Press," *Le Monde Diplomatique*, October 2007.

6. In the interest of full disclosure, I should mention that Gordon is my wife and that I have also contracted with Cornell to write a book about the influence of Sixties radicals within American labor. Gordon is co-editor of an ILR Press series on the "Culture and Politics of Health Care Work" that publishes her own books on caregiving work and others. Gordon's series of books on nursing have sold nearly 100,000 copies, with most of her readers being working RNs and nursing students.

7. Berry's publisher (and mine), Monthly Review Press, is part of a third option available to labor authors interested in bypassing both trade and academic publishers. Left-wing independent publishing houses include MR Press, 106-year-old Charles H. Kerr Publishing in Chicago, and Boston's Sixties-inspired South End Press. MRP has a number of good labor-related titles, including Michael Yates's 20,000-selling *Why Unions Matter* (now available in a new edition) and his more recent, very entertaining *Cheap Motels and a Hot Plate: An Economist's Travelogue* (2007). Kerr's catalogue runs heavily toward "Wobbly classics"—books for and about members of the Industrial Workers of the World. But its list also includes the work of non-IWW writers like Martin Glaberman. South End has published more than 250 left-leaning titles since 1977—among them labor-oriented books like Vanessa Tait's *Poor Workers' Unions: Rebuilding Labor from Below.*

8. See, for example, New York City carpenter Greg Butler's *Disunited Brotherhoods: Race, Racketeering, and the Fall of New York Construction Unions*, published by iUniverse in 2006.

9. At the local level, at least one AFL-CIO central labor council leader uses his regular radio show on WDEV in Vermont to interview authors of a wider range of labor books. Guests of talk show host Traven Leyshon, a *Labor Notes* supporter and president of the Washington-Orange-Lamoille Labor Council, have included Bill Fletcher, Fernando Gapasin, Suzanne Gordon, and other writers.

10. Two Canadian unions have creatively supported and promoted more contemporary portraits of themselves. Despite his own recent criticism of the union leadership, Sam Gindin's book, *The Canadian Auto Workers: Birth and*

Transformation of a Union, is still advertised on the CAW's website; meanwhile, Jamie Swift's *Walking the Union Walk: Stories from the CEP's First Ten Years* is still widely used in the education programs of the Communications, Energy, and Paperworkers to promote solidarity among the disparate elements of that recently amalgamated national union.

11. Les Leopold, *The Man Who Hated Work and Loved Labor: The Life and Times of Tony Mazzocchi* (Chelsea Green Press, 2008). For more on "working-class intellectuals" in the pre-television era, see Jonathan Rose's *The Intellectual Life of the British Working Classes* (Yale University Press, 2001). Rose's study of what one reviewer calls an "enormously energetic working-class reading culture" describes the varied literature that workers read and discussed in twentieth-century Britain.

12. See Associated Press report, June 16, 2008. Also Motoko Rich, "A Book Club Courts Liberals," *New York Times,* June 16, 2008. For more information on how the PBC works, see http://www.progressivebookclub.com.

13. Katrina vanden Heuvel, "Progressive Book Lovers of the World, Unite!" June 16, 2008; available at http://www.thenation.com/blogs/edcut/330135.

INDEX